Smart Moving Calen[dar]

Two Months Before Moving Day

[ ] Get dental checkup and cleaning, see doctor, ve..., ...

[ ] Have antiques, pieces of art, and other valuables appraised for ...

[ ] Make an inventory of your household goods and begin to de-cl... garage, and other storage areas.

[ ] Start using foods and cleaning supplies that cannot be moved.

[ ] Check into reserving a rental truck or start getting estimates from professional movers.

[ ] Stop by the local post office and pick up a set of change-of-address cards.

[ ] Start a file of all your moving paperwork (estimates, receipts, contacts, floor plans).

[ ] Arrange to transfer school records as needed.

One Month Before Moving Day

[ ] Contact phone, power, and other utilities for service disconnection at your old home and connection at your new home.

[ ] Empty a room, the garage, or another area as a staging area.

[ ] Obtain packing materials and start packing items you won't need until after you arrive at the new house.

[ ] Arrange for the cleaning, painting, and preparation of your new home before you arrive, as needed.

[ ] Arrange for special transportation of your pets and plants, if necessary.

[ ] Call your insurance agent to see how your possessions are covered during transit.

[ ] Make any travel plans necessary for your move.

Three Weeks Before Moving Day

[ ] Make child care arrangements for moving day.

[ ] Dispose of items that cannot be moved, such as flammable liquids.

[ ] Have your moving sale.

[ ] Call local charities for pickup of unwanted items, making sure you get a donation receipt for taxes.

alpha books

Two Weeks Before Moving Day

[] Service your car in preparation for the move.

[] Notify creditors of your move.

[] Make sure you have an adequate supply of medications and that they are with you as you travel.

[] Return library books and other borrowed items.

[] Retrieve any loaned items.

[] Transfer prescriptions and medical records as needed.

One Week Before Moving Day

[] If a do-it-yourself move, finish up the packing.

[] Take animals to vet for immunizations, if necessary.

[] Drain power equipment of oil and gas.

[] Drain all water hoses.

[] Check and close your safety deposit box.

[] Transfer your bank accounts.

[] Settle any bills with local businesses.

[] Confirm any travel reservations.

[] Defrost refrigerator and freezer, and then prop open their doors.

[] Disconnect and prepare major appliances for move.

[] Set aside anything that will travel in your car so that it will not be loaded on the truck.

[] Pack a box of items that will be needed first at the new house.

[] Get cash or travelers checks for the trip and to pay the movers.

[] Confirm arrival time of your moving van.

[] If moving yourself, dismantle beds and other large furniture as needed.

Moving Out Day

[] If using a mover, be sure someone is at the house to answer questions.

[] If using a mover, read your bill of lading and inventory carefully before signing. Keep this paperwork in a safe place.

[] Write down all utility meter readings.

Moving In Day

[] Check your belongings carefully and note on the inventory any damaged items.

[] Be ready to pay your mover with cash, certified check, or travelers' checks unless other arrangements have been made in advance.

THE COMPLETE IDIOT'S GUIDE® TO

Smart Moving

by Dan Ramsey

alpha books

A Division of Macmillan General Reference
1633 Broadway, 8th Floor, New York NY 10019

Macmillan Publishing books may be purchased for business or sales promotional use. For information please write: Special Markets Department, Macmillan Publishing USA, 1633 Broadway, New York, NY 10019.

International Standard Book Number: 0-02862126-3
Library of Congress Catalog Card Number: 97-80978

00 99 98   8 7 6 5 4 3 2 1

Interpretation of the printing code: The rightmost number of the first series of numbers is the year of the book's printing; the rightmost number of the second series of numbers is the number of the book's printing. For example, a printing code of 98-1 shows that the first printing occurred in 1998.

Printed in the United States of America

1, Moving, Household

ALPHA DEVELOPMENT TEAM

Publisher
Kathy Nebenhaus

Editorial Director
Gary M. Krebs

Managing Editor
Bob Shuman

Marketing Brand Manager
Felice Primeau

Senior Editor
Nancy Mikhail

Development Editors
Phil Kitchel, Jennifer Perillo, Amy Zavatto

Editorial Assistant
Maureen Horn

PRODUCTION TEAM

Development Editor
Matthew X. Kiernan

Production Editor
Tony McDonald

Copy Editor
Cindy Kitchel

Cover Designer
Mike Freeland

Photo Editor
Richard H. Fox

Illustrator
Jody P. Schaeffer

Designer
Glenn Larsen

Indexers
Chris Barrick
Nadia Ibrahim

Layout/Proofreading
*Cynthia Davis-Hubler, Betsy Deeter,
Terri Edwards, Brad Lenser,
Chris Livengood, Donna Martin,
Shawn Ring, Becky Stutzman*

Contents at a Glance

Contents

i

Appendixes

Foreword

If you're thinking of moving—across town, cross-country or across the international date line—don't let go of this book. You've just put your hands on the most comprehensive sourcebook on moving that money can buy. No matter the size of your estate, a move is a major undertaking.

Here is a wealth of information that will make your move easier than you could have ever imagined possible. The key to stress-free moving, of course, is good planning. With the help of *The Complete Idiot's Guide to Smart Moving*, you won't miss a trick.

You'll start by creating your own Smart Moving Notebook in which you'll be guided to record all the essentials for your move—things you'll need to think about from the home front, and things you need to know about your new hometown. You'll be prepared from the start.

If you haven't yet chosen your new neighborhood, this book will help you consider the host of factors you need to find the community that suits you. How close is the library, grocery store, all-night drug store? Where's the nearest mall, museum, dog pound? If you know where you're going but want to know more, you'll find sources for maps and guidebooks, contacts on the Internet and through the phone. You'll find lists of questions to ask about potential neighborhoods: What are the schools like? Where do the locals go to have fun? Making a list early will help you get acquainted even before you move in.

The Complete Idiot's Guide to Smart Moving doesn't overlook the emotional pitfalls of a move, either. You'll find frank talk and good advice on sorting out the emotional highs and lows a move brings on, and you'll be able to prepare yourself through sound strategies designed to help make your transition smoother. How about a scrapbook on your old neighborhood? A video of friends and family? Plan ahead for new good memories: Have kids make a list of the positive things you can look forward to—new friends, new weekend adventures, a destination for your old friends.

The Smart Mover is ready for all that comes his way. That's why detailed guides to packing, choosing a moving firm or deciding to move yourself, estimating your moving costs, holding a successful moving sale, moving heavy appliances, and preparing a Smart Moving Survival Box are among the many dozens of sound tips you'll find in the pages of this invaluable guidebook.

Even those moving only blocks away will find useful advice in this book. Just cast one thought to all you've accumulated in your home, all the details of your daily life and you'll know why *The Complete Idiot's Guide to Smart Moving* is the right companion for your move. It's like having your mother show you the way—without the guilt.

—Beth Kalet

Beth Kalet is a newspaper editor and writer for *The Times Herald-Record* in Middletown, N.Y. She handled the logistics for her household move of some 100 miles not long ago. Using many of the principles and strategies Dan Ramsey lays out here, her move went rather well. If only *The Complete Idiot's Guide to Smart Moving* had been published when her family of four made their move, she might know where the glass juicer is today, the movers wouldn't have loaded an armoire with boxes of cooking pots and then lugged it up a set of steps, and she wouldn't have unpacked the contents of ashtrays in her new home.

Introduction

America is on the move. In fact, 41,000,000 people move every year—that's 36,000 families every day! (They must really get tired!)

And moving has been voted (by a panel of weary experts) as near the top of the Stress List—right above having your new car stolen while in the dentist's office getting a root canal when he's late for a golf game the day after you lost your job.

I know. I've moved 44 times in the past 35 years! It's been everything from throwing clothes in the back seat to nervously watching as big hairy men packed the cream cheese with the stereo.

I've also been one of the big hairy men. Hey, cream cheese makes good packing material! I know the raw power of packing cherished belongings as families stand helplessly nearby. "Please don't pack my kitty, mister!"

So I have lots of smart ideas—and some war stories—to share with you to reduce the stress of your next move. No, it won't go away. Stress is a part of life. So is moving. But, together, we can put moving in its proper place on the Stress List: just below watching reruns of *Gilligan's Island*.

You can move *smart*!

The Complete Idiot's Guide to Smart Moving includes checklists for getting organized—what to do one month before, two weeks before, one week before, and the day before the move. There are even tips on moving on short notice. This book contains valuable packing and loading advice, tips on how to safeguard the fragile stuff, and a checklist of essential packing supplies.

The Complete Idiot's Guide to Smart Moving offers important information on hiring a mover—from evaluating estimates and negotiating a contract to purchasing insurance and checking for a consumer complaint history. It also shows you how to save big bucks in moving yourself without giving them to your chiropractor. Moving smart!

The Complete Idiot's Guide to Smart Moving is filled with easy-to-follow advice for a stress-free moving day—from packing a Moving Day Survival Kit to keeping the kids and pets occupied (or at least out of harm's way!). This comprehensive and practical book will save readers a truckload of problems.

The Complete Idiot's Guide to Smart Moving offers valuable tips on staying connected during a move—from canceling and starting your phone, cable, mail, and utilities, to carrying a cellular phone (or a prepaid phone card) on moving day.

The Complete Idiot's Guide to Smart Moving also tells you exactly what to do if the move doesn't go smoothly—tips from dealing with difficult movers to getting restitution for damaged or missing items, all while keeping your cool (and your wallet).

The Complete Idiot's Guide to Smart Moving includes practical ideas for moving on: what to do after the move—registering to vote, updating drivers licenses and vehicle registrations, finding new doctors, and getting information on community activities, libraries, schools, and parks. You'll learn how to get on with your new and improved life.

You're going to become a Certified Smart Mover!

Using This Book

There's a whole lot of information you'll need before you become certifiable. Fortunately, it's packed up into logical "boxes" that will be easy for you to unpack and put to use.

Part 1 will help you plan your move. Hey, nobody *loves* to move—not even professional movers. But you can plan not to *hate* it! You'll overcome some of the natural fears of moving, start looking ahead to your new life, start estimating costs and scheduling, and plan the emotional side of your move.

Part 2 helps you make moving decisions. Smart decision making is the key to smart moving. You'll tackle and overcome procrastination, and learn how to get rid of stuff without regrets.

In Part 3 of this user-friendly book, you'll learn how to move yourself the smart way. It covers planning your packing and loading, choosing a moving vehicle, how to pack things, how to move furniture and appliances without a chiropractor, and how to load everything for safe arrival. You'll even learn some inside tips from professional movers on how to use your brain more than your other muscles.

Part 4 is for those lucky folks who will be moved by others—or who just want to consider the option. It offers lots of practical advice on hiring a mover, other moving company options, the legal side of moving, and (ouch) winning disputes with your mover.

Part 5 helps you face moving day without prescription drugs. It offers proven techniques for surviving moving day, helping children and pets survive moving day, and managing the moving crew so nobody gets hurt.

In Part 6, you'll learn about life after moving: how to turn your abode into a home, and how to make your life even better than it was. Tall order, eh?

I've added a couple of other things I think you'll find usesful. There's a glossary of smart moving words at the end of this book. It defines the words that movers use in mixed company. There's also an appendix of information on deductible moving expenses that can save you money on your move.

Extras Just For Thee

As if all that weren't enough, I've included lots of other tips, techniques, asides, and miscellaneous information set off in little boxes, such as:

Back & Back Savers

These bigger boxes include relevant tips, ideas, suggestions, and comments to help you survive the moving process without a doctor or mental health expert.

Making Your Move

These boxes offer short and sweet tips from amateur and professional movers to help you get from here to there without getting lost or injured.

Moving Violations

These boxes include vignettes of painful but relevant moving experiences that illustrate what *not* to do when moving.

Moving Words

These boxes include alternate definitions for words that movers use when not angry or injured.

Acknowledgments

The job of a professional mover is to help others. Many professional (and lots of amateur) movers have helped me help you make your move. They include the American Movers Conference, Allied Van Lines, American Red Ball, Atlas Van Lines, Interstate Van Lines, Paul Arpin Van Lines, Ryder, Stevens Worldwide Van Lines, Wheaton World Wide Moving, and U-Haul. Special thanks go to Blue Bird Transfer, Wheaton, Koplan's Furniture, Hub Furniture, and many of our friends, relatives, and employers who have given me the opportunity—and the necessity—to learn how to move smart.

Dedication

This book is dedicated to our newest team member, Ashley Shea. Yuh-huh!

Special Thanks to the Technical Reviewer

The Complete Idiot's Guide to Smart Moving was reviewed by an expert who double-checked the accuracy of what you'll learn here, to help us ensure that this book gives you everything you need to know about buying and selling a home. Special thanks are extended to Melanie Hulse.

Part 1
Planning Your Move

"Gosh, I'm just so looking forward to climbing up in the attic this warm afternoon and pulling down all those boxes of junk left over from last decade's garage sale!"

"Oh, yes. Me, too! In fact, my job is even more thrilling. I get to lug those antique boxes out to Ned's grungy pickup truck and hang on to them so they don't fall off in transit!"

"I must be on vacation, then. All I have to do is pack up everything from the house, the shed, the barn, BoBo's cage, and Grandpa's mobile home—by tomorrow! Life is just too good!"

Let's get real!

Nobody LOVES to move—probably not even professional movers.

But it's not the end of the civilized world as we know it. Millions of folks successfully move each year without strewing things from here to there. In fact, many of them actually benefit from the move. These are the Smart Movers.

Hey, that's you! Well, maybe not right this minute—but as soon as you finish the first part of the book!

So get a move on!

Chapter 1

Get a Move On: Your First Thoughts about Moving

In This Chapter

➤ Why folks move so much

➤ Planning a smart move: The Smart Moving Notebook

➤ Reducing the stress of moving

➤ Telling friends and family about the move

"Due to an unfortunate decision at the racetrack yesterday, our rent money has been indiscriminately distributed to others. Time to move!"

"The boss says it's Birmingham or nothing. Time to move."

"Hooray! The last kid is off to college. Time to move."

"You're now standing in what will next month be a Wal-Mart. Time to move."

"I want a divorce. Time to move."

"They're predicting another bad winter this year. Time to move."

"I think our business will do much better in Punxsutawney. Time to move."

"Uncle Arthur's been picked up by the police again. Time to move."

"This house is just too big for one person. Time to move."

"I think we can now afford our place in the country. Time to move."

"I think we'll have to sell our place in the country. Time to move."

Like it or not, you're considering moving your household to another street, city, state, region, or country. And moving means stress. Lots of it.

"How are we going to find a regular sitter as nice as Mrs. Johnson?"

"I don't think the schools are as good there."

"It's such a conservative neighborhood. I wonder whether we should invite them to our all-night parties."

"We're going to have to pay more for the same-sized house!"

"How will we ever move your huge beer-can collection?"

"We can't move a lifetime's memories without some help."

"Junior says he's not moving with us."

"How can we be sure that our new town will be better than this one?"

"I hear their crime-rate statistics were recently stolen!"

Moving is one of the scariest things you can do. Are you going to something better or worse? Do you have a choice? How can you make the best of it? How can you afford it? How much of it can you or should you do yourself? Will you find a sympathetic therapist?

The answer to these questions is *smart moving*—making the best decision based on the best information you can get. That's what this book is all about: giving you valuable information and advice gleaned from thousands of successful—and unsuccessful—moves. You will reduce the stress of your move with confidence earned through knowledge. You will save hundreds and even thousands of dollars by moving smart. And you will learn how to move your lifestyle closer to your ideal. You will see moving as an opportunity for growth. You will become a Certified Smart Mover.

In this chapter, you'll consider your reasons for moving, and you'll learn how to find your new home and leave your old one, how to plan a smart move, how to make a smart move, and how to survive the move. All of these elements will be developed in greater detail throughout this book, with specific tips and proven techniques. For now, you'll be doing some brain work to make you more comfortable with the road you're taking. By the end of this chapter, we'll have reduced your moving stress level by about 30 decibels.

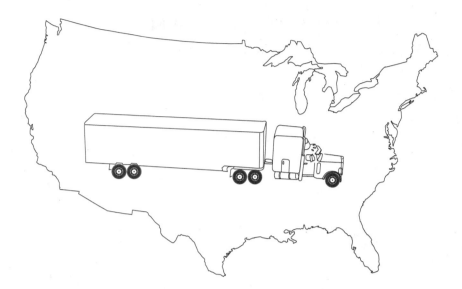

Millions of complete idiots move smart each year.

Famous Reasons to Move

Okay, so why the heck are you moving? Defining your own reasons for moving (there are always more than one) will help you ensure that, from the process, you get what you want—or at least a reasonable facsimile.

Many folks who move really don't have a choice in the matter. If you're lucky, you do. But even if you're being coerced into moving by economics or emotions, you can keep some control over the process and maybe even make some good things happen from it.

There are as many reasons to move your household as there are places to move it. Let's see which ones fit your situation. In the following sections, you'll probably find two or more reasons to move.

New Job: "They Bought the Résumé I Bought!"

Right on top of the all-time list of reasons to move is a new job. You may be moving across town to reduce the commute or moving to a more expensive (or less expensive) home due to a change in salary. In some instances, a new employer's relocation service will pick you up here and move you over there with little fuss or fret. But it won't move all of your relatives and friends (a mixed blessing), so you will have to make some adjustments on your own. You'll probably need to find some new services such as doctors and dentists. You may also need to change NFL affiliations to keep peace with new co-workers. Or not.

And how will you manage all these changes: job, location, neighbors, bankers, services, and teams? Smart moving. In fact, you may find your life is much better because of your move. You'll learn how to turn stress into an opportunity for a better life.

Current Job: Onward and Upward

"You're the new manager of our Phoenix office—beginning this Friday!"

Sometimes a move is required by your current employer. Many IBM executives of a couple of decades ago felt their company's acronym stood for "I've Been Moved!" Maybe your business is similar. Or maybe the chance to move up and away is only offered every decade or so. Perhaps you will have to consider an international move. How's your Tagalog? You've just rung the bell at the top of the stress meter.

More Room: "He Touched My Stuff!"

Families grow. Planned parenthood is an ideal. Aging parents need live-in assistance. Hobbies soon take over spare bedrooms and cry for more space. Garages become crowded with everything except cars. Garage sales become a necessity. Party invitations are limited by available space.

People move to increase space for living. This might not always be the primary reason for a move, but it certainly factors into the decision. A relocation move, for example, can become an opportunity to add more room to the living quarters.

Less Room: "Let's Move Before the Kids Come Back Home"

Downsizing happens in families as well as in businesses. Toddlers soon become teenagers who jump (or are pushed) from the nest. Marriages change membership. Bulky toys that were once important are no longer so. Retirement requires a smaller mortgage and a home to match. The five-acre lawn that you pined for has become a full-time job.

It's time to move to smaller quarters.

Lifestyle Changes: "Let's Be Snowbirds!"

Sometimes the desire for a change in lifestyle requires a move. The retiring Minnesota couple that wants warmer weather. The corporate executive who is tired of the rat race and would prefer life as a country mouse. The Midwest writer who wants to move to New York City as a freelancer. Or vice versa.

It's time to move to a better life.

Finding Your New Place: The Witness Protection Program Loves You!

You've decided to move—or it has been decided for you. Now what?

Chapter 2 will help you reduce the stress of finding your new place, but you should be thinking about the issues involved beginning—now.

Here's my handy dandy list of obvious questions you may not have thought of yet:

➤ What will you need in housing?

➤ What do you want?

➤ How much can you afford?

➤ How can you get more information right now?

Let's get more specific.

Needs List: Gotta!

A book helps you think. It guides your thoughts along organized paths. You can start your own Smart Moving Notebook with a blank notebook. Begin organizing and writing your answers to a variety of questions and concerns that pop into your head as you think about moving. The first thing to write in your Smart Moving Notebook is a list of your needs. Here are some examples to get you started:

➤ A place within a 30-minute commute of Reedsville

➤ A master bedroom and a bedroom for each of the two children

➤ More separation between living and sleeping areas

➤ A utility or back room where Bart can clean up from playing with the gorilla

➤ Wheelchair access to a bathroom for Aunt Tillie's stay during the winter

➤ A place in which we can put a small greenhouse for growing salad vegetables

➤ An uncomfortable sleeping room for out-of-town guests

➤ A neighborhood in which I feel safe

➤ A neighborhood in which the kids can walk to school

➤ A community where I can use my skills as a hospice volunteer

➤ Enough room to hold our traditional family holiday get-togethers

Remember that a *need* is a personal requirement. Something you regard as an absolute necessity in your new location may be only a *want* for someone else. That's fine.

Wants List: Wanna!

For most of us, the Needs List will be much shorter than the Wants List. Both will also be unique. Make sure that you gather the needs and wants of everyone who will be moving with you. Yes, even consider the needs and wants of your iguanas.

To get you writing in your Smart Moving Notebook, here are some popular wants:

➤ A low-maintenance yard so that we can spend weekends at the beaches

➤ Room to entertain friends and family

➤ A place to store my classic car during the winter months

➤ Proximity to Ariakne University

➤ A hobby room for your Peruvian blowdart collection

➤ A cellar or pantry to store Granny's preserves for the next generation

➤ A local Internet provider

➤ A world-class library

➤ A world-class tavern

Making Your Move

Keep a record of all your moving expenses. If your move meets certain criteria, you can deduct the expenses from your federal income taxes. To learn more, call the Internal Revenue Service (800/829-3676) or visit their Web site at **http://www.irs.gov** and request Publication 521 titled "Moving Expenses."

Money Issues: Ain't Got the Dough!

Moving costs money. It may involve the cost of a full relocation service or just a six-pack for your packing crew. If you're lucky—or have an impressive job title—money to move may not be an issue in your decision. The employer will take care of all moving expenses, food and housing costs in transit, and some real-estate fees. For most people, however, money is an issue—and a stressful one.

➤ How are you going to pay for getting from here to there?

➤ Is it really cheaper to hire Two Dopes and a Dolly Moving Company?

➤ Where will you stay if your new home isn't ready?

➤ Can't you just buy an RV and become a nomad?

➤ Should you get full insurance coverage on your beer-can collection?

➤ How much is it going to cost to live there versus here?

The point: Get out your No. 2 pencil again and start making notes about the money issues.

Who is paying for this move anyway?

Are the costs directly billed to an employer or must you pay and request reimbursement?

What costs?

Any limits?

Any advances?

Is there room on your credit card for all of this?

Moving expenses are a legitimate tax deduction for many movers.

Moving Resources: Friends with Pickups

You're going to need lots of friends to pull off this move. Most of your moving friends you haven't met yet. They are movers, moving trade associations, rental equipment companies and agents, real estate and rental agents, chambers of commerce folks, packers, and others.

Who are these people and how can you ensure that they're honest? The search begins today. If an employer hasn't already decided who the mover will be, you have a few important choices to make: Consolidated Amalgamated Worldwide Transfer and Storage...or Billy-Bob's U-Pack We-Hack Moving and Pizza Delivery Service.

Moving Violations
Beware of efficient packers. Our son came in from his last day at school as the packers were working. He laid his coat down for a moment. We next saw his coat when it was unpacked at our destination.

The best place to start looking for good moving resources is with your current friends. Who do you know who has recently moved? Especially, who has made a move similar to yours? A local mover may be unqualified to relocate your belongings to Denpasar, Indonesia. If you are moving to a new city, talk with your employer or other contacts about their moving experiences. You may quickly discover who will make the move a dream—or a nightmare. A real estate agent at either end of the move can serve as an experienced advisor.

Shedding Your Old Place (What to Do when the Sheriff Nails the Notice on Your Door)

Once you know where you're going, it's time to think about getting there from where you are. That is, you may have a home to sell or rent, a lease to renegotiate or assign, or a mansion to donate to charity. We'll get much more specific in the coming chapters, but for now, simply begin getting comfortable with the topic.

Requirements: Mo' Gottas!

In your Smart Moving Notebook, make some initial notes on what you'll need to do with the old homestead.

➤ Is a relocation company buying it from you?

➤ Do you need to sell your home before you can go anywhere?

➤ Are homes selling briskly in your area?

➤ Is your apartment on a lease or month-to-month?

➤ Will you be losing any deposits or fees with your move?

➤ Should you contact a freelance arsonist before or after you call your insurance agent?

Agent or FSBO: Residential Roulette

If you're selling a home, condo, or other financial albatross, you will need to decide whether to sell it yourself or hire it done. An agent can save you (or give you) headaches. Offering it For-Sale-By-Owner (FSBO, pronounced fizz-bo) can save some cash—if you can get a discount on ibuprofen. Here are some questions to consider:

➤ Have you previously sold a home? If so, how do you feel about doing it again?

➤ Are properties in your area selling quickly or slowly?

➤ Do you have a real-estate agent who you are confident will help you get your home sold?

➤ Are you or is someone in your family/living group available to show and sell your current home?

➤ Do you really enjoy weird strangers pointing out the flaws in your home?

Money Problems: Or Is That Redundant?

Maybe you need the money from your current home to move to the next one. Or you have an apartment lease that must be resolved before you can move on. Lots of issues—and they all involve hard-earned dollars.

By listing the money issues specific to your move, you can begin to resolve them. After all, they are certainly not unique. The same issues you face have been successfully solved by hundreds of thousands of smart movers. Think about some of them:

➤ Must you sell, rent, or lease your current property before you can move? If so, how much cash do you need and when?

➤ If you rent out your property, do you require prompt monthly payment from the tenant so that you can make your payment on your new home, or do you have a financial buffer?

➤ Do regulations keep you from leasing your property? Will you need to hire an attorney or a hit-man?

➤ Are you crazy?

Planning the Move: Like You Really Have Any Control!

Your Smart Moving Notebook will be a valuable resource as you plan your move. The notes you've already made in it will help you reduce the stress inherent to moving. Keep it nearby as you read this book and think about your impending move.

Reducing Stress without Pills or Monthly Meetings

As you can see, organization is the most important element of a stress-free move. An organized move will be much easier on the entire family and will save money. It's never too early to start planning your move.

Planning is even more important if you have only a short time in which to prepare for your move. Every hour spent planning your move can save you many hours of work and stress as the move begins. You'll be given numerous easy-to-use planning tools through-out this book to help you minimize stress. Here are a few to get you started:

➤ If possible, schedule your move for off-peak times. Moving companies and truck rental companies are far busier during the summer because approximately 45 percent of all moves take place in June, July, and August.

➤ If possible, schedule your move for off-peak seasons as long as you're not getting into winter, hurricane season, or other bad weather.

➤ If possible, avoid moving on a weekend so that banks, utility companies, and other services will be open.

➤ Run away from home at least three weeks in advance of moving day.

Time Planning

Chapter 4 will help you set up a moving schedule that will be both easy and efficient. For now, begin making notes in your Smart Moving Notebook regarding the time require-ments of your move. Answer questions such as these:

➤ Do you have to be at a new location on a specific date? If so, what is that date?

➤ Do you have any vacation or other time available that you can include in your moving schedule?

➤ Must you or your spouse move first while others finish the moving process from this end? If so, who are they and what will they do?

➤ Do you have a spouse or significant other who must also participate in the moving schedule?

➤ Do you have a child with a school schedule to consider?

➤ If you decide to move in stages, what do you need and when?

➤ Have you completed the preregistration commitment papers for the asylum?

Who's Going Where, When, and How?

This is an important question to ask as you begin considering a move. For example, will some members of your family move before others? Are some simultaneously moving to other places? If everyone is going to the same place, will some drive while others fly?

Also consider *what* will be moved. For example, maybe it's time to disband the petting zoo before you move cross-country. Or sell off some less-valuable antiques rather than attempt to move them.

How and When to Tell Family and Friends (Optional)

One of the most critical parts of your move will be how and when to tell family and friends. Here are some proven guidelines:

➤ Tell the family of the move as soon as possible. A family meeting is a good start.

➤ If you can, involve younger children in the initial discussions too, so that they have time to adjust to the idea.

➤ Don't overload young children with unnecessary details, but be sure all the children know the reasons for the move.

➤ Be prepared to tell the children something about what they can expect at the new location: schools, playgrounds, attractions, weather.

➤ Decide in advance what and when you will tell friends about the move. If they offer to help, make a note of it and thank them. Even if you don't need help, the gesture is a continuation of your friendship.

➤ Decide which "friends" will get the bogus forwarding address.

Chapter 5 will help you with the emotional move. For now, use your notebook to jot down expected problems. A child refuses to move with the family. An aging pet may need special arrangements during the move (or may not be able to make the move). Everyone must leave friends behind. Stresses can build unless foreseen and managed.

Making the Move

Making the physical move will be a piece of cake if you plan to be a smart mover. The majority of this book will cover the details of making the move itself: everything from packing to unloading to settling into your new home.

Moving On

Once you have begun to settle the household following your move, you can quickly make the transition to your new neighborhood or city if you:

➤ Get to know the area.

➤ Get settled in new schools.

➤ Find new banks, doctors, organizations, and churches.

➤ Get your driver's license and license plates (if you've moved to a different state).

➤ Register to vote.

➤ Go to PTA meetings, local sporting events, and other community activities.

➤ Take the kids to visit the museum or the zoo.

➤ Help everyone search out new interests that will keep their names off the police scanner.

The more quickly you become involved in your new community, the sooner you will call it home.

The Least You Need to Know

➤ Smart moving is making the best decision based on the best information you can get.

➤ Even if you don't have a choice in whether or not to move, you still have a lot of options.

➤ Your Smart Moving Notebook can save you time and money.

➤ Organization is the most important element of a stress-free move.

Destinations: Where Do You Think You're Going?!

In This Chapter

➤ Moving within the same town

➤ Moving to a nearby town

➤ Moving to a new state

➤ Moving to a new country

Where ya goin'?

Good question! As soon as you announce that you're moving, friends, family, and bill collectors will begin asking the same question. For you, your destination may be little more than a circled spot on the map. Or it may be "home." It will soon be both.

➤ What's the housing market like?

➤ What are the seasons like?

➤ What's the fishing like?

➤ Are there any vegetarian low-sodium nonsmoking singles bars?

➤ Are there good job prospects for other family members?

➤ What do folks do for fun—symphony picnics or spittoon parties?

Whether your move is cross-town or transcontinental, you want to know what you're getting into. You want to know more about the "location" in "relocation." In this chapter, you'll learn more about moves within the same town, into a nearby town, or into a new state, region, or country. You'll learn where to find information. You'll know before you get there whether it is somewhere you want to be.

So get out your Smart Moving Notebook again and start making notes about your move. Doodling is okay, too.

Same Area: What's the Shortest Move on Record?

Is a move within the same town technically a move?

Sure it is!

And it can be nearly as frustrating as a cross-state move. You still have to pack, load, drive, unload, and unpack—or hire big hairy guys to do it for you. The main difference is that you won't get as many Frequent Mover Miles.

If you're moving from one neighborhood to another in the same town, or to a nearby or adjoining town, you already know some things about your new town. You've probably heard all the rumors about inbreeding there. But you might want to know more specifically what to expect in the new neighborhood—whether it's just around the corner, across town, or in a nearby town.

Peeking Around the Corner

Because you are near your new location, you can easily learn more about it. Drive around to get a feel for the area. If the area is relatively safe, get out of the car and walk, especially the few blocks surrounding your new neighborhood. (If it's not safe, better rethink your move!) Introduce yourself to the local natives—especially those picking up tornado debris in the front yard. Ask them questions:

➤ Is there an annual block party?

➤ Where do the kids play?

➤ Do most residents work away from home, leaving the neighborhood quiet during the day?

➤ Where is the nearest emergency clinic, bowling alley, or tofu snack shop?

➤ Is there a Neighborhood Watch program—or at least a benevolent busybody?

Crosstown Moves

Most cities are a family of towns—and they probably get along about as well. If you want to learn more about the other side of your town, talk with local officials. Call city hall and find out who represents the new neighborhood at the city council. Call your city council representative and ask about issues that concern the neighborhood. Is a plan in place to improve street lighting soon (at homeowner expense)? Is anyone trying to rezone the neighborhood for a paintball range? Ten minutes on the phone can keep you from making a frustrating mistake.

Larger cities have neighborhood newspapers. If you have enough advance time, subscribe to one for your new neighborhood. If not, review back issues at the neighborhood library or newspaper office. Read the ads as well as the stories. The ads tell you what the people in the area are like.

➤ Do they shop the finest stores or the 99-cent sales?

➤ Are they more interested in tennis courts or sports bars?

➤ Does nearly everyone in town have the same last name?

Same State, New Town

Moving to a new town—even if it's just 20 miles away—can be an adventure. Think about all the new things you can see and do—and all the old neighbors you can now avoid. By learning about the city or town beforehand, you can be ready to settle in quickly and become involved in your new home-town. You may not even have to change telephone numbers!

Besides a drive there, you can learn about your new town through maps, booklets, books, tourist bro-chures, and other resources. Dust off your nearly-expired library card and check out the library's resources first. Then try the newsstands and book stores. If you're "wired," log onto the Internet and find out what you can find out.

Making Your Move
If you are moving for a new or relocated job—even if it's just to the next town—ask your employer for help finding information about the town. Many large employers offer help to relocating employees. Or they may be able to direct you to a helpful employee who lives in the area.

Make the new city your own. Start to know it now.

Tips for Easier Same-Area Moves

➤ Try tuning into your new town's radio station to hear the local news, sports, and ads for area businesses.

➤ Ask your friends whether they know people who live in the neighborhood or nearby town to which you're moving.

➤ Remember to pack for a short move as thoroughly as for a long one. Most items damaged in moving happen with short moves.

➤ Short moves can become new beginnings.

New Areas: Have I Been Here Before?

A move from L.A. to San Francisco...Manhattan to Syracuse...Houston to Austin...are all in-state moves to new worlds. How can you make a smart move to a new area?

Learning about a new area is a whole lot like learning about a nearby town. Your local bookstore or library may carry books that include history and current affairs about the new location. Or visit a bookstore or two in your new area.

Order a phone book for your new city or ask someone for a recently outdated one. Or check your local library—some have phone books from different areas. Phone books contain umpteen scads of useful information. What should you look for? Businesses, services, shopping centers, professional offices, police stations, churches—anything that can help you make better decisions about housing and services.

If you have kids, call the schools that your children will attend and talk with a counselor or the principal. Your first questions? Can Junior walk to school, or is it a 45-minute bus ride? How do local reading and math scores rate? Have they just done away with the school band and football team for lack of funds?

Start surveying the medical and other professionals and building your new circle of reference. Are there doctors and a hospital nearby? Can your live-in mother-in-law get to the dialysis center without crossing the county?

How safe is the neighborhood? Can I take an after-dinner stroll without an armed escort? How high are local auto and fire insurance rates? Do all the houses in the neighborhood have bars on their windows? Is there a neighborhood watch group?

Check out the availability of consumer services. Will a run to the local supermarket involve a two-hour drive? Is Acme Cheapo Clothing the anchor store at the local mall? How far away is the nearest bank or hardware store?

And don't forget those quality-of-life issues. Will all the neighborhood teenagers hang out in front of my house in the evening? Is trash picked up or do I have to take it 30 miles to the town dump? Do you really want to live in a neighborhood that has a ham-processing plant?

Speaking with a local minister or priest or rabbi should prove revealing about the potential new neighborhood (and just how God-fearing the locals are).

Order a mail subscription to the local newspaper or magazine. Or find one at a newsstand or library in your area. Read about your new area, the politics, the events, the sports, the schools, and society. You can learn a lot about the people by reading the letters to the editor.

The easiest move is simply throwing your stuff in the car and driving away.

I've Never Seen This Place Before

How can you find out more about your new hometown?

Of course, the best way is to interview people who are moving out! "Yeah, it's okay—if you like police helicopters circling your home at 3 a.m.!" If you can, interview long-term residents as well.

Call or write the chamber of commerce in your destination area. Ask them to send you a package of information about the area. The package will probably include a city map; information about the climate and living conditions; some economic statistics; information about schools, churches, local businesses, and organizations; and facts about utilities.

There's usually some good information in it, but also lots of opinion and just plain fluff. So read the facts and ignore the fancy wording. Ramsey's Rule of Advertising applies here: The more superlatives, the less truth. Ask either for any information that is available or for specific information that will be helpful your family. Or ask for both.

Making Your Move

Don't know much about your new location? Location Guides (P.O. Box 58506, Salt Lake City UT 84158; 800/846-6310) are available for more than 200 U.S. cities and towns. The 100-page guides include local, state, and regional information and contacts. The Internet address for this organization is **http://www.locationguides.com**.

If you or your employer hire a moving company to move your stuff to a new city, ask if they offer any relocation services. Some moving companies will provide information about the geography, climate, government, housing, utilities, education, banks, churches, newspapers, recreation, shopping, transportation, and more.

Meteorology for the Mover

So, what's the weather like?

A couple hundred miles can make quite a difference in weather conditions. There may be more—or less—rain, snow, hail, thunder, sun, or humidity than you're used to. How can you find out what you're getting into? Don't ask the locals, because they are so used to the weekly tornadoes and record-breaking winters that they aren't objective.

The easiest way is to start watching the weather section of a national newspaper, such as *USA Today*, or The Weather Channel on cable. Of course, weather is what's happening today while climate is what typically happens over a period of time. For climate information, contact the National Weather Service office or the chamber of commerce where you're headed. Your new phone book will come in handy!

Tips for Easier New-Area Moves

➤ A relocation service can provide you with extensive information on your new area including assistance with finding new medical professionals.

➤ A cost-of-living analysis compares the costs of products, services, transportation, and housing between where you are and where you are moving.

➤ The Employee Relocation Council (800/372-5952; Web site: **http://www.erc.org**) offers valuable information on moving the elderly. So does Chapter 6 of this book.

Changing Your State of Living

Changing your state? Again, start your search with a bookstore or library. If the shelves contain no useful information, ask about other resources. Obviously, books are available on all 50 states, but you may have to ask a clerk or librarian to order the one you want.

If you're fortunate enough to have a good map store nearby, take advantage of it. A map and a phone book can help you find nearby services, even if you aren't yet nearby.

Even if you aren't moving to a large city in the new state, subscribe to a daily metro newspaper. It will include regional and state as well as local, national, and international news coverage. It may also help you find housing and other living necessities faster and easier.

Regional magazines (*New York*, *Atlanta*, *Southern Living*, and so on) can also give you the flavor of your new location.

So, Who's the Governor?

If you're planning a move to another state and want to get lots of facts, try the official state handbook. You can find it through the state chambers of commerce, department of economic opportunity, or other official office. The handbook for your state may be called the *state handbook*, the *blue book*, or some other title. It will typically include governmental, political, social, and historical information about the state. It may include biographies of members of the legislature, descriptions and telephone numbers of

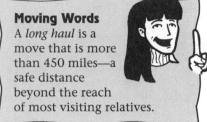

Moving Words
A *long haul* is a move that is more than 450 miles—a safe distance beyond the reach of most visiting relatives.

departments and bureaus, and other useful information. It also may include regulations governing bringing cars, guns, pets, plants, and other items into the state.

Moving costs are based on both mileage and weight.

So, What'll It Cost?

How much will it cost to live in your new location compared to your current one? A variety of cost-of-living sources are available to help answer your questions. Large employers and movers can typically prepare an individual cost-of-living analysis for your family comparing your old costs to your projected costs of the new town. Also, check the classified and store ads in the newspaper to measure whether it will cost you more to live in your new hometown.

Making Your Move

Many moving companies offer a relocation service that includes information about your destination. For example, United Van Lines (800/284-6683) will provide a city or state report that includes government, taxes, geography, climate, housing, and other useful information for movers.

Ask your mover what information services are available and the cost of those services. Some movers and relocation services will also use your information to prepare an individual cost-of-living analysis for your family comparing the costs in your current town to your projected costs in the new town.

Learning a New State Song

Reality check: What do you already know about the state to which you're moving? Your information might not be accurate.

For example, most folks think that each state has a single personality that abruptly ends at the border where the next state's personality begins. Not so. In fact, many states have multiple personalities—separated by geographic boundaries rather than arbitrary lines on a map.

For example, Washington State has many lifestyle regions within it. Seattle (west) is cosmo-metro (lots of BMWs). Spokane (east) is rural-metro (lots of sports utility vehicles). Walla Walla (southeast) is plain isolated (lots of rusty pickups). In fact, life in western Washington is more like that in western Oregon than it is in eastern Washington. Other states with an abundance of geography (mountains, rivers, lakes) also seem to develop multiple personalities.

The state's department of tourism can be a good source of information. Call or write them and ask for maps and general information about the state, as well as for specific information about the region of the state you will be moving to. Learning about other parts of the state will help you create a list of fun things to do on weekends after you get settled into the new house.

Tips for New-State Moves

➤ For children, find out whether their new school has a service club (Teen-to-Teen) that will welcome and help them make new friends.

➤ Obtain a travel video on your new state through your mover, a library, or a chamber of commerce.

➤ Make up a going-away video of your current home, neighborhood, schools, and friends to later help satisfy pangs of homesickness—or remind you why you left!

Moving to a New Country

Moving somewhere else in the world can get scary. Will the natives understand me? Will I understand them? Should I learn a foreign language? What's that funny green stuff everyone puts on their food? Should I take along Pepto-Bismol? Will I get homesick—or never want to come back?

Hablan Inglés—or Not?

An international move means adventure. Each step of the moving process will be more complex and many may include language barriers. And more paperwork. An international move will probably require a passport and other documents. Good schools may be harder to find. Cultural differences may be difficult to overcome. Even your small appliances will probably require special adapters to get along with the local plugs. And finding new doctors, dentists, and other medical specialists can make you ill.

The whole thing can be either a problem or a challenge.

No, Don't Tell Me What's in the Food!

Before you decide to make your home in a foreign country, you'll want to know mucho about the country, the people, the food, the customs, and a million other details. Once again, books offer mucho answers. Head directly for the travel section at your bookstore or library. Search for books aimed at the long-term resident rather than the four-day tourist. Look for current titles because laws concerning work permits, visas, and other topics can change quickly. You need up-to-date information.

You'll probably need advice on the legal aspects of working and living in another country, as well as social customs, educational opportunities, shopping, language, and much more. The more informed you are about the country you are making your new home in, the more quickly you will feel at home and the more quickly you will be accepted.

Tips for New-Country Movers

➤ If you are planning to move your pet internationally, make sure you're aware of all applicable laws. Some countries require a lengthy quarantine; others want documentation of the pet's health. Very few will let you bring your pet in at will.

➤ Make sure you have the appropriate work and residence permit before you move to a new country.

➤ If you live in a metro area, you may find an ethnic restaurant nearby that serves the type of food you'll soon be eating. Try it out before you decide to have kimchee flown in weekly.

➤ Remember to bring your important papers with you: passports, visas, birth certificates, and marriage certificate, as you move to a new country.

➤ The United States State Department can tell you about passports, visas, export permits, and more. You also can contact the embassy for the country you are going to. Check the white pages of a nearby metro phone book.

The Least You Need to Know

➤ A cross-town move can be nearly as difficult as a cross-country move—just less expensive.

➤ Moving to a new state or country requires attention to new laws, taxation, licensing, regulations, and climate. But millions of people do it successfully every year.

➤ International moves require more planning, but can go smoothly with the help of relocation services and/or government offices.

Chapter 3

Moving Mountains: How to Estimate Moving Costs

In This Chapter

➤ Figuring the size of your move

➤ Calculating the distance of your move

➤ Estimating the cost of your move

➤ Planning for fun

Moving isn't cheap!

Even if you're moving your household around the corner, you'll need to spend some money. In addition, you'll probably lose some time and money as you pack, transport, and unpack your belongings—however humble they may be. The more stuff you have and the farther it's going, the higher the cost.

Even if your current or new employer is picking up the moving bill, you may have to pay other costs associated with the move—cleaning fees, temporary housing, lost time, maybe some food and lodging. And even if your benevolent boss pays these, too, you still will need to buy your own sedatives!

Buck & Back Savers

Negotiate with your employer for coverage of moving costs. Of course, the company can say no—but it may also say yes. If it won't pay for a moving company to move you, maybe it will pay for you to move yourself with a rental truck. Or maybe it will pay a set amount toward your relocation. It's worth a try to ask the question!

This chapter will help you keep medication to a minimum by helping you consider and prepare for all moving costs. It will also offer dozens of tips for reducing costs. Best of all, it will help you find ways to make moving an adventure—or at least a cheap thrill.

How?

Knowledge. Included are tips from my own professional and personal moving experiences, as well as those of other survivors. Together, we offer practical advice for estimating and reducing your moving costs. And we plan to have some fun along the way.

So get out your Smart Moving Notebook again, grab a pen or a crayon, and start making notes.

How Big Is Your Mountain?

That's the first and most important question: How much are you moving? It could be personal belongings from your 10-by-10 apartment or everything from your 40-bedroom mansion and polo stables. It's probably something in between.

The best way to calculate how much you're moving is to take an inventory of what you have. A moving company agent can do this inventory for you. You can do it yourself. In fact, it's a good idea to take your own inventory before you have a moving agent do one. You can then decide what you will move and what you won't. As you do your inventory, you can envision what will fit into your new location and what should be thrown out, donated, or put in storage.

Use these rules of thumb to do a quick calculation of how much you're moving:

➤ Small boxes are about 3 cubic feet in size.

➤ Large boxes are about 6 cubic feet in size.

➤ Beds and large appliances are about 30 to 40 cubic feet in size.

➤ Couches and buffets are about 30 cubic feet in size.

➤ Recliners and medium appliances (washer, dryer) are about 20 cubic feet in size.

➤ TVs, chests, and tables are about 10 cubic feet in size.

➤ Six-foot-wide closets will take about 30 to 40 cubic feet of space.

Chapter 9 contains more specifics on planning your packing.

Most households are easy to estimate. For example, a typical two-bedroom apartment will take up about 750 cubic feet when packed. However, many folks have also accumulated hobby items, collections, special knickknacks, and home computers or business equipment that must also be moved. These items may require special packing or handling. Write down these items in your Smart Moving Notebook.

Chapters 10 and 11 cover the details of selecting, packing, and moving everything from appliances to zithers.

How Far Are You Moving?

Of course, another important part of estimating moving costs is distance. A neighborhood move probably won't entail mileage costs, but it probably will require a vehicle. Whether you pay for a moving van, rent a truck, or simply buy gas for your own vehicle, distance is important.

Are We There Yet?

Calculating cross-town miles is easy. But how far is it from Santa Fe, New Mexico, to Reedsport, Oregon? A moving company will figure transportation costs from a schedule of fees that gives the mileage between two points and the transportation charge per mile. It may be something like $1.00 per mile per 1,000 pounds. So getting the correct mileage is important.

A rental truck charge will be based on estimated mileage as well as the number of days it will take to get there, unload, and return the truck somewhere. Again, the correct mileage is important.

How long will it take you to get there? Larger road atlases include estimated time as well as mileage between points. If you estimate traveling 50 miles per hour, you will be allowing for stops every couple hours. A day's driving should be limited to 500 miles in a car or 400 in a rental truck. Your mileage may vary.

Making Your Move
The shortest route between points may not be the best. Remember to consider road conditions, mountains, rivers, weather, and other obstacles as you plan your move from here to there. Map books are available at truck stops and will show you the preferred truck routes and help you calculate mileage. They will also identify routes that aren't open to truck traffic.

Is It on the Map?

Not only is mileage to your destination important, but the location is also important. For example, a 1,000-mile move to North Carolina may be more expensive than a 1,000-mile move to North Dakota. Why? Because two-thirds of the North Carolina moves are *into* the state while about two-thirds of the North Dakota moves are *out of* the state.

What that means is the moving van or rental truck in North Carolina might have to travel a bit for the next moving job. And guess who pays for the "deadheading"? Yup, you! That's why moving companies and rental truck firms charge a premium or offer a discount for moves between certain locations.

How can you tell if you live in a lopsided state? Ask a moving agent or moving truck rental firm. They have the latest facts and figures regarding what the move may cost you.

Pricing the Moving Company Move

Calling a few moving agents will net you a rough estimate of the price of your move or an appointment for someone to come out and make a written estimate. Check the phone book's yellow pages under "Movers."

Your moving agent will estimate the space required in the van and the net weight of everything you're moving. These figures will then be multiplied by the mileage to come up with your estimated cost. The price of packing materials (boxes, crates) and services (packing, unpacking, appliance preparation) will also be added. Insurance costs are extra.

If you have access to the Internet, go online and search for moving companies and truck rental companies. Many have Web sites with information you can download, and some offer online assistance and cost estimates.

Pricing the Do-It-Yourself Move

Ready? Here's Ramsey's Unreal Formula for Pricing the Do-It-Yourself Move:

> Miles × cubic feet × days on the road × current price of a Big Mac Meal + distance between your location and Puckerbrush, Nevada + distance required to avoid driving by Aunt Martha's / rental fee for videos in your new hometown. Reverse the formula if you cross a longitudinal line during your move. Margin for error: 100%.

Estimating the cost of a do-it-yourself move is actually pretty easy. Be sure you figure in the size truck or trailer and any other equipment you will rent, such as dollies, furniture pads, tow bar, and automobile transport. You also need an estimate of how much packing material (boxes, tape, rope, plastic peanuts) you require. And add in the cost of labor you must hire to help you pack and load.

Here's a list of expenses that might be involved in a do-it-yourself move:

➤ Truck or trailer rental

➤ Tow bar or car-carrier rental

➤ Drop-off charges, if applicable

➤ Other equipment rental (dollies, furniture pads)

➤ Packing materials (boxes, tape, rope)

➤ Any labor you employ to help pack, load, or unload

➤ Insurance

➤ Fuel

➤ Mileage

➤ Motels

➤ Meals

➤ Storage

So Ya Wanna Be a Truck Driver?!

The biggest expense of your do-it-yourself move will be the charge for renting a truck or trailer. Here are some guidelines:

➤ A small (14-foot) rental truck will hold about 750 cubic feet of stuff—a one- to two-bedroom household.

➤ A medium (18-foot) rental truck will hold about 1,000 cubic feet of stuff—a two- to three-bedroom household.

➤ A large (24-foot) rental truck will hold about 1,400 cubic feet of stuff—a four-bedroom household.

➤ A professional (40-foot) moving van will hold about 4,000 cubic feet of stuff—enough for everything from the attic to the basement including the car in the garage.

That's a Wrap!

You can save money on packing materials by getting free grocery and liquor boxes from your favorite market. Also, check fast-food restaurants for non-food boxes. However, using them can be false economy. Moving boxes are sturdy and of uniform size, making them easier to handle and stack than assorted grocery boxes. Special dish packs, wardrobe cartons, mirror boxes, and other containers will keep your things safer during the move.

Newspaper is cheap and works for packing around things in boxes, but it is dirty. The ink will rub off on your hands and clothes as you work and on the things you pack it around. Consider purchasing clean wrapping paper instead.

Making Your Move
To save money, wrap your dishes in clean paper so they don't have to be rewashed. You can wrap other things in newsprint.

You also can buy bubble wrap and packing peanuts. If you know ahead of time that you will be moving, you can save original packing materials from items you purchase.

You also will need packaging tape to seal boxes and rope for tying off your load. Many suppliers will let you return any unused materials for a full refund.

Working Hard or Hardly Working?

Unless you're going to do all of the packing, loading, and unloading yourself, you'll need some help. And help costs money. Even free labor isn't really free.

Moving Violations

You can save a couple hundred—or lose a couple thousand—dollars by using inexperienced packers. For best results, use this book to train your packers, and then watch them as they pack. Alternatively, pack everything except your fragile or valuable items, leaving them for an experienced packer.

If you need to hire help, remember that a small, efficient crew will work better than a large, disorganized group. Ask your truck rental agency. They may know of some unemployed movers who could use a day job. Or call the local employment office for day laborers. Also check with moving companies. Some may have a crew that needs work and can make you a good deal.

How much will you have to pay? Ask around. Typically, paying $1\frac{1}{2}$-times–minimum wage will get you good but inexperienced help. Paying twice the minimum wage should get you experienced, but otherwise unemployed, laborers. Pay a reasonable wage and you should get good work. If boxes are packed and the household prepared for moving, two laborers can load a medium truck in four to six hours or a large truck in less than a day.

Six Days on the Road

Okay, folks. How are you going to get you and your entourage from here to there? If "there" is simply around the corner or across town, the convoy isn't a big deal. But if you're relocating to Ma-po Ku, Korea, you have a problem. You also have lots of options.

"What Do You Mean, We're Out of Gas?"

If you're moving yourself, your vehicle will deliver both you and the goods to your destination.

Your car must have enough gas and oil to transport you from the old house to the new—another legitimate moving expense. If you sent your household goods off in a moving company van, you can drive to the new house in your own car. You can set your own route and schedule, as long as you are on hand at the new house on delivery day.

If you don't know what kind of gas mileage your car gets, check a tank or two before your move. Note the odometer reading when you fill up. Then, the next time you fill up, note the new odometer reading and the number of gallons of gas you put in. Subtract the beginning reading from the ending reading to learn how many miles you drove on that tank of fuel. Divide that number by the number of gallons it took to fill the tank the second time. There you have the number of miles per gallon (mpg) you drove your car.

Next, multiply the number of miles you will drive from your old home to the new one by your car's mpg and you can estimate how many gallons of fuel you will need for the trip. Multiply that number by the average cost per gallon of fuel for an estimate of your fuel costs for the trip.

Making Your Move

If you are moving cross-country and driving, you can save by making the drive as quickly as possible. A couple of drivers will mean you can put in longer days on the road, saving a night or two's motel bills. This strategy will also save several restaurant meals, which do add up quickly.

Remember to allow mileage for any side trips you are making.

What kind of mileage will your car get if it's pulling a trailer? First, estimate the weight of the fully-loaded trailer. Your rental agent can give you a good guesstimate. Then divide that number by 100. The resulting number is the approximate percent of reduction in fuel the trailer will cause when pulled. Here's an example:

> A trailer with 3,000 pounds gross weight will reduce your mileage by 30 percent (3,000/100 = 30). If you now get 30 miles to the gallon (30 × .30 = 9 mpg), you will probably get about 21 mpg (30 - 9 = 21). Your mileage may vary.

How much fuel will your rental truck need to get there? Ask the rental agent approximately how many miles per gallon the truck gets, loaded. Assume they are optimistic and subtract a couple of miles per gallon. You can then figure your estimated fuel cost of the truck as you did for your car.

Leaving on a Jet Plane

If everything from the house, including your car, is being moved on a moving company van, you and the family might opt to fly or take a bus or train to the new town. Flying makes a quick transition, while the train or bus will allow the family to get a real sense of change.

If you know well enough in advance, you may be able to take advantage of special airline discounts such as kids-fly-free, advance-purchase fares, or other promotions to help keep your travel costs down.

Making Your Move

For information on Amtrak train routes and schedules, call 800/USA-RAIL or visit them on the Internet at **http://www.amtrak.com**.

Gorging and Snoring

Longer moves require overnight lodging along the way. You can budget as little as $40 or $50 per night, or you may spend upwards of $200 per night. If you own a tent, you can camp along the way for just a few bucks a night. If you know your route and schedule, make reservations ahead of time.

Has eating become a habit? Set a food budget for your trip. You already have a good idea what your family likes to eat. Do you all need three full meals per day? Can you make a breakfast of granola bars and fruit? Carry a cooler or ice chest filled with snacks, breakfast, and lunch foods, and stop for one full meal per day. Or you can eat a big, late lunch (usually cheaper than dinner menus) and finish the day with lighter fare such as a salad.

To estimate your food costs for the move, decide how you will eat, determine approximately what it will cost per day, and multiply that by the number of days you will be on the road.

Fun, Fun, Fun!

While they are not tax deductible, you may decide to add a fun category to your moving budget. Everyone in the family has worked hard to get ready for the move. They've earned a reward.

Moving Violations

For our 1985 move, we decided to drive one of our two cars from Oregon to Iowa while the moving van made its own way. But the better of our two cars was a 1949 Plymouth I was restoring. There we were—two adults, three pre-teens, two dogs, a cat, and a guinea pig—halfway across the country in a 36-year-old vehicle. I thought it was a blast—but my family has yet to forgive me.

Want some real fun? Stop along the way to visit relatives. If you'd prefer, you can spend a day at Six Flags over Somethingorother. Or take a few hours to drive through a national park. Or visit the Smithsonian or Gettysburg.

Our family's 2000-mile trip took five days to drive and gave all of us an invaluable look at our country.

Get a book on national parks and check entrance fees. Call toll-free numbers for major attractions along the way. What's the price of a one-day pass to Disney World? What's the cost of a few hours at an attraction in a city on your travel route? Many cities offer sightseeing tours by bus at a reasonable cost. Or you can see the downtown area in a horse-drawn carriage. Look around. There's something fun to do almost everywhere.

And remember, you can do lots of fun things for free. Most parks are free. Lots of small museums ask only for a donation. Short side trips to see country lanes, fall colors, or spectacular waterfalls cost only a little fuel. During the summer months, many towns along your path may be holding festivals, which offer interesting things to do and a variety of foods to try.

You all deserve a little fun in between the work of moving out and the work of moving in.

The Least You Need to Know

➤ Rules of thumb and mover's estimates will help you figure the amount of truck space you'll need for your move.

➤ Carefully plan your moving route, whether you're driving the truck or riding in the back seat of your limo.

➤ Estimate the cost of your move by adding up labor, materials, transportation, and incidental costs.

➤ Plan to have some fun along the way, no matter what your moving budget!

Chapter 4

Time to Move: Planning Your Moving Schedule

In This Chapter

➤ Organizing your move with a moving calendar

➤ Putting it all down in your Smart Moving Notebook

➤ Countdown to moving day checklist

"Grab the beer and the kid, hon. The sheriff's on the way and he's got a warrant for Junior's arrest!"

Some moves include advance notice—and others don't. In either case, this chapter will help you plan for the actual, the inevitable, or the unforeseen move.

If you have a Smart Moving Notebook, keep it nearby. If you don't have one yet, I'm going to pester you until you do.

How Much Time Do You Have?

"Lessee, there's the stuff stored in Ma's chicken coop, the stuff Uncle Chester borrowed and never returned, and the stuff in the back of the pickup. Okay, inventory's done!"

Do you have enough time to sort and give away or pack all that stuff? You'll soon find out as you decide what to move and what to donate to the recycling center.

The ideal move includes not only someone else to do the work for you, but also lots of time. The two usually don't occur together. You may have a moving company to do the work, but with only ten days notice, or you may have a couple months notice, but have to do it all yourself.

The amount of time you have before you move makes quite a difference in how you plan it.

Yesterday

"The boss says we have to move to Cedar Rapids this afternoon!"

Not much planning time here!

I am hopeful that you saw the change coming and began making notes in your Smart Moving Notebook. If not, read "The Least You Need to Know" information at the end of each chapter in this book and start packing now!

Next Week

"Got the job! It starts in two weeks but it's 500 miles away. We have to move next week!"

How much planning time you have somewhat depends on whether you're moving yourself or being moved. Also, who is hiring the mover: you or a relocation service?

The best way to plan for a "next week" move is to review this chapter, writing needed steps in your Smart Moving Notebook depending on who's in charge of your move. For example, if you or a spouse is managing a do-it-yourself move, you should estimate, select a truck, start packing, gather the crew, and go. If a relocation service is handling the move, you still have lots to do: prepare, sort and make an inventory, notify, travel, and move in.

This chapter covers all of these steps.

Next Month

Okay, we have a little breathing room here—but just a little. You can still save some time and energy by moving smart. You may even have time for a garage sale or a few trips to a charity clothing store.

Where to start?

Scan the list and suggestions in this chapter, noting those that apply to your situation and schedule. The list is for an ideal move where there's lots of time for preparation. You may wind up spending evenings and weekends "on the move" instead of at a leisurely pace. But your smart planning will make a smart move.

Stay tuned for some good news!

Next Season

Some folks get plenty of advance notice for their move. A relocation may start at the beginning of the new fiscal year. A government or military move may be known well in advance. A move into retirement may be planned months or even years in advance of the actual date.

Don't let the long-term deadline encourage you to procrastinate. Start planning your move right now. Doing so will give you confidence and reduce the worry factor for your upcoming move.

Keep reading!

Who Knows?

In some cases, folks know for certain that they will be moving, but aren't sure of when. It may be next week, next month, or even next year. This situation can be frustrating. Should I pack everything in marked boxes and unpack if I need something? Should I get a quote from a moving company, knowing that rates will probably change by the time I actually move?

The answer depends on many factors including who will do the actual moving of your household goods: a van line, a rental truck, or your Uncle Harry. Based on your decision, you can develop a chronological list of things to do toward your move. You then work through the list, completing tasks that you think you probably won't have to undo—or unpack. For example, let the mover know that you need an estimate now and an update when you're actually ready to move—whenever that is.

> **Moving Words**
> A moving agent's *estimate* of the cost of moving your goods is based on weight, mileage, and service requirements (up a flight of stairs, and so on).

Smart movers don't have to live out of boxes!

Your Moving Calendar

There's so much to do and so little time.

You might feel overwhelmed as you begin planning your move. But once you know what needs to be done (based on the type and distance of your move), planning becomes much easier.

A moving calendar will really help reduce stress. Sketch out a rough moving calendar in your Smart Moving Notebook. Or use a wall or desk calendar. Or get one from a moving company or a truck rental outfit. The important thing is to get a clear image of the tasks that need to be completed and an idea of timing. As moving day moves closer you can fill in more details and begin to cross off completed tasks.

Use a calendar or your Smart Moving Notebook to start planning now.

Where to start?

Start your moving calendar with moving day and plan backward, allowing ample time to complete each task. No task is too small to list. Your calendar should include everything from "decide on a moving company" to "notify milkman to stop delivery" to "get Fido's shots up-to-date" and "return the library books."

Moving is a group effort, so get the whole family involved in creating the calendar and in completing the scheduled tasks. After something is written on the calendar, you can forget worrying about it and know that it will be remembered and done at the proper time.

The Best Moving Calendar

So what kind of calendar should you use to keep track of your moving project? A Garfield calendar? Dilbert? Miss Spare Parts? Hunks of Holland?

Whatever works!

For example, we have used a 24" × 36" 60-day organizer plastic-coated wall calendar. It has 2" × 3" day boxes that cover two months of planning—lots of room to write things. Erasure is easy. And you can see the whole moving project at one time. These calendars cost $10 to $15 at larger stationery stores. Other sizes are available and will fit most moving schedules.

Or you can use a computer scheduling program, a free calendar from your insurance company, an executive calendar notebook, or a few sheets of paper and a ruler.

An easily accessible moving calendar, for example, enables your family to check information or make notes easily. Moving becomes a group adventure and everyone can participate.

Using a Calendar to Plan the Move

Your moving calendar gives you a place to personalize and prioritize the suggestions in this book. You can use the calendar to make the suggestions specific and timely.

What will you write on your moving calendar? Contacts, deadlines, steps, appointments, reminders, estimates, costs, and other useful info.

Keeping It Current

"I already did that!"

Make sure you keep your moving calendar up-to-date—especially if more than one person is using it. You don't want to duplicate efforts or overlook something important because someone forgot to update the calendar.

If you are the primary planner, consider using a notebook or other more portable calendar. You can then update the calendar while waiting for the dentist, riding the bus to work, or waiting in a restaurant for your late-great-date.

Your Moving Notebook

Test time!

You were introduced to the Smart Moving Notebook in Chapter 1. If you've been remiss and haven't started it yet, you are forgiven. But don't let it happen again! Start your Smart Moving Notebook right now and begin making notes in it. It will save you many hours of worry.

Use your Smart Moving Notebook to make all kinds of notes about your move as they occur to you. The notebook also can be used as a daily reminder of errands that need to be handled and for lists of people to contact to stop services at your old house and start them at the new house. You can use the notebook to record addresses of people to notify of your move. Add in lists of resources about your new home town, state, or neighborhood. The Smart Moving Notebook will become an invaluable helper in your move.

How to Organize

You can organize your Smart Moving Notebook in many ways. Here are a few suggestions:

➤ By room (living room, dining room, bedroom)

➤ By type of task (packing, cleaning, buying, selling)

➤ By date (page per day, week, month)

➤ By resource (mover, rental agent, employer)

➤ By person (named, with cross-references to tasks or dates)

How to Use

You can use your Smart Moving Notebook in many effective ways. Here are a few suggestions:

➤ Review it at the beginning of each day.

➤ Tape useful business cards to the inside front or back cover.

Moving Words
An *agent* is a local moving company with a franchise from a national moving company. Some are also known as road agents!

➤ Make notes of telephone conversations with moving agents, relocation services, truck rental agents, real estate agents, airlines, travel services, and others involved in your move.

➤ Use your spare time to review your moving process.

➤ Make reminders as they occur to you: shots for pets, contact new DMV on arrival, visit Waldo World.

➤ List moving expenses, as well as how and when they need to be paid.

➤ Write down questions for your new employer, new supervisor, new landlord, and new psychiatrist.

Start planning how and when you will be packing.

Countdown to Moving Day

Many tasks are involved in the moving process, depending on who, what, where, and how. So the remainder of this chapter outlines a plan for making a smart move. To make the process easier, check off any [ ] that you feel apply to your move. The tasks are listed in approximate order of a typical move with a typical timetable. Because no move is "typical," your list will be differ somewhat. And you'll add many more things to the list as you decide how, when, and where you're moving.

Two Months Before Moving Day

Let's get started.

[ ] Secure a new place to live.

[ ] Get dental checkup and cleaning; see doctor, vet, and other professionals so that you don't have to make these visits immediately after the move.

[ ] If necessary, make arrangements for storage.

[ ] Ask doctors and other professionals for referrals.

[ ] Have antiques, art objects, and other valuables appraised.

[ ] Start cleaning out closets and drawers.

[ ] Start using foods and cleaning supplies that cannot be moved.

[ ] If you will be using a professional mover, start getting estimates from at least four agents in your area.

[ ] If you are moving yourself, get costs from at least two truck rental companies, and reserve a rental truck, especially if you plan to move during peak times.

[ ] Pick up any available literature, moving tips, and worksheets from moving agents and truck rental agents.

[ ] Sketch out a floor plan of your new home for furniture and appliance placement.

[ ] Stop by the local post office and pick up a set of change-of-address cards.

[ ] Subscribe to the newspaper in your new home town.

[ ] Order address labels with your new address.

[ ] Make an inventory of your household goods and begin to de-clutter, starting with the basement, attic, garage, and other storage areas.

[ ] Start a file of all your moving paperwork (estimates, receipts, contacts, floor plans).

[ ] Arrange to transfer school records as needed.

[ ] After you have the information you need, choose a mover or a relocation service.

One Month Before Moving Day

[ ] Contact phone, power, and other utilities for service disconnection at your old home and connection at your new home.

[ ] Empty a room, the garage, or another area to use as a staging area.

[ ] Arrange for the cleaning, painting, and preparation of your new home before your arrival, as needed.

Making Your Move
Arrange for utilities to be disconnected the day after you leave and connected the day before you arrive. If you're a day early arriving at your new home, it will be ready.

[ ] If you are packing yourself, obtain packing materials and start packing items you won't need until after you arrive at the new house.

[ ] Arrange for special transportation of your pets, plants, and fragile or valuable items, if necessary.

[ ] Call your insurance agent to see how your possessions are covered during transit.

[ ] Make any travel plans necessary for your move.

[ ] Set a date and start planning for your moving sale (see Chapter 8).

Three Weeks Before Moving Day

[ ] Find out about auto registration at your new location.

[ ] If you are moving in or out of an apartment, arrange for use of the elevator.

[ ] Find new homes for plants and pets that will not be moved.

[ ] Make child care arrangements for moving day.

[ ] Dispose of items that cannot be moved, such as inflammable liquids.

[ ] Have your moving sale.

[ ] Call local charities for pickup of unwanted items, making sure you get a donation receipt for taxes.

Two Weeks Before Moving Day

[ ] Service your car in preparation for the move.

[ ] Cancel current newspaper delivery.

[ ] Notify creditors of your new address.

[ ] Make sure you have an adequate supply of medications and that they are with you as you travel.

[ ] Return library books and other borrowed items.

[ ] Retrieve any loaned items.

[ ] Transfer prescriptions and medical records as needed.

[ ] Start collecting a file folder of information to leave for the new owner of your home, such as appliance manuals.

One Week Before Moving Day

[ ] If you are moving yourself, finish up the packing.

[ ] Take animals to vet for immunizations, if necessary.

[ ] Drain power equipment of oil and gas.

[ ] Drain all water hoses.

[ ] Check and close your safety deposit box.

[ ] Transfer your bank accounts.

[ ] Settle any bills with local businesses.

[ ] Confirm any travel reservations.

[ ] If using movers, stand by to answer questions while movers pack your belongings.

[ ] Disconnect and prepare major appliances for move.

[ ] Set aside anything that will travel in your car so that it will not be loaded on the truck.

[ ] Pack a box of items that will be needed first at the new house.

[ ] Get cash or travelers checks for the trip and to pay the movers.

[ ] Confirm arrival time of your moving van.

[ ] If moving yourself, dismantle beds and other large furniture as needed.

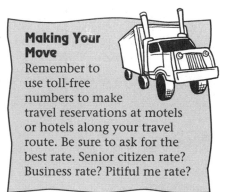

Making Your Move
Remember to use toll-free numbers to make travel reservations at motels or hotels along your travel route. Be sure to ask for the best rate. Senior citizen rate? Business rate? Pitiful me rate?

Moving Violations
Be ready to pay the mover for your shipment as agreed, often *in cash*, upon delivery. If you don't, the shipper can hold your shipment and charge storage fees.

The Day Before Moving Day

[ ] Drain your water bed.

[ ] Defrost refrigerator and freezer, and then prop the doors open.

[ ] Have your landlord or building superintendent look at your place to determine if some or all of the cleaning deposit can be refunded.

Moving-Out Day

[ ] If using movers, be sure someone is at the house to answer questions.

[ ] If using movers, read your bill of lading and inventory carefully before signing. Keep this paperwork in a safe place.

[ ] Write down all utility meter readings.

[ ] Load 'em up and head 'em out!

Moving-In Day

[ ] Load 'em out and head 'em up!

[ ] Supervise unloading and unpacking.

[ ] Check your belongings carefully and note on the inventory any damaged or missing items.

[ ] On an interstate move, you must pay the driver before your possessions are unloaded.

[ ] Be ready to pay your mover with cash, a certified check, or traveler's checks unless other arrangements have been made in advance.

The Least You Need to Know

➤ You can make a smart move no matter how much time you have to plan—but the more time the better.

➤ Your Smart Moving Notebook and Moving Calendar will help you organize your move efficiently.

➤ Encourage others in your entourage to help plan a smart move.

Chapter 5

Moving Moments: Making the Emotional Move

Moving can be tough on a person's psyche. Besides all the physical stuff, you may be saying good-bye to friends and family, neighbors, and even the paperboy whom you finally trained to hit the porch. It's not so much that change is taking place, but that so many changes are happening all at once. No wonder you can't sleep at night.

Here are some of the emotional factors that can go along with a move:

➤ Changing jobs

➤ Changing schools

➤ Changing church and organizational affiliations

➤ Changing recreation settings

➤ Changing social activities

➤ Changing work hours or conditions

➤ Changing proximity to friends and family

➤ Changing finances

➤ Changing languages

➤ Retirement

➤ Divorce

➤ Death of a family member

➤ A new mortgage

➤ Leaving pets behind

➤ Need I go on?

Change is good—but moving can be overload!

This chapter offers dozens of proven methods for facing, surviving, and even enjoying the emotional side of moving. No, moving won't replace a hobby—but at least this chapter will help you grow out your fingernails.

Fortunately, Dr. Dan can help you sort through the issues and resolve your conflicts—or at least help you feel warm and fuzzy again. Keep reading!

Making Your Move

There must be lots of good things to remember about where you are. Okay, maybe just a couple. Treasure them. They will become a part of your new reality. If you ever return to "the old place," it will have changed and become a part of someone else's life. So use your Smart Moving Notebook to list the good memories you want to treasure: the kids' tree swing, the backyard picnics, the view, the nice neighbors (who moved away first).

Cherish the good memories.

Controlling Chaos

Have you ever wished you could start over? Maybe you want to dye your hair or wear a hat until the plugs grow in, without all your friends' sarcastic comments. Or maybe you plan to clear up your bills and never get into debt again once your house is sold. Or you want a good excuse to get rid of that living room furniture that Grandma Beatrice willed you.

Here's your chance!

A move can be an excellent time to get rid of old furniture, clothing, habits, emotions, and even attitudes. Take advantage of it. And offer the same opportunity to those who will be moving with you. Discussions over dinner or at family meetings can start everyone thinking about what to keep and what to get rid of. Adopt the attitude that you're not just moving, you're moving on.

For example, maybe you have a teenager who wants a new start at making better friends. Or maybe you or your spouse want to get more involved in sports, recreation, civic activities, or other pastimes.

Again, here's your chance!

A move isn't an ending as much as it is a beginning.

Don't Give the Boogeyman Your New Address

Here's your chance to leave behind any bad memories: a divorce, a death, a bankruptcy, a bad job experience. Plan to leave them all at the city limits as you go.

Give yourself and your life a fresh start.

Moving a family from here to there involves many emotions—and lots of stuff.

Chin Up!—The Positive Side of Moving

If you look, you and every member of your household—even the one least happy about moving—can find a number of benefits to moving.

Moving can offer a new start, an adventure, an avenue to new friends, hobbies, and interests, and a learning experience.

It's all in the attitude.

Here are some positive things to consider about moving:

➤ New friends

➤ New opportunities

➤ New experiences

➤ New stores for shopping

➤ New neighbors

➤ New places to go on the weekend

Anticipating the good things about your move can help you reduce the stress and soothe the emotions.

Turning Your Move into a Vacation

Moving is an adventure. With a little luck, your new house won't soon be called the Temple of Doom!

Even if you are simply moving to a new house within the same town or neighborhood, you can make the moving experience an adventure. There will be a new home, yard, or maybe even acreage to explore, get to know, and make your own.

Try this: Spend some time in the empty house before anything is unloaded from the truck. Wander through the house. Search for each room's personality. Get everyone's ideas and suggestions, discounting none of them. You may be surprised at all the ideas that emerge! Most will probably never materialize, but even if just one or two become a family goal, you will be well on the way to making the new house your home.

Life is still an adventure.

You can relieve some of the emotional apprehension of the move by visiting the new town before the actual move.

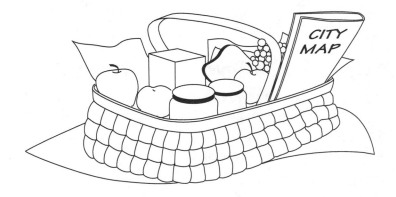

We're Off to See the Wizard!

There will be many new things to see and do in your new location. Finding them can help you reduce the anxiety of your decision to move—even if the decision was forced.

Make the trip to your new home a mini-vacation—even if it's across town. Here are some ideas:

➤ Take the scenic route to your new town.

➤ Ask the others in your wagon train where they want to stop along the way.

➤ Plan a picnic at a state or national park.

➤ Stop at a lake on the way and rent a canoe for a couple hours.

➤ Go horseback riding for an hour.

➤ Visit a science museum in your new town.

➤ Visit a local history or art museum.

➤ Whether driving, flying, or training, try some food you have never tried before.

Making Your Move
You just never know where you'll find some fun. On one move, we discovered a fantastic clock museum in Spillville, Iowa, and an interesting Norwegian museum in Decorah, Iowa. We discovered both through a regional brochure picked up in a restaurant along the way.

The longer the distance, the better the chance of finding fun activities along the way. If possible, leave an extra day—or at least a few hours—for exploring. Ask the locals where they take out-of-town guests. Slip off the Interstate highway for awhile and drive an older state highway that wanders through small towns.

Learn things about the area you're going to or through and its history. Then let the kids be Plains Indians, or Lewis and Clark, or astronauts on the way to lift-off.

Even if you're flying to your new home, you can probably schedule a layover somewhere interesting en route. For example, flying coast to coast, schedule a plane change in Denver, Minneapolis, or Dallas. Come in one day and fly out the next, using the evening and morning to see the sights.

If you have teenagers traveling with you...pray for guidance. In addition, consider letting them plan your itinerary. Really! You may find that their ideas will give you a fresh look at your trip—and help them feel more in control of the process. Give them some cash to spend along the way.

I Hope Uncle Clarence Keeps His Teeth In

Sometimes there are friends or relatives living along your path who you want to visit. Or maybe other family members have friends who have moved away that they want to see again.

In addition to giving you a chance to see relatives and friends, you can save some money on motel bills!

Even if you're flying, you can plan to visit with friends and relatives at the airport during layovers.

Saying Good-Bye to People and Places

No doubt about it: Moving is a time of saying good-bye.

Psychologists tell us that neglecting to say good-bye to the old home, friends, and town can leave an emotional gap. Saying good-bye can help bridge the gap and speed the process of settling happily into your new home.

So start making lists in your Smart Moving Notebook of people and things you want to say good-bye to before you move. Encourage others in your entourage to do the same.

Let's Do Lunch

The hardest good-byes are those to the important people in your life who will not be nearby after your move. How can you say these farewells before you're swamped with work and buried in the confusion of packing?

➤ Have lunch with old friends and co-workers during the few weeks before your move.

➤ Plan to have a backyard barbecue for the neighbors a month before you leave.

➤ Host a family potluck get-together.

➤ Take cookies and say good-bye at a meeting of your church group, civic organizations, and youth sports teams.

Going Away Parties

Moving is a good excuse for a party!

Maybe you should plan a party for the others in your moving group. Here are a few party ideas:

➤ Young children may want to take cupcakes, cookies, or fruit and vegetable snacks to school, day care, or a play group.

➤ Pre-teens or teens may want to plan their own weekend evening going-away party.

➤ Teens may prefer treating friends to a day at a nearby amusement park.

➤ Plan on buying pizza and pop for co-workers' lunch.

Saying Good-bye to the Old Pad

Some homes (houses, apartments, condominiums, lean-tos) can be easy to bid adieu. Others can be more difficult. And some family members have better memories about a house than others.

So how can you say good-bye to This Old House?

The best way is to give folks a chance to talk, remember, and share memories of the house. For some groups, a family meeting is best. For others, a one-on-one good-bye is better. And for some, it's "good riddance!"

Memories are transportable. And new ones will be custom-made at your new home.

Save Thousands of Words: Pictures and Videos

Photos can keep good memories alive. Make sure you have or get pictures of friends, family, the old house and neighborhood, and favorite spots around town. If you don't already have them, dust off (or borrow) a camera or camcorder and get moving. Take a couple rolls or a whole videotape. Put the photos in an album.

Here are a few photo opportunities:

➤ Flowers and plants in your yard

➤ Your favorite restaurant

➤ Children's schools, friends, and hangouts

➤ Your workplace

➤ Your church, synagogue, temple, or meeting hall

➤ Your neighborhood

➤ Pets you're leaving behind with friends or new families

➤ Your old boss without his toupee

Buck & Back Savers

Ask your photo processor if digital prints are available. If so, your photos will be copied to a diskette. You can then use software to attach photos to your electronic mail messages to friends back home.

Telling children about the move can be difficult, so tailor your talk to the needs of each child.

Good Counsel

Sometimes we need some help—a good listener—to get us through the stresses of life. And moving is at the top of the stress list. Talk with a professional counselor, pastor, rabbi, priest, mental health expert, or good friend about your emotions during the moving process. Another person can often offer a fresh perspective and sound advice. A good listener can also let you voice your feelings and sort out your emotions for yourself.

Buck & Back Savers

A nervous breakdown is expensive. If your move is too stressful on you or others, consider hiring more of the work done now rather than later paying a shrink to deal with the emotional consequences.

Keeping in Touch

You're not going off to Alpha Centauri or another galaxy! Keep in touch with friends, relatives, and other important folks in your life. In this highly mobile society, you'll probably see—or at least hear from—many of them again.

Or are you offering no forwarding address?

One Ringy-Dingy: Phone Options

Want friends to call you more? Call your long-distance telephone service about getting a personal toll-free number. Then give your number to folks who you'd like to call you.

Want to call friends more? Contact your long-distance telephone service about special rates at certain times or to specific area codes. You may find a package that lets you call nearly as frequently as before your move.

If you're making an international move, remember that your telephone number will be longer. Contact your long distance telephone service about how the folks back home can easily dial your new number in Djakarta. And remember to let your friends know when to call—or you may be awakened in the middle of the night by a caller who's having lunch.

Of course, you can call them back during your lunchtime!

"I Promise to Write!" Right!

"Write if you get work!"

People don't write letters as often as they used to—or as often as they promise to. How can you help them write to you more? Buy them stationery, postcards, and even stamps. It's a moderately subtle way of saying: WRITE TO ME!

And you can encourage correspondence by buying postcards from your new town and sending them to your friends and relatives back home. Set aside a time on Sunday evenings, for example, to correspond with people. Make it a family event and get the kids into the habit of writing their friends as well. The letters don't have to be lengthy. A note or even a postcard will be appreciated by those who want to stay in your life.

me@lonesome.com: Electronic Options

What was the world like before e-mail? Some retort, "a lot better off!" Others ponder, "I don't know how we got along without it!" Many folks respond, "so what's e-mail?"

E-mail is electronic mail, messages sent electronically using the Internet or other computerized delivery services. Businesses rely on e-mail as an important method of communicating quickly and easily. Many individuals are learning the same. In fact, e-mail may be reviving the dying art of letter writing.

If you're already an e-mail user, you know how it's done. Gather the e-mail addresses of your friends and relatives so that you can keep in touch when you move. If you have a computer and modem but know nothing about e-mail, talk to someone at a local computer shop about finding an Internet provider (ISP) and setting up an e-mail account.

The Least You Need to Know

➤ Moving is an emotional stress as well as a physical one. It's also an opportunity to clean house in your life, get rid of things and habits you don't want, and replace them with ones you do.

➤ Memories are transportable, and actually improve with distance.

➤ "Good-bye" can mean "see you later." There are many ways of staying in touch.

Part 2
Making Moving Decisions

Aaarrgh!

Decisions, decisions!

Should I turn down the job offer from Bora-Bora?

How am I ever going to move all that junk in the garage?

Grandma doesn't want to move with us. Should we tie her up or sedate her?

Should we move our home-based business and maybe lose customers?

Should we move before the baby is due?

Planning a move can go on forever. It's now time for decisions. And making smart decisions is the key to smart moving.

What kinds of decisions?

➤ *How much of the move to do yourself and how much to hire someone else to do.*

➤ *How to find and use the best moving resources and not regret your decision.*

➤ *What to keep and what to get rid of.*

That's what the second part of this book is about: making smart decisions. And making them easier.

So quit biting your nails!

POKE POKE

Chapter 6

It's Your Move: Putting Off Procrastination

In This Chapter

➤ Deciding how much you can do yourself

➤ Solving moving problems

➤ Deciding what goes and what stays

➤ Dealing with second thoughts about moving

➤ Helping others involved in the move make moving decisions

"I've thought about moving, but I just can't bring myself to a decision."

"I know we can't afford it, but I just don't want to mess with the hassle of moving. Call a mover."

"We have so much junk in the garage that I'd rather stay here than try to move it."

"Let's move. No, let's not. Alright, so we're moving, right?"

Making the decision to move may be the most difficult part of moving. Or so it seems. In fact, there are many good reasons—and a few lame ones—for not making a move when logic says otherwise.

This chapter walks you through those reasons to stay put and, if possible, helps you overcome them. The chapter can also help you handle second thoughts about your move.

The key to making a smart decision about moving is seeing problems as challenges and solutions as opportunities.

Challenges and Opportunities (Translation: Problems and Solutions)

To decide how much of the job to do yourself, you need to make choices based on what you learned in Part 1.

➤ Where are you going?

➤ How much will it probably cost?

➤ Who's going to pay for it?

➤ What's the limit of your moving budget?

➤ What's your moving schedule?

➤ What special moving problems will you have to solve (disabilities, health, children, business)

➤ How much of the physical work of moving can you and your crew do?

Each of these so-called problems is really a challenge that can be overcome. The solutions are opportunities. For example, the challenge of moving on a limited budget offers the opportunity of traveling by car rather than airplane. Moving an elderly member of your family becomes an opportunity to participate in their life and make some good memories for everyone. Moving with physical limitations becomes an opportunity to let others help you.

It's How Many Miles?

Sometimes the most difficult obstacle to overcome in a moving decision involves perceptions. That is, making a 1,000-mile move can sometimes seem to require travel through outer space.

For our foreparents, of course, a 1,000-mile move was a once-in-a-lifetime relocation for only the bravest of complete idiots. But today, the trip is just a couple hours by plane or a couple days by car or van. It's not really the end of the world. In fact, you'll find that CNN's *Headline News* and *I Love Lucy* reruns got there before you. Life in today's electronic age isn't really that much different in Texarkana than it is in Twisp.

So relax. You'll most likely be able to get Chinese takeout, a Big Gulp, and ESPN where you're moving—even if it's to another country. And that makes the decision to move a little easier. Some of the familiar things in your life are already where you're going!

Is All That Stuff Ours?

Some folks can pack a suitcase or two and be ready to move next door, across the country, or halfway around the world. Others need the largest moving van available—or maybe even a fleet of them. Most of us fall somewhere in between. How much do you have to move? A room full? A house full? A whole farm full? Your decision of how much you do yourself in the move depends somewhat on how much stuff you have to move.

The apprehension of a moving decision can come from the overwhelmingness of it all. There's just so much stuff! What goes and what stays? How do you get rid of it? Should you just walk away and replace it all at the other end?

Moving Words
Items packed by the owner are known in the trade as *PBO*; a.k.a., "pile of broken objects."

These decisions are important in the moving process. Chances are you already have the facts you need to make the decision; trying to come to a firm decision, however, becomes overwhelming.

How can you decide?

Here are some "opportunities" for making a smart move based on the "challenges" of your type of move.

Swing Sets and Sand Boxes

If you're moving a young household:

➤ Get rid of toys no longer used.

➤ Replace that bulky swing set or sand box at your destination rather than move it.

➤ Sell or give away youth beds and get standard beds for your new home.

➤ Give away some of the numerous toaster ovens you got as wedding presents.

➤ Hand down hand-me-down clothing to cousins, neighbor children, or charities.

Old Folks' Home

If you're moving a mature household:

➤ Start emptying your nest now, giving heirlooms to children and other relatives who have the room for them.

➤ Turn your junk into someone else's treasure—hold an estate sale and let them move it.

➤ Go through your stuff asking, "Is there someone I know who can use this more than I?" If so, give it to them.

➤ Rethink what makes you really happy and what is ultimately important in your life.

➤ Plan to make room in your new home for lots of visitors.

I'm Moving Out!

If the membership of your living group is changing (marriage, divorce, death, boarding school, college, felony conviction):

➤ Decide whether to keep or get rid of items that belong(ed) to others.

➤ If necessary, ask for help with the physical and emotional aspects of splitting the sheets or reviewing the memories.

➤ Relax and try to find some good things about the situation.

Cottage Companies

If you have a home-based business or a second office in your house:

➤ Review your business objectives to decide whether they should be continued, modified, or eliminated with your move.

➤ Decide how you want to change your business' communication system as it is moved: more phone lines, a fax machine, call waiting.

➤ If you have an inventory, consider renting a separate location for it near your new home.

➤ If you have a bulky desk, consider selling it here and getting a new one there.

No, You Decide!

Decisions are tough to make, and making them is harder for some folks than for others. But they still have to be made. How?

First, remember that few decisions are irreversible. You moved away—you can move back. You got rid of a bedroom set—you can buy another. You took a new path that was difficult—it may be easier than the one you were on. Reversing a decision may be difficult, but it usually isn't impossible. And it probably doesn't signify the end of the world.

Of course, you don't want to reverse decisions—you want to benefit from them. And the key, of course, is making the best decision you can based on the information you have. It will probably be the right one.

Baseball fans know that nobody bats 100% (1,000). In fact, anything over 30% (.300) will get you a multimillion dollar contract. Don't expect all your decisions to be home runs. Sometimes, just getting to first base is quite an accomplishment.

Here are some useful tips on making good decisions.

What Ifs

One way to develop a number of good moving options is to play "what if..."

➤ "What if we leave most of the large household goods in a storage unit here and rent furniture until we are sure we will stay?"

➤ "What if I offer to repay the moving expenses if I leave the job in the first year?"

➤ "What if I take an apartment near my new job and plan to move the family out in six months?"

➤ "What if we keep a summer retirement home here and a winter home there?"

➤ "What if we just call a freelance arsonist!"

Coming up with a variety of moving options is a good first step in making a good decision.

Buck & Back Savers

If you move to a new job, your moving expenses may be deductible on your income taxes. Talk with your tax advisor, review IRS publication 521, and keep good records of your moving expenses. Which ones are deductible? Refer to the Appendix B, "Deductible Moving Expenses," for more information.

Smart Moving Advice

Most free advice is worth what you pay for it—but some is invaluable. The best advice to consider is that from people who have experience rather than just opinions. If you're considering a move to Nebraska, for example, ask around your family and friends for people who have made the move. The same goes for empty-nesters who have become snow birds, executives who have made international moves, and young couples who are moving away from family and friends.

➤ Would they do it again? Why?

➤ What would they change about the move?

➤ Which mover would they use?

➤ How have they handled some of the challenges of the move?

➤ Are they divorced yet?

You certainly don't have to take all the free advice you get from experienced smart movers, but you can use the most valuable tips in your own decisions.

Decisional Elasticity

One of the greatest tools in the decision to move is an eraser.

"Nope, scratch that idea!"

"A house is too expensive to rent, so let's consider leasing a condo."

"Come to find out, the job only lasted two months! Time to move again."

If you believe that

1. Most decisions are reversible

2. Free advice can sometimes be invaluable, and

3. The more ideas you have, the better the ultimate decision will be,

You must also believe in flexibility. If you only have one option, losing it means that your bag of options is now empty. But if you're resourceful, you will have considered the many factors, found good advice, and come up with lots of good options. One less option doesn't mean the move is canceled—especially if you stay flexible:

"I'm glad the lease fell through because we may now be able to buy a home."

Second, Third, and Fourth Thoughts

Having second thoughts about moving away from family, friends, and your favorite yogurt bar?

Those thoughts are natural. Most people have second thoughts about significant decisions. And moving certainly qualifies as significant.

So what can you do about second thoughts? First, don't ignore them. They are usually legitimate points that you may or may not have considered in the decision process. If not, do so now. If you have already considered them, ignore them—now and in the future.

Most second thoughts are borne of our own insecurities. We've made good decisions in the past. Why do we only remember the ones that weren't so good?

Do I look like a $300-an-hour shrink?

Just remember that second thoughts can serve a purpose of reminding you why you made your decisions in the first place. Once they've served that function, send them packing!

Moving Special People

Sometimes, the decision to move means helping others make decisions, or making decisions on their behalf.

Children can *participate* in the decision to move, but they typically don't *make* the decision (see Chapter 19). Elderly relatives, too, may need to be active in the decision but not able to make it. Or they are quite capable of making the decision, but not executing it alone. People with disabilities may be willing, but not physically able, to make the move without help. Each of these situations means more decisions.

You can help. By being a smart mover you can help others with the important decisions in moving. You can offer ideas, present options, perform tasks, and make contacts. You can help others feel in control of their lives while maintaining their self-dignity.

Moving the Disabled

Thousands of people live nearly normal lives despite disabilities. And many of them are on the move. Some are limited in what they can physically do during a move. Others have mental or emotional challenges. Nearly all with disabilities can participate in the moving process. Talk early in the decision process with social workers, therapists, doctors, or other professionals who are involved in care.

If you're using a moving service, let them know of the special needs that must be considered. Many movers are familiar with the needs of the disabled and will be able to help plan a move that requires the least disturbance and discomfort for the disabled person. They can better do their job without obstructing wheelchair access or disrupting important routines. They also can help you make sure that special equipment is moved and set up with the least hassle.

Your decision to move with a disabled person should also include seeking services at your new location. Professionals and support groups can help you get settled and make the transition easier for the disabled person.

Mobile Rockers: Moving the Elderly

Many of today's families are multigenerational. Mom and/or dad live in the family home or nearby. Moving the family means moving elderly members as well.

If the elderly are part of your moving decision, help them participate in that decision—or let them make that decision on their own. Bodies and minds don't always mature at the same time. Nor do they decline cooperatively. An 80-year-old person with many physical limitations may have a sharp mind that can make important decisions as well or better than younger folks.

Life is dignity.

For more information on moving with the elderly, contact one of the following organizations:

American Association of Retired Persons
1909 K St.
Washington, D.C. 20049
tel. 202/872-4700
Web site: **http://www.aarp.org**

National Council of Senior Citizens
925 15th St., NW
Washington, D.C. 20005
tel. 202/347-8800

National Council on Aging
600 Maryland Ave., SW
Washington, D.C. 20024
tel. 202/479-1200

Moving in the Third Trimester

Should a pregnant woman move during the third trimester or wait until after the baby is born? That, of course, is a question for the doctor. However, moderate moves can be made quite late in the pregnancy without problems as long as professional advice is followed about stress, lifting, and travel. In most case, the decision is a personal preference.

Which of these two tasks do I want to complete first: birth or moving?

Avoid doing them simultaneously!

The Least You Need to Know

➤ Deciding how much of the move you do yourself depends on where you're going, who's going with you, how much it will cost, and who's paying for it.

➤ To make good moving decisions, consider all options, get good advice, and be flexible.

➤ Use dignity and common sense to help others make good moving decisions.

Chapter 7

Move It or Lose It: Getting Rid of Stuff

In This Chapter

➤ De-cluttering your move

➤ Having a successful moving sale

➤ What to donate

➤ What to dump

Move it or lose it...that is the question!

"Should we move that old player piano with the bellows missing?"

"Should I move that disassembled 1959 Studebaker or get rid of it here?"

"Will I ever refinish that old bedroom set stored in the attic?"

"Should we move those boxes we haven't unpacked since our last move?"

These can be tough questions for those on the move. On the one hand is Ramsey's Rule of Mass: Everything you get rid of now is something you won't have to move yourself or pay to have moved. But, on the other hand, "I might need it someday."

So how often can you make the tough decision between move it or lose it? A thousand times? Without lots of regrets?

This chapter is all about how to efficiently decide what gets moved and what to do with what doesn't.

De-cluttering Your Move: Treasures or Trash?

Where did all this junk come from?

The Junk Fairy!

Yes, there is really a being who travels house-to-house late at night distributing other people's junk to unsuspecting and otherwise neat folks. That's why attics bulge, garages have no room for cars, and storage unit rental is big business. The Junk Fairy is busily at work! (Kind of a demented Santa!)

What can you do to combat the Junk Fairy?

You can start today to de-clutter your home, apartment, or other abode. If you have plenty of time before your move, begin to de-clutter your home as soon as you even think about moving. The longer you have lived in your current home, the more important this step.

Making Your Move

Get out! As the moving date draws near, reduce stress by regularly taking a break from the confusion and activity. Take an hour a day for yourself. Use it to exercise, go out for lunch, read a good book, or relax with a friend.

A few years ago, our family was stuck in a location it wanted to leave. Winters were too cold, summers too humid, and family too far. So we decided to make the move back "home" in the next year. The problem was that, in our five years in the middle of nowhere, we had accumulated stuff to keep us occupied. Lots of stuff. And we knew we would have to either move it or lose it.

So we had garage sales and trips to the recycling and donation centers. But we still had lots of just plain old junk that nobody wanted. Trash may be a better term. So we purchased a new 30-gallon trash can and promised to fill it up each week for the next year. That's 1,560 gallons of trash!

Well, maybe we only got rid of 1,000 gallons, but that was 1,000 gallons that we didn't have to move halfway across the country! And, years later, there wasn't one item that we wished we hadn't thrown or given away. We really didn't need it.

So how can you begin de-cluttering? If you are lucky enough to know about your move months in advance, you can begin examining your belongings to determine which are really valuable enough to move. If you have just a short time to prepare, getting rid of at least some of the big extras will simplify your job. Set up your own criteria for what to save, what to send to the dump, what to sell, and what to give away.

Here are some proven tips for de-cluttering:

➤ If you haven't used it or worn it in the past year, will you use or wear it again?

➤ If it needs repair, will you fix it or should it be replaced after the move?

➤ If it costs you $1 a pound to move it, do you really need it or want to move it? (Such as a 120-lb. barbell set that cost you 60 bucks.)

➤ Will that clothing match the climate to which you're moving?

➤ If it hasn't been unpacked since the last time you moved, it's probably time to get rid of it.

If you find parting with anything difficult, invite a friend or relative to give you a hand. Sometimes it's easier to make the decision with someone else asking the question: move it or lose it? But always, the decision is yours. It's valid to keep some things (but not everything!) just because you want to.

Moving just might provide a welcome opportunity to replace some of that old furniture and replenish your wardrobe. Besides, it feels good to de-clutter and simplify.

Everyone can help de-clutter! Every member of your living group (excluding infants, of course) can go through his or her belongings and find lots of items to dispose of. Small children may need help. Give everyone containers to fill with disposables. You should be the arbitrator who finally decides what is bound for the dump and what might sell at your moving sale.

Where to start? Start with the attic and the basement (if you have them). Go through every drawer and every closet in every room. Consider each piece of furniture and every appliance. Do you plan to have another baby or is it time to sell or give away the stroller, high chair, crib, swing and car seat? Have you ever used that fondue pot Grandma Florence sent you last Christmas (because somebody gave it to her ten years ago and she's since moved)?

What about the kids? Give away or sell toys that are not used. Ask the child if he or she would like to share the toy with a child who doesn't have any. Offer a child one new special toy at the other end of the move. You may save enough on moving costs to pay for it.

So-called "empty nest" couples often need another step in the moving process: notifying the young adults that they must remove their belongings from the old family home. Somehow, when young adults leave the nest, they leave many things behind for mom and dad to store. The family garage becomes a U-Store-It unit.

Give them a deadline! If it isn't gone by that deadline, you will dispose of it as you see fit.

Making Your Move

If your move is within a month or two, take some time now to prepare and freeze several meals to serve during the last couple weeks before moving. You're going to get tired of take-out! Casseroles and other one-dish meals are good choices and easy to prepare. Just add a packaged green salad, bread, and fresh fruit for dessert for an easy and satisfying meal.

Unlike the Junk Fairy, de-cluttering doesn't happen overnight. Consider getting rid of things in stages. Go through once, then again later if possible.

Of course, if your move is just across town, your de-cluttering will probably be simpler than if you're moving from one coast to another—or across an ocean.

Another tip for de-cluttering: Use photos or a video of your new home (if selected) to decide now what will probably fit and what probably won't. If possible, decide who will get each bedroom and how storage will be used.

And don't forget to use a 25-foot or longer tape measure to help you figure what fits.

If your move is temporary, especially out of the country, consider putting some items in storage. It's more expensive than getting rid of them, but less expensive than moving them.

Tossing Stuff for Fun and Profit

Sometimes the most merciful thing you can do with extraneous possessions is to throw them away before they breed.

You can become a source for the Junk Fairy!

But how can you decide when to throw something away as opposed to giving it away or selling it? Here are some guidelines:

➤ Is it broken? If so, do you have a clue of how to fix it?

➤ Is it outdated—but not enough to be a collectible?

➤ Did it ever do what you bought it for?

➤ How many do you have?

➤ How many do you need?

➤ Will someone else get any use out of it? Really?

Donations Gladly Accepted

Most of us have so many things that fall into the category of too-good-to-toss-but-not-good-enough-to-move. You know you should really give it away—but you just can't bring yourself to do so.

So how can you decide what to give away? Ask yourself: Would someone else really get use or enjoyment from this? If so, give it to them now. If so, but you're not sure who, donate it to a charity that can benefit from finding it a good home. Or plan on having a moving sale.

And who will take all this stuff?

➤ Household items and clothing to Goodwill Industries or St. Vincent de Paul

➤ Books to your local library or school

➤ Clothing to a local shelter, church, or Red Cross center

Maybe Another Complete Idiot Will Buy It

If you've decided that the junk you're not moving has value to others, you must then decide whether to sell or donate it.

Donating it offers a warm fuzzy feeling, but it's not the same as cold hard cash!

For economic reasons (read: you're nearly broke!), you may decide to sell anything that you're not throwing away. We'll cover how to have a successful moving sale in a few pages. Meantime, consider whether your stuff is salable:

➤ Would I buy it (a moot point as you probably already did!)?

➤ Have I seen them for sale somewhere in used condition?

➤ Is there someone who will come in and buy it (books, collectibles, old kitchenware)?

➤ Do I want to mess with selling it?

➤ Will it bring me enough money to pay for the hassle?

Wrapping Your Junk as Gag Gifts

Of course, you may have the world's largest collection of white elephants! Bean-bag door-stoppers. Wine bottles with colored wax-drippings on the outside (and nothing on the inside!). Plastic back-scratchers with Wile E. Coyote handles. Psychedelic lava lamps. The list goes on.

So have a going away party for yourself and give away these unique, one-of-a-kind albino pachyderms. You can wrap them and require each guest to take one home...or you can give them to friends and enemies who you think will best enjoy or hate them.

Heirlooms and Other Junk

There may be a few things that you don't want to sell, give away to strangers, or throw away. You might even consider them heirlooms: things you want family members to have once you've shuffled off this mortal coil.

If there's any of your things that you truly believe that others will like, give these items away now while you can enjoy others enjoying them. The family Bible. Photo albums from when the kids were growing up. Grandpa Bill's pocket watch. The items don't have to be of value to anyone but your family; they have sentimental value. They are gifts from you. And they will help others think of you after you've moved away.

A garage sale cannot only help you move less stuff, but it can also give you more money to do so.

Guide to a Successful Moving Sale

Okay, you've been piling stuff up something like this:

➤ To move

➤ To give away

➤ To throw away

➤ To sell

You're now wondering what to do with that massive mass of stuff to sell.

It's time for a moving sale!

When you are getting ready to move, a moving sale may be an excellent way to pick up some cash while you get rid of stuff you no longer need—or shouldn't have bought in the first place. Most folks hesitate to dispose of never-used, seldom-used, worn out, or even broken or ill-fitting items. Moving offers the perfect excuse to get rid of it all, reduce the work and cost of shipment, and even earn a little cash in the process.

A moving sale is smart moving.

So you probably have a good supply of things to sell, right? It includes everything from clothing to kitchen gadgets to exercise equipment to snow shovels and lawn mowers. As a reality check, remember that anything you do not get rid of has to be packed, loaded, unloaded, unpacked, and placed in your new home.

If you've never held or attended a moving sale, you may be surprised at how many of your unwanted items will find paying homes. And your sale can be even more profitable if it is well organized.

Before planning your moving sale, check with local authorities for regulations on personal sales. In some towns you will need a permit. In other areas, the posting of signs is limited.

When should you have your moving sale? As soon as possible. Idea: Ask your neighbors and friends whether they would like to combine sales. Shoppers like to see lots of goods at one time.

Saturdays are the best days for a moving or yard sale, but be sure to avoid holiday weekends when many people have other plans. If you can, hold your sale for two or three days, beginning on Thursday or Friday. Establish a rain date if necessary. Set your sale hours early, as early as 7 a.m. if you can, because bargain hunters are notorious for starting early. Even with early hours, be prepared for a few early birds. Most moving sales aren't productive after about 3 p.m.

Come One! Come All!

What should you call your sale?

"Garage Sale" says you have lots of unusable junk you've been storing in the garage and want to get rid of.

"Yard Sale" says the junk in the garage (if there is one) has now spilled out into the yard.

"Moving Sale" says I'm moving my better stuff, but these things are pretty good. Make me an offer.

"Estate Sale" says I hate to get rid of this fine stuff, but I'm moving on. Make me an offer.

Moving Sale has a little more desperation to it than Estate Sale, but either name is better than Garage or Yard Sale.

Publicize your moving sale like crazy! A community newspaper may have a classified section for moving, garage, and estate sales. Include the days, hours, and location of the sale. Call it a moving sale to create extra interest. List a few of the major items you have to sell.

In smaller communities, a local radio station may have a call- or write-in program with announcements of personal items for sale.

Signs are good, too. In fact, they may be your best source of impulse buyers. Post signs wherever you can, at church, work, restaurants, laundromats, grocery stores, and other businesses. Be sure that any signs you post along the street are easily readable. Use large letters and dark waterproof ink.

And don't forget to tell neighbors, relatives, and friends about your moving sale.

Mark pricing on all items to increase sales.

The Price Is Right!

The pricing issue is often one that keeps otherwise sane folks from having moving sales. How much should I charge?

The best way to price your stuff is to know the pricing used by successful moving sales in your area. To get a feel for pricing, drive around a week or two before your sale, visiting sales and making notes.

You will also have a better idea of how to price if you know what the item would cost new. You can then use a formula for pricing, depending on your desperation to sell:

➤ 50% of original price (want to, but don't have to sell it)

➤ 25% of original price (will probably sell it soon)

➤ 10% of original price (first come, first served)

I Wonder Whether Anyone Will Show Up?!

There's an art to setting up a successful moving sale. You want to draw in lots of folks, have ample parking, and simultaneously enable people to buy easily and discourage theft.

So here are some ideas for your Smart Moving Sale:

➤ Move your own cars down the block or otherwise out of the way to allow for ample parking.

➤ Save or gather plastic and paper bags and a few boxes for shoppers' convenience. It will help people select and carry more items. And you don't want to move all those empty bags you've saved anyway.

➤ Decide where you will hold your sale. More people will stop at your sale if items are clearly visible from the street. If you have large furniture to sell, you can leave it in the house/apartment and have one of your co-inhabitants stationed inside to help.

➤ Clearly price all items to be sold. Remember that buyers will probably want to negotiate a lower price than you set. If your sale involves more than one family, color code, initial, or otherwise mark each item so that proper credit is given.

➤ Be sure that items not to be sold are clearly separated from sale items. Make sure the cashier knows what is NOT for sale. Otherwise, Pop's favorite fishing rod may become someone else's favorite.

➤ Group like items together with signs designating categories, such as "infant clothing" or "games."

➤ Offer a table of giveaways to draw people and make the sale look busier to passersby.

➤ If possible, hang clothing for best display. Make sure they are hung on something sturdy or they will soon be on the ground.

So, Whaterya Doin' This Weekend?

How can you get help for your moving sale?

Ask for it. Sometimes there's a neighbor or coworker who owes you a favor. Or someone else who will do anything to help get you out of town faster. You may have to bribe kids with a percentage of the take, but it's worth it to 1) get the help (however minimal), and 2) keep them busy.

Everyone in your moving group gets a job. Designate a greeter, a cashier, a bagger, and a carry-out person. The more people you have working the sale, the busier it looks to passersby—unless everyone is grouped in conversation.

If your sale is more than just a few hours long, have your help periodically trade off jobs. But make sure they pass on what they've learned so that everyone is working efficiently.

Tell Ya What I'll Do

Here are some additional hints to help you get the most from your moving sale:

➤ Some successful sales offer coffee, tea, ice-water, or lemonade to customers. It not only keeps customers longer, but they may feel more obligated to buy.

➤ Make sure the cash box has plenty of change.

➤ Never leave the cash box unattended.

➤ If you accept local checks, get identification, including phone number and address.

➤ Buy an inexpensive receipt book from a stationery store because some customers may want a receipt.

➤ Consider using a notebook for writing purchases down, especially if you have more than one seller (such as children who have been offered the proceeds from any of their items sold).

➤ If you're selling electrical appliances, make sure you have an electrical outlet nearby or available so customers can test items.

Marketing Techniques for the Truly Desperate

As the sale progresses, cut prices. At the halfway point of your sale, consider slashing prices by 50 percent. Everything left after noon of a one-day sale or the second day of a two-day sale is marked down by half.

Or put two or three dollars' worth of things in a bag, seal it, and offer it for a buck. Some people love grab bags.

And add more items to your giveaway table. Don't forget that your goal is not to get rich with a moving sale, but to reduce the bulk of items that you need to move.

So, What's Left?

Finally, donate leftovers from your sale to your favorite charity. And make sure you get a receipt for tax purposes.

If at all possible, try to have fun at your moving sale! Involve everyone in your moving group. Make your sale day a social event in the neighborhood. Help your customers enjoy their time at your sale—and maybe they'll feel sufficiently benevolent to buy your junk at ridiculous prices!

Down in the Dumps

You still have stuff left over? Send it to the dump! If nobody else wants it—family, friends, customers, charities, recyclers—then put it out of its misery and get rid of it for good. Don't pack it into a box and move it!

Don't think of these things as junk, but as fewer things you're going to have to move yourself!

The Least You Need to Know

> ➤ De-cluttering your home in preparation for your move starts today.

> ➤ You can have a Smart Moving Sale that not only reduces what you will have to move, but also brings in extra cash for moving expenses or mad money.

> ➤ If someone else will benefit from things more than you, sell it or give it away. If no one will, just toss it.

Chapter 8

Move Aside: Planning Your Packing and Loading

It's time to get moving!

No, no. Put the boxes down. We're going to move on paper. Less chance of a hernia!

Actually, moving on paper—planning your packing and loading in advance—can save you time, money, physical ills, and mental stress.

Do-it-yourself doesn't really mean do it *all* yourself. It means deciding which parts of the moving process you will do and which you will manage others to do. You may even decide (Smart Mover that you are!) to make your move without moving a thing yourself.

This chapter offers proven ideas on how to plan packing and loading for an easy and safe move. Coming chapters will get more specific on the *doing*.

So sit back, relax, and get moving.

Dilemma #173,926: Packing It Yourself Versus Hiring People

Should you pack everything yourself or have it packed by big, hairy men (or women, you sexist!)? Yes, the amount of junk and money you have may dictate your answer to this question. And your physical conditioning and aversion to work also play a part in your decision. But there may also be the lingering doubt of "I can't do my own packing because I've never done it before."

If you can talk and watch cable at the same time, you can do your own packing!

Don't Let Strangers Break Your Stuff—Do It Yourself!

Never packed anything that survived?

Well, don't worry about that aspect. Even the best professional packers had to start somewhere. They weren't born into the trade with immediate packing skills. They had to learn how to pack well, just like you can. And, as promised, the skills to do so are offered in the next few chapters.

The point: Pack the stuff yourself or hire to have it packed based on your budget, available time, and other factors rather than just your own experience.

Don't let the fact that you've never done it stand in the way of doing it!

What You Need to Plan Your Own Catastrophe

The real trick to good, safe packing lies as much planning as it does in skill. Throwing your belongings helter-skelter into the back of a pickup is sure to result in something broken or lost. But thinking about placement can make a difference.

Here are some common sense rules about moving:

➤ Boxes should be packed and sealed tightly, but should not be too heavy to carry.

➤ Soft things should be wrapped around clean, hard things.

➤ Tie things down so that they don't move around when transported. (Friction can mar surfaces.)

From these basic rules, you can figure out what you'll need for an easier move:

➤ Properly sized boxes

➤ Packing materials and wraps

➤ Ropes

Of course, you can go out and buy these materials or you can come up with them through more creative means. More on both options later in this book.

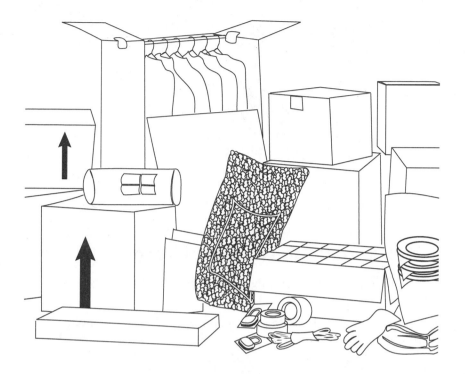

You can buy good packing materials from movers or moving equipment rental retailers.

Professional or Procrastinator?

Planning smart packing means working like the pros do. Their "secret"? Professional packers are generous with materials, using lots of packing material to cushion all your belongings. That isn't just because they sell the packing material to you. Actually, the materials are cheap compared to the loss of damaged goods or insurance claims. Packers use lots of boxes, materials, wraps, and straps because it's faster and safer in the long run.

So, if you plan to do your own packing and loading, work like a pro and plan on lots of packing materials.

Specifics forthcoming.

Making Your Move

Avoid false economy in your move. Using cut-rate equipment and materials can end up costing more in the long run. Cheap materials might not protect your valuables, increasing the chance of costly damages. Deal only with reputable companies with dependable equipment.

The 1.5-cubic-foot box is ideal for books and other small, heavy stuff.

Surviving Packing Day without Recreational Drugs

Have lots of stuff to pack? Just a few things? Packing day will go more smoothly if you approach it with a plan.

If you have lots of time between now and moving day, you may have a number of partial packing days. The first round may be packing everything that's now in storage. Next time, it's books, hobby items, and other things you may not need for a few weeks. Finally, it's the essentials: housewares, clothing, bedding, television.

And plan to label everything that isn't obvious. Book boxes should be marked so. If you have lots of books, group and mark them: "Judy's books," "cookbooks," "kids' books," "heavy box"!

You don't have to start packing up yet; just start planning.

Who's in Charge Here?: Moving Yourself Versus Hiring People

Making Your Move

Plan ahead. If you have the information, sketch a floor plan and decide upon furniture placement. If something won't fit, don't go to the expense of moving it.

Okay, so how much of this superfluous junk are you going to lug out to the trailer yourself?

Of course, you can hire to have any or all of it done, from packing to loading. But consider how much of it you can lug before lifting your wallet.

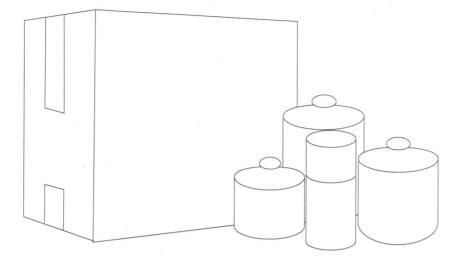

The 3-cubic-foot box is useful for kitchenware and other small, medium-weight stuff.

How to Lug like a Born Lug

Even if you're not Arnold Swartzenwhatever, you'd be surprised how much of the packing and loading you can do yourself with a little know-how.

Chapters 11, 12, and the ever-popular 13 offer techniques for lifting, moving, and packing big and little stuff without a note from your chiropractor.

But let's be smart about this. Moving a household full of heavy boxes, furniture, and appliances takes strength and stamina, even with the help of a few advanced techniques. If you're in good health, are you in good condition? Make an honest appraisal of your physical abilities. Maybe you can carry lots of boxes and smaller items, but feel virtually useless for moving large furniture and appliances. If so, start planning now to have a couple of big, hairy persons of whatever gender on hand to give a hand.

Santa's Moving List

So, how many boxes are you going to need for your move? We kinda talked about this in Chapter 3 on estimating moving costs. It's time now, moving fans, to get more specific.

Here's a cool chart for estimating how much stuff you have, how many boxes you'll need, and what supplies are necessary to get it all shoved into the moving vehicle. Figure basements and storage buildings separately.

The 4.5-cubic-foot box is great for lamp shades and medium-sized stuff.

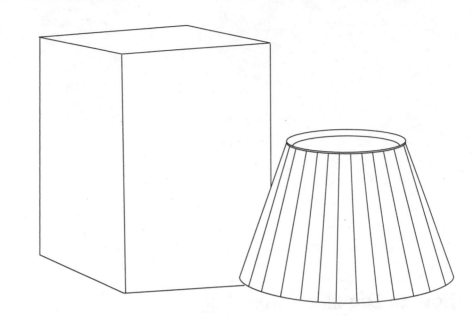

These recommendations are just a starting point. They are averages. You may need more or fewer boxes than estimated here. You'll probably also need wrapping material, such as bubble wrap, packing peanuts, cream cheese, and/or newspaper. In many cases you can also use towels, blankets, and other linens as some of your packing material. Old coats are okay as long as the buttons or zippers don't scratch anything.

Size of Your Home	Boxes	Supplies
small apartment (250 sq. ft.)	8 small boxes	1 roll tape
1–2 rooms	4 medium boxes 4 large boxes 1 dish pack 2 wardrobe boxes	1 roll tape 1 roll rope
1–2 bedroom up to 1,200 square feet	15 small boxes 10 medium boxes 8 large boxes 4 wardrobe boxes	2 rolls tape 1 roll rope
2–3 bedroom 1,200–1,600 square feet	20 small boxes 15 medium boxes 10 large boxes 6 wardrobe boxes	4 rolls tape 2 rolls rope
3–4 bedroom 1,600–1,800 square feet	30 small boxes 20 medium boxes 15 large boxes 8 wardrobe boxes	5 rolls tape 2 rolls rope

Size of Your Home	Boxes	Supplies
4 or more bedrooms 2,000 or more square feet	40 small boxes 30 medium boxes 20 large boxes 10 wardrobes	6 rolls tape 3 rolls rope

For folks who haven't the foggiest notion of how many square (or any other shape of) feet their abode contains: multiply the width of the entire living area by the depth. A 24' × 24' apartment has 576 square feet. A 75' × 90' home has too many square feet to clean!

Making Your Move

Make a room-by-room inventory of the goods you need to move. A couple of hours making an inventory will help you enormously in your planning and budgeting.

Want to get more specific, you say? Well, here's a more comprehensive chart (Table 8.1) of how much space stuff will take. Use the third column to add up the number of cubic feet of space you'll need in your moving vehicle(s). A cubic foot is simply a square foot (width times depth) times the height (1' × 1' × 1' is 1 cubic foot). Cubic feet is a standard measure for moving, whether you're a do-it-yourselfer or a professional mover.

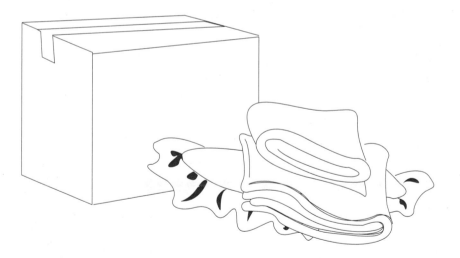

The 6-cubic-foot box is fine for lighter stuff.

Table 8.1 Number of Square Feet by Item

Item	Cubic feet	# pieces
Living Room		
Bookcase (3 x 6 foot)	15	
Bookshelves	5	
Chair—arm	10	
Chair—recliner	20	
Chair—rocker	12	
Couch	30–40	
Desk	20–40	
Fireplace equipment	5	
Grandfather clock	20	
Lamp—floor	3	
Lamp—table	2	
Magazine rack	2	
Piano, upright	50–70	
Stereo components	3	
Stereo console	20	
Table—coffee/end	4	
TV—console	15	
TV—portable	10	
Kitchen/Dining Room		
Bar—portable	15	
Buffet	20–30	
Cabinet	20–30	
Chair	5	
China cabinet	25	
High chair	3	
Hutch	25	
Stool	3	
Table	10–20	
Bedroom		
Bed—king	75	
Bed—queen	55	
Bed—double	45	

Item	Cubic feet	# pieces
Bedroom		
Bed—single	30	
Bed—water	20	
Cedar chest	10–15	
Chair	4	
Chest/dresser	20–30	
Night table	5	
Wardrobe/armoire	35	
Children's Room		
Bassinet	4	
Bed—youth	20	
Changing table	5	
Cradle	5	
Crib	10	
Playpen	6	
Toy chest	5	
Appliances		
Air conditioner	15	
Clothes dryer	25	
Dehumidifier	10	
Dishwasher	15	
Freezer, chest or upright	45–60	
Microwave	5	
Range	25	
Refrigerator	40	
Sewing machine	10	
Vacuum cleaner	5	
Washing machine	25	
Home Office		
Bookcase	10–20	
Computer	5	
Filing cabinet	8	

continues

Table 8.1 Continued

Item	Cubic feet	# pieces
Garage/Outdoor		
Barbecue	5–10	
Bicycle	6	
Canoe	50	
Garden cart	5	
Golf bag	2	
Hose and tools	10	
Lawn chair	3	
Lawn mower	7	
Lawn swing/glider	20	
Picnic table	25	
Sandbox	10	
Stepladder	5	
Swing set	20	
Tool chest	3–10	
Tricycle	4	
Wagon	5	
Wheelbarrow	7	

You've estimated the number of boxes and other stuff you'll be moving. Congratulations! Now what?

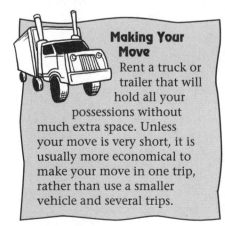

Making Your Move

Rent a truck or trailer that will hold all your possessions without much extra space. Unless your move is very short, it is usually more economical to make your move in one trip, rather than use a smaller vehicle and several trips.

Add up the cubic feet of these items to get a good estimate of the size of the moving load you will have. Should your household include hobbies (like collecting Greek statuary) or a business (like selling Greek statuary) with an inventory, these will anywhere from slightly to greatly increase the load.

How much packing material should you plan on getting? The best packing materials are available through your mover or through a rental truck company. They will offer square cartons in several sizes, as well as many specialty cartons. You can purchase dish packs, wardrobe boxes, mirror packs, tape, straps or rope, and even a lock for securing your items once they are all loaded into the truck or trailer.

The dish pack has dividers to help minimize damage.

How many boxes will you need? Wardrobes? Rolls of tape? Unless the supplier is far from your home, remember that you can always purchase more supplies if you run out. Also remember that some moving services will buy back unused materials at full price.

Buck & Back Savers

When you buy packing materials, ask whether the supplier will buy back unused materials. Most will. You may even be able to sell most of the boxes to a moving company after your move is completed and everything unpacked. If you move often and have the space, break the boxes down and store them for the next move. Many families that relocate frequently use those sturdy moving boxes many times over.

Another way to save on moving supplies is to purchase used boxes when available from your truck rental or moving company. Make a few phone calls. Good used boxes are just as sturdy and usable as new.

*A wardrobe box has a
hanging rack for
clothing.*

Calling on Your Friendship and Other Forms of Coercion

Ah, friendship is a wonderful thing to share...especially on moving day!

Thousands of do-it-yourself moves each year depend on the benevolence or conscience of friends and relatives.

So can yours!

Don't Have Any Friends to Call?

To have a friend, be a friend.

This is good advice, especially when considering making a move. So, as your friends, relatives, and neighbors plan their moves, help them. Then, unless they've moved to The Hague, Holland, you can call on them for reciprocity.

And as they thank you for your help, say "Glad to do it...and I'm sure you'll be there for me when I move next Thursday!" "Uh, yeah, right."

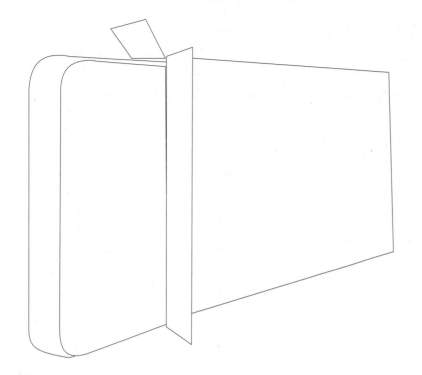

A mattress box is a special box for keeping a mattress or box spring clean and safe during transit.

Call on a Friend

Okay, so you're not a socialite and you don't have a long list of chums to call on when planning your move. There are other likely candidates:

➤ Fellow church, synagogue, mosque, or ashram members

➤ Fellow club or association members

➤ Your teenager's friends

➤ The high school football or wrestling team

➤ Neighbors who have asked when you're moving

➤ Co-workers who owe you a favor

➤ Acquaintances who will do anything for a case of beer

➤ Folks who flash their "will work for food" sign as you drive by

➤ Local groups who want to raise money with donated labor

➤ People you know who are unemployed

Smart Packing for Complete Idiots

Smart moving means planning your packing for efficiency. And that means having lots of space, lots of materials, and lots of good help.

We'll cover the specifics of smart packing in Chapter 10. For now, let's plan.

Lost in Space

Few things are more frustrating than trying to pack stuff up for a move when there's little room to do so. You wind up moving things out of the way two or three times. What you need is somewhere else, and things don't get packed efficiently.

So what can you do to make sure you have lots of packing space? Plan ahead.

Here are some proven planning tips:

➤ Clear out a location near the door where packed boxes can be placed without getting in the way.

➤ Make space in the center of each room where you can pack a box efficiently.

➤ Use a strong end table or other short and sturdy surface on which you can pack a box without having to stoop over.

➤ Designate a central location for packing materials.

➤ Keep open paths through the area so that you and others can easily get in and out.

➤ If lifting is a problem, get a dolly or handtruck for moving boxes as well as appliances.

She's Just a Materials Girl!

Running out of materials can waste lots of time in your moving process. So begin planning right now to have adequate boxes, tape, paper, cushioning materials, and other packing supplies on hand.

Here are some tips for planning moving materials:

➤ Store flat packing boxes on a side edge leaning against a centrally located wall.

➤ Group boxes by size so that they can be efficiently selected and monitored for availability.

➤ Have extra packing materials (blankets, towels, old clothing, carpet samples) nearby for easy access.

Help!!!!!!

Smart moving means using cranial mass to elicit or coerce others into helping you. Guilt works well, too. Here are some suggestions for planning good help with your move:

➤ Schedule your packing and moving help. ("Can you help between 2 and 4 p.m.?")

➤ Use your help by estimated abilities. (Bob can help with the big boxes and his young son can help tape the finished boxes.)

➤ Offer food and refreshments to sustain workers' morale and energy levels.

Planning the Best Way to Get Loaded

This is going to sound like an idea from a complete idiot, but I've been accused of worse. Here it is:

To load safely, empathize.

That is, to pack and load an antique dresser, first think of yourself as an old but beautiful object of aged wood and fragile surfaces.

Now *you* think I'm crazy, too. True story! In fact, this is similar to what the moving companies teach new packers: Empathize with what you're packing. Think of yourself as the object being packed and you will be more sensitive to its needs. This viewpoint, in turn, ensures that objects are packed for safe travel and arrival.

After all, you wouldn't stand up in the back of a pickup truck for a thousand-mile move, would you? And, as a dish, you wouldn't want to be exposed to the friction of rubbing against some dumb old coffee cup for a thousand miles, would you?

A coffee table will need padding so that other moving objects don't mar the table's thin finish.

Let's carry this odd but effective concept a little further and show you how an object would prefer to be moved.

Look at Me! I'm a Vase!

If you were a valuable vase that had to move, whether cross-town or cross-country, you would want to be kept away from hard objects that could push or rub on your surface. You would probably also want to be packed snugly into a container that would not easily flex when lifted.

Thinking like a fragile vase can help you plan your packing of similar items: glassware, knick knacks, fragile jewelry, lamp bases, valuable dishware.

Being of Sound Mind

Okay, now you're a stereo! How does it feel, getting plugged in, your buttons pushed and your dials twisted? You will welcome the restful sleep within a dark box, won't you?

Actually, as a stereo system you will want to be packed with padding to protect your electronics and your finish. You don't want to spend a month or two in the repair shop! It's no vacation, being poked and probed. But you do want to be packed with related components, speaker wires removed and carefully wrapped, exterior dusted and amply padded.

You will also want the box you're in to be accurately marked so that you can quickly get back to work in your new home.

Holstering Your Upholstered Furniture

And now you're an overstuffed chair! Nothing personal! But considering how specific furniture would want to be packed if it could speak can help you plan on a safe move.

Cloth-covered furniture will want light protection so that objects of lower social order (tables, garden tools) don't rub against it in transit. A plastic sheet will do the job.

As a sleeper sofa, you will want to make sure you don't open up and smack one of the movers in the head as you're placed on end in the moving truck. You will want them to tie your innards together so that they don't move around.

Hey, you get the picture. To safely pack and load your stuff, commiserate!

The Least You Need to Know

➤ The more you plan your self-move now, the more time, money, and effort you'll save on moving day.

➤ Call on your friends, relatives, neighbors, co-workers, and other victims of your charm when you're ready to move.

➤ Plan an efficient working area to make packing easier.

➤ To efficiently move stuff, think like stuff.

Chapter 9

Keep on Truckin': Choosing Your Moving Vehicle

In This Chapter

➤ Renting a truck

➤ Renting a trailer

➤ Renting a car hitch or dolly

➤ Renting other equipment

➤ Insuring your move

Nothing is more frustrating than getting to the end of your moving vehicle before you get to the end of your stuff.

"So, what do we leave behind: the dining room set or the bedroom set?"

And maybe you're afraid of having to drive a moving vehicle that's larger than the home you left!

"Looks like we're eating at truck stops all the way!"

Or maybe you're concerned about loading a pickup truck with stuff hanging off the sides!

"We look like the Joads in *The Grapes of Wrath*!"

What kind of a vehicle will you need for your do-it-yourself move?

Good question. And this chapter offers good answers.

Should you rent a truck? Rent a trailer? Borrow a pickup? Use a car?

This question has no universal answer. Your family's moving needs are different from those of your neighbors. You may need a 26-foot van to hold your furniture, appliances, tools, and toys, while your neighbor may be able to move in a small, enclosed trailer—or in the backseat of a borrowed car.

Let's consider your options.

Rental moving trucks come in a variety of sizes.

I Wanna Be a Trucker, Like Mom!

"Gimme 40 acres and I'll turn this rig around!"

Those lyrics from a popular song of yesteryear express the feeling of many folks who consider renting a truck for their move. In other words, "It's so big! How will I ever drive it?"

Later we'll get to the art of driving the truck. For now, know that driving most rental moving trucks isn't inordinately difficult—just different. In fact, in most states, you can drive a pretty big truck without any special license. Scary, huh?

If those 90-year-old folks in 90-foot motorhomes can drive their rigs cross-country, so can you!

Renting a truck can make sense for many moves:

➤ If you don't have other moving vehicles available

➤ If you are moving more stuff than will fit in a trailer

➤ If the land distance is too great to make more than one trip

After you decide to use a rental truck for your move, the obvious questions come to mind:

➤ Whose truck?

➤ How big a truck?

Let's take on those two fascinating topics right now.

That's a Pretty Color Truck! Let's Rent It!

How will you choose a truck rental company? Should you rent one of the yellow ones, the orange-and-white ones, or some other color?

Maybe the decision is easier than you think. If you live in a small town, you may either have to use whichever company has trucks available locally or travel a ways to pick up and drop off your unit.

If you live in a city, you'll have more choices. Call several companies and ask lots of questions:

➤ How many trucks/trailers do they have?

➤ How old are the vehicles?

➤ Do the vehicles have automatic or manual transmission?

➤ Do the trucks have gas or diesel engines?

➤ Is the cab air conditioned?

➤ How many adults can ride comfortably?

➤ How many miles to the gallon will the truck get when it's full of stuff?

➤ How's road service if the truck breaks down? And who pays for the charges?

➤ Does the truck have a ramp or hydraulic lift?

➤ Does the truck have a spare tire and emergency flares?

➤ What packing and loading materials does the company provide or sell?

➤ Are there mileage charges or drop fees on the vehicle?

After a number of calls, you should have a pretty good idea of who has the right equipment for your move.

Next? Go look at the equipment. If you are moving across the country, you will be spending several days in the cab of that truck. It will be worth a few dollars more to have a clean, comfortable ride and a working radio. You don't want to be in the middle of the desert in August without air conditioning or Montana in February without heat! And check to make sure the windows work.

Then? After you have a firm moving date, reserve your truck and other moving equipment. Here's what the truck rental agent will ask for to reserve a truck:

➤ Your name

➤ Your telephone number

➤ A major credit card number

➤ The date of your move

➤ Your current address

➤ Your destination address

➤ The size of truck or trailer you need

➤ The name of your grandmother's first boyfriend

Make sure your rental truck has a ramp for easier loading and unloading.

Making Your Move

Make reservations early for your truck or trailer rental. If you don't reserve early, you might have to pick up a truck in a neighboring town, and this type pickup can be costly.

When should you reserve your truck? Make reservations early, especially in the summer when truck rental companies are busiest. Most folks move on Friday or Saturday, and end-of-month weekends are the busiest. If possible, schedule your move between Sunday and Thursday when more rental trucks are typically available. Make your reservations at least a month before your move for a better chance of getting the truck or trailer you want. If you rent from a national truck rental company, the company must schedule the vehicle you want because their fleet travels the entire country. When you rent from a national firm, however, you can pick up the truck in your current hometown and, when you finish the move, return the truck to the nearest dealer in your new hometown (for a fee).

If your move is local, check out small, local rental companies; they are more apt to have smaller trucks and trailers available. In addition, any trucks rented out will probably be back in a few days and probably won't need a reservation.

My Truck's Bigger'n Yours!

After working through Chapter 8, you have a good idea of the size truck you need. This section explains how to determine the type of truck you need.

Making Your Move

Don't move worn-out appliances. These heavy and bulky items add significantly to the cost of moving. You might find selling or donating them (for a tax deduction) more cost-effective than moving them.

In addition, a truck rental firm can offer you advice and assistance in selecting the best size for your move. They can tell you how much mileage-per-gallon you can expect from the truck. Be sure that you ask for *loaded* mileage—the mileage the truck gets when full; an empty truck takes far less fuel than a filled truck. Most companies can furnish brochures that graphically instruct you on the best and safest way to load your truck or trailer. You should also get information about what to do if the truck breaks down while you are using it.

Do you want an automatic or a manual transmission? Most do-it-yourself movers prefer an automatic transmission. Larger trucks require a five-speed transmission, some with two-speed differentials and sometimes a three-speed auxiliary transmission. In theory, these vehicles have 30 potential gears. Intimidating! Automatic transmissions do most of the thinking for you.

Gas or diesel? If you've never driven a diesel vehicle, stick with gasoline-powered trucks. It's not that diesel-powered trucks are trickier; they're just a little different to drive. Starting them requires that you wait a few seconds for the glow plugs to warm up the engine's combustion chambers. Diesel trucks also differ in other ways from gasoline trucks, and you probably have enough adventure in your life that you don't also need to master diesel trucking.

The advantage to diesel is that fuel costs will probably be less for a diesel truck than for a gas one. The cost difference isn't significant, but it does make diesel trucks a better option for those who have experience with them.

Even if your move is just across town, it may be more efficient to rent a truck that will hold everything in one trip. When you compare costs, remember to add in fuel—and remember that your time is valuable. It's more exhausting to make several trips than to pack up one truck and get all your stuff at your new home in one trip. Making several trips rather than one or two may even mean that you end up paying for a second day's rental on the truck.

Making Your Move

When you are figuring costs, be sure to include the cost of fuel for your rental truck. If you ask the rental agent how much mileage the truck gets, be sure to specify that you want to know what the mileage is when the truck is loaded. Just to be safe, increase the figure a bit more when you make your calculations.

If you fell asleep during Chapter 8, here's a quick summary: You may be able to move out of a condominium or apartment using a small truck, up to about ten feet in length. This truck should hold the furniture from a small dwelling, plus about 15 boxes of personal items.

The contents of a one- or two-bedroom home of up to about 1,200 square feet can usually be loaded onto a 14- or 15-foot truck, with room for furniture, appliances, and about 35 boxes.

If you are moving out of a two- or three-bedroom home of up to 1,600 square feet, you will probably require a 17- or 18-foot truck, allowing for about 50 boxes in addition to large items.

A three- or four-bedroom home of up to 2,000 square feet will require a truck of about 24 feet to hold furniture, appliances, yard gear, and garage items, as well as about 70 boxes.

If the home you are leaving is a four-bedroom home of more than 2,000 square feet, you will want to rent a truck of at least 26 feet to hold everything, including as many as 120 boxes of personal and household items.

Saving Money by Renting a Trailer

Sometimes, renting a trailer is the best option available. It's a less expensive option than renting a truck because your vehicle is supplying the power.

Will It Hold My Mother-in-Law?

How big a trailer will you need? If you're moving away from your parents' home for the first time, if you are moving into a furnished retirement home, or if you've sold most everything at your moving sale, you may be able to move all your possessions in trailer as small as 4×6 feet. Of course, a closed trailer protects your belongings far better than an open trailer. Open trailers should have a tarp securely covering your precious cargo.

A small, open trailer is best for short moves from apartment to apartment—on a sunny day.

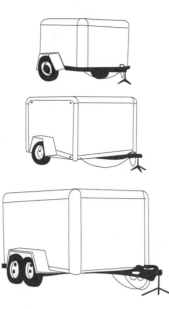

Three common sizes of moving trailers.

If you are moving out of a two-room residence, you should be able to get everything into a 5×8 foot trailer, including about 20 boxes. Possessions from a three-room home, including approximately 35 boxes, should fit into a 6×12 foot trailer.

Our Car's Following Us!

Before renting a trailer, consider the type and condition of your tow vehicle. Check the radiator. Even if it has not given you any previous trouble, your car may overheat when pulling a loaded trailer over a mountain pass. Check your brakes. They will be expected to stop a heavier-than-normal load. Be sure the car is tuned up and in top condition. Everything you save by moving yourself with a borrowed or rented trailer can quickly be eaten up with the expense of a car breakdown.

Remember, too, that some cars should not pull a trailer. Check the owner's manual for towing information.

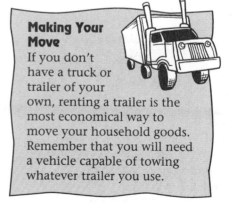

Making Your Move

If you don't have a truck or trailer of your own, renting a trailer is the most economical way to move your household goods. Remember that you will need a vehicle capable of towing whatever trailer you use.

Say, Can I Borrow Your Truck?

If you're moving a short distance—across town or to a neighboring town—you may be able to accomplish it all in a few pickup truck or trailer loads, depending on how many possessions you have accumulated. If you don't own your own truck or trailer, a good friend may loan you one for a day or two.

Be sure to return the vehicle cleaned out, washed, and with a full tank of gas.

Need Insurance?

When you borrow any vehicle, check on insurance coverage for it, yourself, and the goods you are moving. If your auto or household insurance does not cover the move automatically, you may be able to purchase short-term special coverage. Get all these insurance questions answered before the day of the move.

What If It Breaks Down?

Don't borrow a vehicle that isn't in good running condition. Think how frustrating it would be to be stuck at the side of the road for several hours while your unloading crew waits at the new house. And then having to pay to repair something you don't even own!

There's Always a Hitch!

If you're going to use your car to pull a trailer, you'll need a hitch to connect the two. If your car isn't equipped with a hitch, you'll need to rent or purchase and install one. Check your owner's manual to determine the size trailer your car can safely tow. Install only a hitch that meets your car's specifications. Be careful not to exceed the weight limit of the trailer or hitch.

Hitches are grouped into classes:

➤ Class I hitches have a maximum rated capacity of 2,000 pounds.

➤ Class II hitches have a maximum rated capacity of 3,000 pounds.

➤ Class III hitches have a maximum rated capacity of up to 5,000 pounds.

➤ Class IV hitches have a maximum rated capacity of 7,500 pounds.

There is a wide variety of trailer hitches classified by the amount of weight they can safely tow.

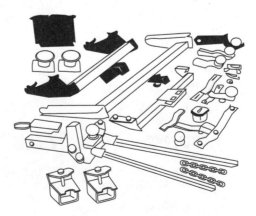

In most cases, the Class I and II hitches have a receptacle ball of $1^1/_4$ inches in diameter, while the Class III and IV hitches use the 2-inch ball.

Some truck rental companies sell and install hitches, but you can also install it yourself or have it done elsewhere.

Transport a car on a special trailer with tie-downs.

Maybe It's a Carrier!

If you move in a borrowed or rented truck, you may need to tow your car to your new home. The easiest way is with a car carrier trailer, available from truck rental companies. You can easily load and unload your car, and the trailer causes no wear on tires or any other part of your car. You can also rent tow bars and tow dollies.

For extra storage, you can install a car-top carrier on your car. You can also pack your towed car with stuff—as long as you don't exceed weight limits.

Tiedowns

If you decide to transport your car on a flatbed trailer or car dolly, don't neglect tiedowns. Any object set on an open, flatbed trailer will move around in transit—especially if that object has springs and round tires! Tiedowns are straps with hooks on the ends to anchor the car to the trailer. The tiedowns are then cinched tight to remove any slack and prevent movement.

> **Moving Words**
> *Gross weight* is the fat removed during liposuction. It's also the weight of the truck and contents after your goods have been loaded.
>
> *Tare weight* is the extra pounds put on after the holidays. It's also the weight of the truck and contents prior to loading your shipment.

I've Got Four Bucks Left! What Else Do I Need?

So what other equipment are you going to need for your move?

If you're pulling a trailer, you can rent or buy hitch balls, wiring, automatic transmission coolers, safety chains, extended side mirrors, trailer brake controllers, sway controls, and other products.

Appliance Dollies

Appliance dollies are heavy-duty two-wheeled dollies with straps and cinches to hold major appliances in place for a move. You don't have to buy an appliance dolly for your move; you can typically rent them where you rent your moving truck or trailer.

When you rent a dolly, make sure you get clear and complete instructions on how to use it. Some dollies have cinching mechanisms that seem to defy logic. Once understood, they can be safely used to carry appliances, furniture, and heavy boxes into or out of a house, upstairs into an apartment, or nearly anywhere.

Chapter 11 covers using appliance dollies.

Furniture Wraps

Solid furniture such as tables, dressers, and entertainment centers need a cushioning wrap around them to minimize abrasion. You typically can rent furniture wraps in dozens from the rental center where you get your truck or trailer.

Straps and Ropes

Straps and ropes are useful because they help keep things from shifting. If you're loading a larger moving truck, you may want to tie a strap across the van every six feet to keep furniture and boxes from shifting. Ropes are useful for tying off loads on open trailers. In most cases, straps can be rented, but rope will need to be purchased at a local hardware store.

Feeling Lucky?

Be sure to check into insurance coverage whenever you rent or borrow a vehicle. Check your homeowners and auto insurance to determine comprehensive and collision coverage of the vehicle and coverage of the contents you are moving. If you rent a truck or trailer, be sure you understand the extent of the coverage the rental company offers and compare it with extra coverage you may be able to purchase from your regular insurance company.

Neglecting to obtain adequate insurance coverage can be a costly oversight.

The Least You Need to Know

➤ Renting a moving truck means figuring out how much stuff you have, and then finding and reserving a truck to fit your needs.

➤ If you have a good towing vehicle (or can borrow one), renting a moving trailer can be the most cost-effective way to get a medium-size household from here to there.

➤ Make sure you know what other tools and materials you need and arrange to rent or borrow them before moving day.

Making Your Move

Be sure any truck or trailer you rent or borrow is insured. Know what is covered by the truck rental agency. Talk to your insurance agent about coverage of the truck's contents.

Part 3
How to Move Yourself

"I don't no nuthin' about movin' no boxes!"

For one reason or another, you're considering moving yourself.

Maybe your new boss is too cheap to move you.

Maybe you're moving because you told your old boss he's cheap!

Maybe you're a masochist.

But, because you're not a complete idiot, you've decided to hire me to give you the lowdown on moving yourself.

Smart move!

You don't have to have hairy arms to be a mover. In fact, you can manage your move from an easy chair by learning how to move smart. Or you can pitch in to do some of the work and hire big hairy arms to do the rest. You have choices!

This part of the book force-feeds you ideas and tips on

> ➤ *Planning your packing*

> ➤ *Choosing your moving vehicle*

> ➤ *Packing anything*

> ➤ *Moving furniture and appliances*

> ➤ *Learning professional moving techniques*

> ➤ *Loading your moving vehicle*

Now, aren't you glad you decided to move it yourself?

Chapter 10

*&^%$#@!!!!!!

Cream Cheese and Stereos: How to Pack Anything

In This Chapter

➤ Use the Five Tips for Smart Packing

➤ Learn how and where to save money on packing supplies

➤ Learn the right way to pack everything in your home

"Hey, don't pack the cream cheese with the stereo!"

Most do-it-yourself movers are intimidated by the thought of packing fragile or valuable stuff—with good reason. Valued treasures of a lifetime can become so much junk because of poor packing.

"Okay, who put the lawnmower in with the bedspread?!"

"Hon, exactly how many pieces should we have in our 12-place dinnerware set?"

"No, FRAGILE isn't Italian for 'stack heavy stuff on this box!'"

"That painting of Grandpa has a hole in the head!"

Smart packing is really easy.

Count 'Em: Five Tips for Smart Packing

Over the years as both an amateur and professional mover, I've learned dozens of useful techniques for smart packing. Here are my top five.

Find a table for packing and keep packing materials together.

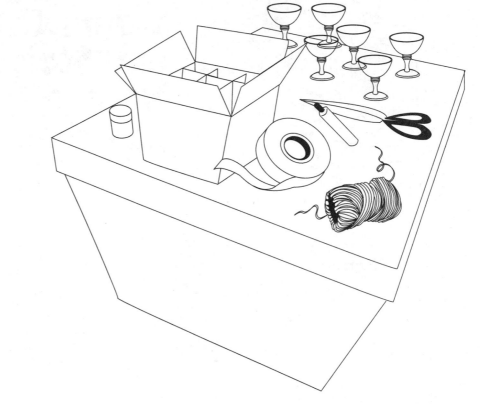

Smart Packing Tip #1: Plan Your Move Before You Start

Making Your Move
Even if you have a moving company move your possessions, you can save money by doing part of the job, such as the packing, yourself.

Yes, PLANNING. I devoted Chapter 8 and lots of other verbiage in this book to the important first step in moving: planning smart. Planning each stage and task of the moving process really will make the ordeal easier. Here are some plan-ahead questions to ask yourself before the move. Jot the answers in your Smart Moving Notebook for future reference:

➤ How many boxes will you need?

➤ What size?

➤ How many special boxes will you need for lamps, dishes, and your wardrobe?

➤ How much tape will be necessary to seal the boxes?

➤ What kind of marking pens?

➤ What cushioning materials will you use?

➤ How much cushioning material will you need?

Smart Packing Tip #2: Get the Best Packing Materials You Can Afford

If your moving project is on a tight budget, you can make the rounds of grocery and liquor stores several times to acquire usable packing boxes, but they will be of varying sizes, shapes, and durability. If you can, purchase new packing boxes from a moving company or truck rental company. Also consider purchasing used moving boxes and material. You can cut costs somewhat by packing your "stuff" in grocery boxes (with tops on them) and your valuables in purchased boxes.

For example, if you pack your hanging clothing carefully in professional movers' wardrobe boxes, they will arrive at your new home still clean, pressed, and ready to wear. And you can pack other items at the bottom of the wardrobe box, underneath your hanging clothing.

Using professional movers' dish packs will ensure that your best dinnerware will arrive without chipping or breakage (or at least with less damage, depending on how you load and drive).

What about packing materials for a computer, stereo, VCR, or other delicate items? If possible, repack them in their original cartons with the original packing material. If you've long since thrown away the original boxes, ask your favorite computer or electronics store for discarded boxes and packing materials.

Making Your Move
You can sometimes purchase used moving boxes from a moving company. If your budget just won't stretch at all, you can visit local grocery and liquor stores and fast food restaurants for sturdy cartons with lids. Or check with local offices for photocopy paper boxes.

Making Your Move
Careful packing will save money because items that are packed carefully and appropriately are less vulnerable to breakage. Use good packing materials and take the time to pack well.

Smart Packing Tip #3: Start Packing Early

Starting the packing process early will reduce the stress of moving day!

When to start? You can start packing as soon as you know you will be moving. Start by packing seldom-used items from storage areas such as the attic, basement, or garage. Move on to closets, cupboards, and pantries. Next, pack up decorative items, such as collections, figurines, framed photographs, paintings, and other items that aren't essential for daily living.

And make sure you follow the next tip!

Smart Packing Tip #4: Label Everything!

"Hey, what's in this box?"

"Where's my raincoat?"

"Who packed the boa constrictor?"

All good questions! If you've marked everything well, you'll have good answers.

Mark what?

Use a wide-tip, bright-colored, waterproof pen for marking boxes. Professional movers' boxes include spaces for noting the box's contents and the room to which those items belong. Mark each box in the same place on two sides with the same information.

Mark how?

Label more than one side.

Indicate which room the box should be unloaded into: kitchen, nursery, the boys' bedroom, garage, attic, basement, storage. (Use different colored markers for different rooms—yellow/kitchen, green/bathroom, and so forth.)

In addition, list the contents: computer, books, games, dishes, coffee maker, toaster, household tools—whatever's in there. Be specific. You don't necessarily need to list every item in the box ("pile of pennies from bottom drawer, Pez dispenser, broken sunglasses"), but if the box contains small appliances, do list each of these; you'll want to organize your kitchen as quickly as possible.

"Kitchen: Coffee Maker. OPEN ME FIRST!"

Smart Packing Tip #5: Set Up a Staging Area

You'll need a place to put all of those boxes you're packing. Choose a seldom-used room or a portion of the garage as the storage area. If possible, select a room that is near where your moving truck or trailer will be loaded so that on moving day you will easily be able to bring in a utility dolly and load stacks of boxes onto the moving vehicle.

110

In addition, by keeping a dedicated moving area, you will more easily be able to find a packed item if you determine you need it before the move—especially if you mark boxes with the room and contents, as suggested in Smart Packing Tip #4.

Now that you've been tipped off about smart moving, let's get specific on how to pack a box safely and efficiently.

The Inside Story: How to Pack a Box

As with most things, there's a right way and a wrong way to pack a moving box. Of course, how you pack depends on what you're packing. For example, you pack books differently than you pack glassware: Books are packed flat rather than on edge so that the spines aren't damaged. Glassware and other breakables, called *fragiles*, are packed with material to cushion them.

Moving Words
Fragiles are glassware and other breakables. You protect fragiles by packing them with cushioning material.

Remember that it's easier to move more lightweight boxes than fewer heavy boxes—especially up or down stairs.

Here's how to pack fragiles:

Making Your Move
If you have many books to move, research alternative ways of shipping them, such as book rate through the post office.

1. Place a layer of packing material, such as packing peanuts or a towel, in the bottom of the box.

2. Wrap the heaviest items in paper, linen, or bubble wrap and place them in the bottom of the box.

3. Wrap lighter items with paper, linen, or bubble wrap and place them in the box, separated from the heavier items with more packing material.

4. Fill any empty space in the box with peanuts, paper, or other packing material to keep contents from shifting and to keep box firm.

5. Use strong packing tape to close and seal the box. Mark on two sides of the box the room the box is to go into when the boxes are unloaded.

Remember not to underpack or overpack boxes. An underpacked box can be crushed in the move, damaging its contents. An overpacked box can burst and allow contents to be damaged.

From A to Z: How to Pack Everything Else

Moving your place of residence from here to there will mean packing many boxes—maybe a hundred or more. The instructions in this chapter will help you do it efficiently and safely.

In addition, you will need to pack some things around your house differently. So the remainder of this chapter offers specific instructions on packing everything from antiques to tools.

Valuable furniture with fragile, non-removable legs should be packed in specially built cases to minimize damage.

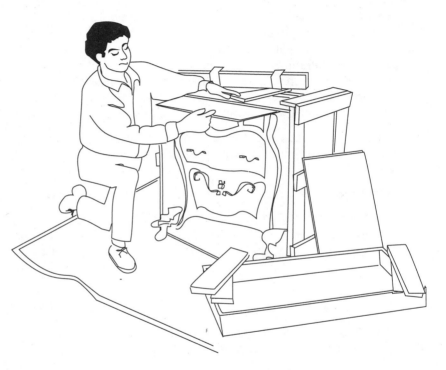

Antiques

No, don't pack your mother-in-law in a box marked "Antique"!

If you really own valuable antiques (and not just old stuff), before you move, have your antiques appraised by a qualified professional appraiser so that you can adequately insure the items. Your insurance agency may be able to recommend an appraiser.

If your antiques are truly valuable, consider having a professional packer make specially designed cartons to hold your pieces. In most cases, following the rules for safe packing and loading will probably be sufficient. Make sure you adequately mark the boxes so that they get special treatment throughout your move.

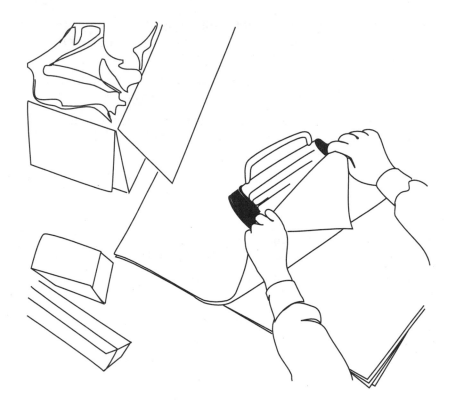

Wrap small kitchen appliances separately and pack securely in a box marked "Kitchen."

Small Appliances

Chapter 11 covers preparing larger appliances for the move, but what about your cabinets full of small appliances such as coffee makers, toasters, toaster ovens, and dehydrators?

The carton or box the appliance came in is the best packing material. If the box does not include molded packing material or if you do not have the original carton, cushion the appliance with packing peanuts or wadded newspaper as described earlier in this chapter in the section, "The Inside Story: How to Pack a Box."

Audio Equipment

Packing your stereo, tape player, CD player, or other audio equipment is relatively easy. Because most electronic equipment serves as a dust magnet, clean the equipment before packing it. You can clean the inside of audio cases by using a can of compressed air blown through the ventilation slots in the back of the appliance.

If you are moving an entire stereo system, first draw a diagram of the wiring (or take a Polaroid) before disconnecting the components. This drawing will save you hours of time at the other end when you're ready to set up the equipment.

If you are moving a turntable, first secure the arm with a rubber band or twist-tie. The changer can typically be cinched down by turning two screws on the top of the unit. Then wrap the dust cover in a large towel, small blanket, or soft tissue.

To move a CD player, first remove all CDs from the unit. Remove stacker or multi-play cartridges. If the unit includes a transport screw, tighten the screw before packing.

If you have the original box and packing material, repack the player in it. If not, use a box slightly larger than the unit, so that it can be surrounded by packing material. Pack tightly so that the unit will not shift within the box.

Finally, place the units in one or more boxes marked "Audio" and "Fragile."

Bedding

Clean bedding can be packed or used as packing. Soiled bedding from your last night in the old house should be packed separately if you've already packed the washer and dryer.

Lighter bedding items such as pillows and blankets can be placed in furniture drawers. Heavier items, such as comforters, should be placed in clean cartons.

Bedding can also be used as packing material to cushion breakable items. Use older bedding as furniture wraps.

Books

At my house, once all the books are packed, the moving job is half done!

Books are heavy. Pack them in small, strong boxes. Book boxes are typically about 1.5 cubic feet in size. Place the books flat in the box, cover to cover, alternating bindings.

If you have especially old or valuable books, pack them separately with padding.

Canned Food

Chances are, you're not going to be able to eat all the canned food in the house before you move. If you're moving very far, consider donating unopened food containers to a charity rather than pay a buck a pound or more to move things that cost sixty cents a pound.

Like books, canned food is heavy, so it should be packed in small, strong cartons. About 25 food cans (15 juice cans) is the maximum you should pack in a box. If necessary, fill the rest of the box with lighter durable items or packing material.

Carpets and Rugs

The best way to pack loose carpets and rugs is to roll them up for the shortest length and tie them. If you use tape, make sure it is strong enough to keep the carpet from opening. Remember: The tighter the roll, the easier it will be to carry.

Clocks

Some clocks, especially those with moving parts, such as grandfather or anniversary clocks, need disassembly before moving. Remove the pendulum or secure it to the base of the clock. Attach the clock's key to the back of the clock with tape. Wrap and place the clock in a cushioned box. Mark "Fragile" on the box.

Chapter 11 covers moving grandfather clocks.

Clothing

Moving (if not before) is a good time to clear out your closet of clothing that you haven't worn in a while. You can even use discarded clothing as packing material.

Pack hanging clothing in wardrobe boxes, which each holds about 25 garments. Pack other clothing items in the bottom of the wardrobe, under the hanging clothing.

Lightweight clothing can be left in dresser and bureau drawers, packed in suitcases or in clean cartons.

Collections

So how are you going to pack your beer can collection? Or your butterfly collection?

Very carefully!

Most collectable items should be wrapped separately in clean wrapping paper or bubble wrap and packed into small to medium cartons, depending on the size and weight. Fill any empty space in the carton with peanuts or other cushioning material. And remember to mark the box "Fragile" as well as to identify the box's contents.

A computer can be wrapped and packed as components.

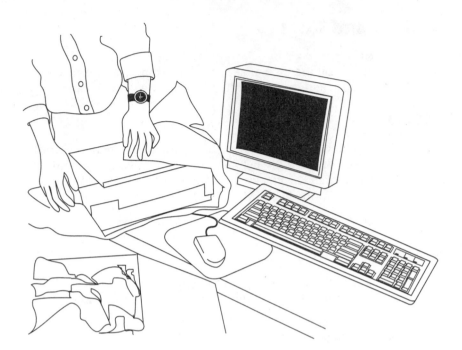

Computers

Moving a computer from here to there can be relatively easy if you treat the computer like the expensive piece of electronics that it is. Chances are it's traveled from Taiwan or Timbuktu to your place, so a thousand more miles won't hurt it—if you prepare it for the move.

First, back up all the files on your computer's hard disk. Store this backup disk with your original computer disks.

Next, remove disks from drives and insert a cardboard diskette or an old, disposable diskette into the drive. If the drive holds 5¹/₄-inch disks, close the drive door. (3¹/₂-inch drives latch themselves.)

Check your computer manual for the exact procedure for preparing your hard disk for moving. Some hard disks will need to park the recording heads for transport. If so, a program called SHIPDISK.EXE, included in the operating system, will park the heads. The hard disk will automatically unpark when you turn it back on.

Finally, turn off the system. Remove all cables from the back of the unit, labeling each cord for position. Mark the cords and wrap them separately. If possible, place the main computer unit in its original box with packing material. If you no longer have the original packing material, use sturdy moving boxes and good packing material such as bubble wrap, packing peanuts, or a small blanket.

Pack the monitor, keyboard, and printer in the same way. If you didn't save the original boxes, use sturdy moving boxes and pack securely with bubble wrap and/or packing peanuts. Remove ink cartridges from the printer.

Make sure you mark all computer component boxes so that you can find them when you arrive at your new place.

Curtains, Draperies, and Shades

The last things you'll pack as you move out are curtains and drapes. If they're yours, don't forget them in the rush to move.

Curtains can be folded and placed in drawers or clean cartons. If you have draperies cleaned and your move is within the same town, have them delivered to your new home, or hang them in wardrobe boxes, still in the cleaning bags. Schedule cleaning the drapes one week before the move; otherwise, you probably won't have the cleaning bags to hang them in when the wardrobe boxes arrive.

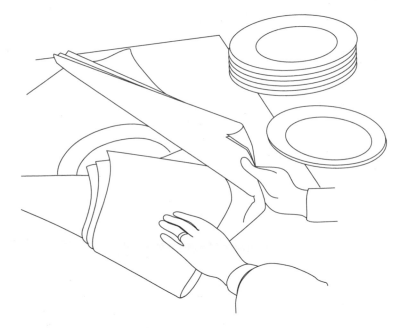

Plates are wrapped flat by folding packing paper edges over.

Dishes

You can pack dishes in regular boxes or in dish packs: special boxes available through movers.

117

To safely pack dishes, line a dish pack or a medium-sized carton with crumpled packing paper or newspaper, and then wrap each piece separately. Start with a stack of commercial packing paper or newspaper. Place a plate in the center of the paper. Grasp about two pieces of paper at one corner and pull the paper over the plate. Place a second plate on top of the first one. Take a second corner of the paper and pull over the two stacked plates. Stack a third plate on top of the other two. Grasp the third corner of the paper and pull it over the plates. Repeat with the fourth corner.

Now, turn over the stack of wrapped plates and place the stack in the center of the stack of paper. For added protection, rewrap the bundle in paper or towels. Grasp one corner of the wrap and pull it over the bundle of plates. Repeat for the second, third, and fourth corners. Seal the bundle with packing tape and place it in a carton with the plates with the narrow edge down.

Wrapped plates are placed in individual compartments within a dish pack or stacked flat with extra paper between plates.

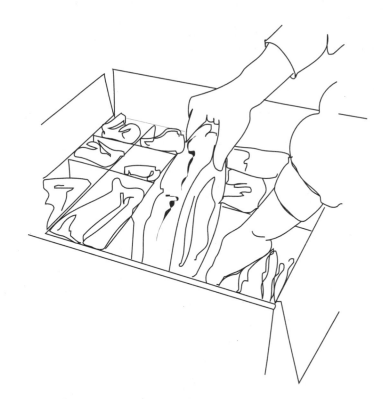

To pack the box, place larger items on the bottom and smaller items toward the top of the carton, with cushioning between layers and over the top layer. You can avoid getting newsprint on the dishes by either packing with clean packing paper or by slipping each dish into a clean plastic bag before packing with newspaper. Mark the box as "Kitchen: Dishes" and "Fragile."

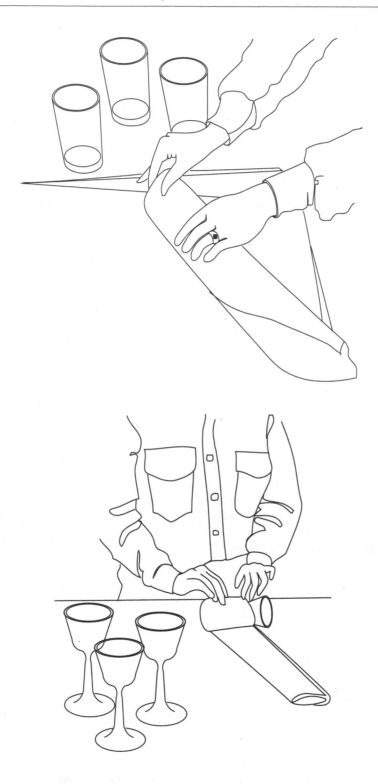

Start at the corner of the wrapping paper and roll the glass to the center, then fold the ends over.

Wrap stemware glasses using a thicker pad to protect the stem.

Glasses and Cups

You can also pack glasses and cups easily by using smaller boxes or dish packs. First, place crumpled paper inside each glass or cup. Either wrap each piece separately or nest three or four cups or glasses together, depending on the value of the objects versus the cost of your packing material.

Cups can be wrapped similarly to glasses and other small, round objects.

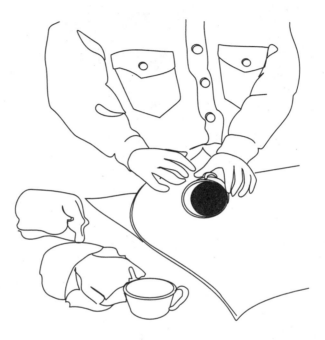

Next, place three or four wrapped glasses or cups together and lay them on your stack of paper, diagonally. Grasp a corner of the paper and wrap it around the glasses. Repeat with each corner of the paper. Roll the glasses into a bundle and secure with tape. Place glasses toward the top of the box and above dishes, on their sides. Mark the box as "Kitchen: Glassware" and "Fragile."

Kitchenware

Nest pots, pans, and similar unbreakable items with paper between pieces. Place heavier items at the bottom of a sturdy carton and lighter items, such as the pot lids, on top.

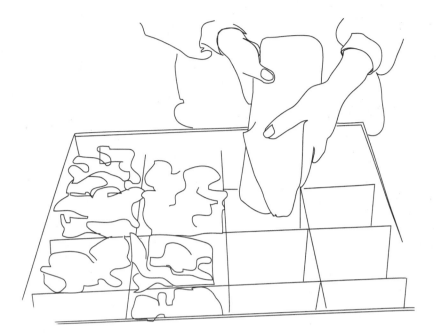

Dish packs include compartments to keep items from damaging one another.

Lamps

Lamps take a little time to pack, but they can be safely moved with the right packing procedures.

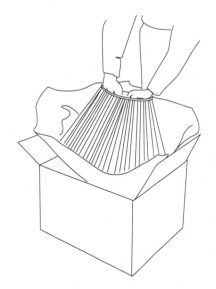

Wrap the lamp base and place it in a box separate from the shade.

First, remove any shades on the lamp by unscrewing the clips on the wire harp that attaches the shade to the lamp base. Next, remove bulbs for the lamp and wrap them separately. Wrap lamp bases in bubble wrap or with towels and place in boxes. Wrap lamp shades in clean, white tissue paper or bubble wrap in individual cartons. Mark the box: "Lamps" and "Fragile."

Alternately, you can place wrapped lamps and shades in your disconnected freezer or washing machine with adequate padding.

Medicines

You'll probably need lots of sedatives for your move, so remember not to pack them up with the things going in the moving vehicle.

Actually, you or someone in your moving party may need medications nearby either as you move or as soon as you arrive. Pay special attention to packing medicines.

After you've determined which medicines get packed in boxes and which in luggage, find a box that will easily hold the packed medications. If you expect that the box will be jostled during the move, stuff cosmetic cotton balls in the containers to keep the pills intact. Then tape the caps of medicine bottles, wrap the bottle, and pack it upright in a small carton. Mark the box: "Medicine."

Mirrors, pictures, and other fragile flat items are packed in mirror packs.

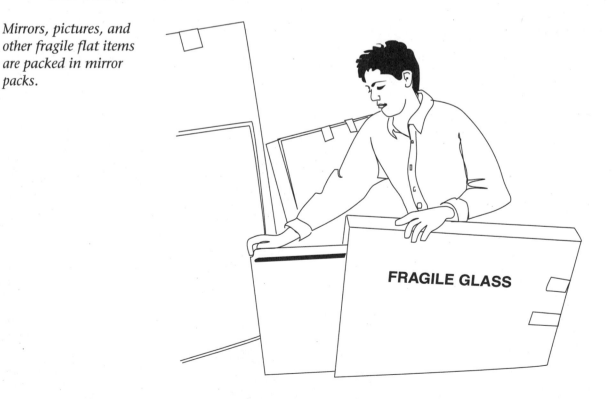

FRAGILE GLASS

Mirrors and Paintings

If you're moving very far, consider crating valuable mirrors and large paintings. Less valuable mirrors and paintings can be packed in mirror cartons available through your mover or truck rental agency. Alternatively, you can protect mirrors or paintings in the truck or trailer by wrapping them in blankets or rugs and loading them on edge between mattresses. Smaller mirrors and paintings can be packed in heavy cardboard boxes.

Photographs

Photographs often have value beyond what an insurance company can cover. Your treasured photos will be safest in boxes with soft cloth to reduce movement. If the photos are in frames, pack them as you would mirrors and paintings, as I covered in the preceding section, "Mirrors and Paintings."

Plants

Most professional movers will not move household plants, which are too fragile to be packed and transported in the typical moving van. Even moving plants in your rental trailer or truck can be hazardous to their health.

Your climate-controlled car is a better choice for moving plants. If you are moving to another state, be sure to learn whether there are any restrictions on importing plants. California, Arizona, and Florida are the most finicky states regarding this issue. Check with the Agriculture Department or Department of Natural Resources of your new state for current information about any restrictions. If you cannot move your plants, you may be able to take a cutting. Put the cutting in sterile soil or in a plastic bag with a damp cloth and vent holes. Most plant cuttings packed this way can survive for several days.

On moving day, pack your plants in a box sufficiently large and strong for safe transport. Pack paper around the pots to keep them in place. Use soft paper to cushion branches and leaves. Punch air holes in the sides of the box and fasten the lid loosely.

Records, Tapes, and CDs

Most records, tapes, and CDs are easy to pack into a box. The real issue is climate control. Make sure the items don't get too cold or hot, because they may crack, melt, or warp. Pack them in small cartons, first placing tapes and CDs in their holders. Bundle records and place them in a box on edge so that they don't break or warp. Mark the box: "Records, CDs."

Silverware

If your silverware is really silver, use cloth or low sulfur–content paper to wrap them and prevent tarnishing. Stainless silverware doesn't require special care. If the silverware is in a chest, wrap the chest in a blanket or moving pad. Place the wrapped chest in the bottom of a carton of similar items. Mark the box: "Silverware."

Garden tools can be tied together while hoses can be boxed.

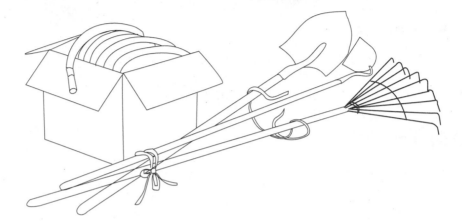

Tools

You may have only a few tools or a whole shop full of them. Hand tools can be wrapped individually in paper or packed loose in tool boxes or in small cardboard boxes. Add crumpled paper to make sure that they don't move around much.

Tools that are dirty or oily should be wiped off and wrapped in plastic before being packed. Then be sure to keep them away from things you'd prefer not to have dirty or oily.

You can pack power tools in the same way you do other household items, wrapping in newspaper and packing tightly in a sturdy box. Make sure the boxes are marked "Garage: Power Tools," for example.

The Least You Need to Know

➤ Plan well, use good materials, start early, mark boxes, and use a staging area.

➤ Follow the five easy steps to pack a box efficiently and reduce or eliminate breakage.

➤ You can pack like a pro if you use proven packing techniques.

Hello, Dolly: Moving Furniture and Appliances

> ## In This Chapter
>
> ➤ Preparing furniture and appliances for the move
>
> ➤ Moving furniture and appliances without injury
>
> ➤ Professional tips and techniques for moving big stuff

"How am I ever going to get the grand piano down seven flights of stairs?"

"I would rather use a moving company, but we just can't afford it."

"I'm afraid to do much lifting or my back will go out again."

"Is liniment a tax-deductible moving expense?"

Many otherwise confident people go weak in the knees when thinking about moving large things like furniture and appliances. Certainly, a 97-year-old grandmother can't handle these items, but you may be quite surprised at how many of your larger possessions you can move—once you know how.

Tools and techniques. That's what this chapter is all about: how to use common moving tools and professional moving techniques to move larger and heavier items.

But first, a word of wisdom. Before deciding to move that old refrigerator from one coast to another, consider the wisdom in the decision. The refrigerator may cost you $100 as its share of the moving vehicle, fuel, equipment, and your time. Is it really worth a hundred bucks? Or should you sell or donate it here and buy another one (not necessarily new) there?

For example, if you're moving a long distance for a short-term stay, consider selling off, storing, or donating appliances, and then, if needed, renting what you need at the other end. Your best bet might be to get rid of larger items now.

Something to think about.

How Are We Feeling Today?

Yes, moving large stuff can be hazardous to your health. With good planning, good tools, and good friends, however, moving a sofa, dresser, or refrigerator really isn't that strenuous for a person in typical condition. Even if you're older or have physical limitations, you can sidewalk-supervise others to do the actual work.

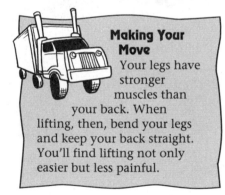

Making Your Move

Your legs have stronger muscles than your back. When lifting, then, bend your legs and keep your back straight. You'll find lifting not only easier but less painful.

Assorted and Sundry Tools of the Moving Trade

A number of valuable tools are available to professional movers, most of which can also be rented or purchased by the do-it-yourself mover.

One Dolly Is Worth Three Strong Men

The appliance dolly is on top of the moving tool list. Not only is it handy for moving major appliances, you can also use it to move stacks of boxes and even sofas and other furniture.

A good appliance dolly is 60 inches high or taller. It has a cinch strap that can be wrapped around an appliance and cinched tight with a locking mechanism. The last thing you want as you move that refrigerator is to have the strap come loose halfway down the stairs!

An appliance dolly should be rated for a load of at least 500 pounds. More is better. If you can, select a dolly with a slider or stepper located between the two wheels. A slider is two small wheels with a rubber track around them. A stepper is three small wheels on a rotating shaft. The slider or stepper can help you make your trip down a set of stairs easier.

Legal Things You Can Do with a Piano Dolly

Another useful moving tool is the four-wheel or piano dolly. This dolly is approximately 30×30 inches and about 60 inches high with wheels on each of the four corners. Be sure to rent one rated for a load of at least 500 pounds.

A piano dolly is useful for moving, yes, pianos. For uprights: One end is lifted, the dolly is placed under the center of the piano, and the lifted end is lowered. The piano can now be rolled away. For grand pianos, the piano is first placed on its side, and then the dolly is placed under that side. Grand pianos should be strapped to the dolly for secure movement.

As you can imagine, a piano dolly can also be useful for moving other big pieces such as cabinets. Wrap the item and the dolly with a cinched strap to keep the item from moving.

Other Friendly Moving Tools

Other useful moving tools include a pry bar, a couple of four-foot two-by-fours, and a blanket. You can use the pry bar to get under the edge of a large piece to help lift it for insertion of a dolly.

You can use a two-by-four board as a fulcrum under the center of the pry bar or to hold the item off the floor after the pry bar has lifted it.

Moving Words
When talking about a dolly, a *slider* is two small wheels with a rubber track around them. A *stepper* is three small wheels on a rotating shaft.

Moving Violations
Don't use a smaller two-wheeled dolly (called a *stock dolly*) to move appliances. It isn't built for the job. Stock dollies are typically 36 to 60 inches tall, but have no cinch strap for holding the appliance in place.

And the blanket? Yes, a thick, tightly woven blanket, mover's quilt, or carpet scraps are excellent tools for moving couches, chairs, tables, and other objects that are more bulk than weight. Here's how.

To move a couch across a room, for example, place half of the blanket under the two side legs. Then grab the other end of the blanket and carefully pull. Your success depends on the weight of the couch and the surface underneath it. If the floor is a firm surface, place another blanket or some carpet samples (carpet-side down) under the other legs to reduce friction.

Your hands are your best moving tools. Here are some tips for smart carrying:

- ➤ Wear gloves. Gardening gloves with rubber dots on the fingers and palms provide adequate protection and a nonslip grip.
- ➤ Larger objects (chests, cabinets, refrigerators) should be tipped to keep the carriers from bumping knees on the furniture. Lower end goes out the door first.
- ➤ If the edges of heavy objects are sharp (such as on a washer), use a towel or gloves to protect your hands.
- ➤ Always carry large objects by the bottom edge so your fingers don't get crushed or bruised as you go through a tight doorway.

Okay, so let's go through the house or apartment, searching for smart ways to move your furniture and appliances.

Moving Bedroom Furniture for Fun and Profit

Moving bedroom furniture really isn't as difficult as you might imagine. In fact, most bedroom furniture is made up of components—frames, drawers, box springs—that can be taken apart and moved separately, making the job easier.

The next sections tell you how to disassemble and relocate your bedroom.

What You'll Find When You Move a Bed

Remove all bedding and pads before trying to move the components.

To remove the mattress, push it to the side of the bed nearer the bedroom door. Then stand the mattress on edge.

The easiest way to move a mattress is with two people: one at each end of the mattress. Stretch a rope from the right hand of the person at one end, underneath the middle of the mattress, to the right hand of the person at the other end. (Reverse hands if you have two left-handed folks. Flip a coin if one's a righty and the other a lefty.) The rope hands lift and the alternate hands steady the mattress.

Alternatively, you can move a mattress by having the person at each end use both hands to press the mattress from each side; then lift the mattress off the floor and walk.

The same techniques can be used to move a box spring.

Remove the bed frame from the headboard and footboard. Some frames are connected with bolts while with others the frame's rails simply slip into slots in the board posts. Disassemble the bed frame, placing the screws and bolts in a zip bag (freezer bags are best—they can be relabeled) and taping the bag to the frame. Bed frames typically have a twist connector that locks the cross-brace in place. Turn it to remove.

Ugh! Moving Dressers and Chests

Dressers and chests may look difficult to move, but they really aren't—if you look at them as components. If the furniture includes a mirror, remove the mirror bracing from the back or top of the chest. The bracing is usually fastened with screws. Then remove all drawers. Finally, use an appliance dolly, piano dolly, or two-person carry to move the chest. Once in the truck or trailer, reinstall the drawers. Pack the mirror in a mirror carton or wrap it in blankets and place it on edge between two mattresses in your truck or trailer.

Waterbeds: I Slept in One Until I Was Three!

Remember to always drain a waterbed before attempting to move it!

But how? As there are several types of waterbed mattresses, follow the instructions for the type you have (from your purchase literature or a local waterbed store). In most cases, you need to unplug the waterbed heater, then drain the bed using a siphon, faucet adapter, or drain pump. A drain pump can cut the emptying time in half! Rent one from a waterbed or hardware store.

After the mattress is drained, grasp the baffle system along with the external vinyl and fold the mattress about 20 inches at a time. Place the mattress in a large plastic bag and pack it into a large carton. You can use a blanket to provide more padding and protection to the mattress.

Disconnect the heater from the control and carefully roll and fold the pad. Wrap it and place it in a carton where it will not be crushed.

Moving Living Room Furniture for Aches and Pains

There's probably lots of furniture in your living room to move: couch, recliner, tables, entertainment center, and maybe some antiques or special-care furniture.

Moving Upholstered Furniture the Easy Way

You can move couches, recliners, cabinets, and other typical living room furniture by following the suggestions earlier in this chapter on moving larger objects by hand or by dolly. Here are some additional suggestions:

➤ By standing a couch on end and wrapping it with an old (but clean) blanket, you can use an appliance dolly to move a large couch. (Watch out for hanging fixtures.)

➤ If your sofa is a sleeper, make sure you use a short rope to tie the sleeper unit to the frame before attempting to move it. Otherwise, the unit might decide to open up into a bed halfway through the doorway!

➤ Before you put that nice upholstered furniture into a dusty old truck and drive it cross-country, cover the furniture with plastic covers or at least some old sheets.

Moving the Television: Open Me First!

First step to moving the television: Disconnect it from the cable!

As life may seem to end when the cable is disconnected, make this one of the last things you move.

(Actually, our home has been without cable for more than six months due to a difference in valuation with the cable company, and we seldom miss it!)

If the original TV carton is available, pack your television in it. If not, place the TV in a box slightly larger than it and pack soft things around it—especially in front of the screen.

Some experts recommend service before and after moving. Read your owner's manual to determine whether your TV's manufacturer recommends such service.

Moving Tables and Cabinets

Some tables can be disassembled for easier moving. Turn over the coffee or end table and look for nuts that can be removed behind the legs. Box or tape them together with the hardware.

If you are moving a cabinet with doors, tie the knobs together or carefully use packing tape across the doors to keep them shut in transit.

As you load the tables or cabinets into your truck or trailer, wrap them in moving pads to protect their surfaces.

Moving Grandfather Clocks and Other Neat Stuff

In this age of digital time, not everyone has a grandfather or grandmother clock. If you do, however, you need to take special precautions with it. Here's how.

First, remove chimes, weights, and pendulums, wrapping them in moving pads. Then tie or tape the door closed so that it won't open in transit.

If you feel uncomfortable preparing your grandfather clock or other heirlooms or antiques for moving, consider hiring a professional mover to pack them for you.

Dining Room Furniture

Dining room furniture is relatively easy to pack. Depending on the available space in your moving vehicle, you might want to remove the legs or base from a dining table. If it has a glass top, carefully remove it and pack it in a mirror box or wrap it in moving blankets and place between mattresses.

Dining chairs can be disassembled or stacked. Low-back kitchen chairs can be stacked with the second chair upside down. High-back dining chairs can be stacked with a box on the seat of the first chair. Then the second chair is placed upside down on the box so that the chair back doesn't touch the floor. Place moving blankets between and around chairs to minimize abrasion.

You can move dining room cabinets by removing all loose shelves, securing doors, and, if possible, removing legs.

Remember to use moving pads to wrap dining room furniture for extra protection. Make sure that pads cover edges, corners, and other places that can rub or be rubbed.

Moving Kitchen Appliances without an On-Call Chiropractor

The kitchen is the center of a home. And your new abode won't feel quite like home until you get all the appliances in place and working.

Can't Live without It: Moving Microwave Ovens

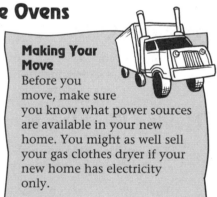

What did we ever do before the microwave was invented? Today, it is a vital part of many kitchens, so you want to pack it up last and set it up at your new home first.

To move a microwave oven, remove all loose items from inside the oven. Wrap them and pack in a separate carton. Next, tape the door shut, using an X pattern to keep the door closed. Use any type of sturdy tape that will come off later without removing finish.

Making Your Move
Before you move, make sure you know what power sources are available in your new home. You might as well sell your gas clothes dryer if your new home has electricity only.

If possible, place the microwave in the original box with original packing material. Otherwise, choose a sturdy packing carton slightly larger than the oven and pack tightly with packing material. Make sure you mark the box "Kitchen: Microwave" and "Fragile."

Moving Refrigerators and Freezers

Wouldn't it be nice if you could simply put the refrigerator in the moving truck or trailer, plug it in and not worry about all the leftovers inside? Won't happen! So you'd better learn how to prep it for the move.

First, follow the manufacturer's directions for defrosting your refrigerator or freezer. Dry the interior of the cabinet thoroughly with towels. Leaving the doors open for several hours will help air it out.

Next, remove drawers, shelving, ice trays, and that old bottle of ketchup. Pack them as you would other kitchen items.

To keep the interior smelling fresh, pour a cup of fresh coffee grounds, baking soda, or charcoal in a clean sock and place it in the cabinet. The cabinet can be packed with large, lightweight items such as wardrobe or lighter boxes.

When you move the unit, use an appliance dolly or some professional wrestlers. Place the unit upright in the truck or trailer—laying it on its side or back can damage the unit.

What's Cookin'?: Moving Stoves

Stoves are for cooking—when the microwave's broken. But, in case you need it someday, here's how to move your stove or oven.

If gas, shut off the gas line. Disconnect the unit from the gas line or unplug it from the electrical outlet. Remove any burners, coils, oven racks, or other loose components and pack separately. Tape the electrical cord to the back of the stove. Finally, wrap and move the range as you would the refrigerator.

Moving Other Big Stuff You Should Have Sold

You probably have some other big stuff in your life that you now feel you cannot live without: washing machine, clothes dryer, ergonomic recyclator. Whatever. Here's how to move other big stuff.

Moving Washing Machines

The washing machine will be one of the last things out the door as you move—and one of the first in at the other end. Here's how to move it easily.

First, turn off faucets and disconnect and drain hoses. Then place plastic bags and rubber bands securely over the ends of each hose to prevent leakage. Check your washing machine's instruction manual for specifics on how to brace the tub and secure the motor. Some have set screws while others simply require that you stuff something soft into the tub to reduce movement. No, you can't use pets for this step!

Moving Dryers

Where there's a washer, there's a dryer. Or so Mr. Maytag says. Dryers are relatively easy to move—especially if you have lots of relatives to help!

First, disconnect the unit from the power source: electricity, gas, or gerbil motor. Then check the dryer's instruction manual or your appliance service man to figure out how to secure the motor from excessive movement.

Air Conditioners

Air conditioners, dehumidifiers, and other air filtration units can easily be prepared for moving. Disconnect the unit from the power source, then remove parts that can fall off or damage other things. Make sure that water or condensation is drained from the unit. Wrap the unit with moving pads.

Exercise Equipment

Most modern homes have one or more pieces of exercise equipment that need to be moved. In most cases, the first step is to dust it off. Then refer to the unit's instruction manual to disassemble or fold the unit down to a compact size. Use rope or sturdy tape to keep everything together. Finally, wrap the unit in a moving pad to keep it from scratching things around it in the moving vehicle.

Outdoor Stuff

So, what's left?

Probably all those toys in the back yard: hot tub, canoe, surfboard, skis, bicycles, unicycles, et al. How to pack them for the move?

Just as you would any items of similar size and weight. That is, the hot tub can be packed as you would a large refrigerator: clear out, disconnect, and wrap for protection. Bicycles, skis, and surfboards are tough to wrap, so can be tied or taped to minimize abrasion, then packed where they won't be in harm's way.

The list of stuff you could pack is endless. Fortunately, once you've packed a few boxes and major appliances, you'll be an expert. You can then apply what you've learned to packing the oddball stuff that we all seem to accumulate.

The Least You Need to Know

➤ Find and use a professional mover's dolly for both appliances and stacks of boxes.

➤ Use a piano dolly for moving large, bulky items.

➤ Learn how to lift correctly before trying to hoist a heavy object.

➤ Knowing how to move specific furniture and appliances can make the move easier and safer.

Chapter 12

Professional Moving Techniques for the Amateur Mover

In This Chapter

➤ What works well when moving yourself

➤ What *doesn't* work when moving yourself

➤ Moving vehicles the easy way

➤ Packing your Smart Moving Survival Box

"Remember to lift with your legs."

"Pack the mirror like this so you won't get seven years of bad luck."

"No, don't stack the refrigerator on top of the stereo!"

Don't you wish you had a professional mover advising you as you planned and packed?

You have the next best thing: this book. This chapter, especially, offers dozens of tips and techniques from professional movers on how to get from here to there without stops at the nut house—or the poor house.

No, you won't learn to *love* moving. But it can become relatively tolerable!

The pros say: Lift with your legs, not with your back, and carefully use dollies on slopes.

A Mover's Dozen Tips from the Professionals

"Gosh, I didn't know!"

Knowing how to do things the first time as if it weren't your first time is the key to most tasks. Moving, too.

And professional movers have plenty of experience to share with others. They've learned what to do and what *not* to do when moving.

Here are a mover's dozen (that's 11) tips for Smart Moving as offered by professional movers.

➤ Train your helpers on safe lifting and moving before they load your truck or trailer.

➤ Pack heavy items in small, sturdy cartons and lightweight items in large cartons.

➤ Pack each box tightly so that contents will not shift; then seal each carton securely with packing tape.

➤ Invest a few bucks in good packing materials to protect your belongings.

➤ Label every box on two sides, in the same position on each box, with destination room and contents.

➤ Use towels, linens, and out-of-season clothing as packing material to cushion breakables.

➤ Protect mirrors, framed pictures and other breakables by wrapping them in moving pads or packing them in mirror cartons.

➤ Don't pack flammables or plants. (We'll cover what to do with combustible stuff later in this chapter.)

➤ Plan early how you're going to get not only your stuff but all your vehicles from here to there. (Upcoming topic alert.)

➤ Pack one box of essentials that will be the first thing unloaded at your new home. (We'll cover this topic, too, later in this chapter.)

➤ Pack your truck or trailer for even weight distribution with the heaviest items over the axle, not at the end. (And we'll cover this one in the next chapter, folks.)

Grab the Extinguisher!: What Not to Pack

For a variety of reasons, there are a few things that you shouldn't pack and move your-self—or at least not in the back of a moving truck or trailer.

Some items might explode or leak. Living things might discontinue living. You get the point.

So what can you do about it?

Do You Smell Something?: Dealing with Flammables

Whether you are driving the truck yourself or having a mover transport your goods, some items should not be moved because of the danger of fire or explosion.

Here's a list of stuff you either shouldn't move or should at least be especially careful about moving:

➤ Aerosol cans (hair spray, shaving cream, deodorants)
➤ Ammunition
➤ Bleach
➤ Car batteries
➤ Cleaning products
➤ Gasoline
➤ Other automotive fluids
➤ Insecticides
➤ Kerosene
➤ Lighter fluid
➤ Matches
➤ Oil-based paints
➤ Oxygen tanks
➤ Paint thinners
➤ Paint strippers
➤ Propane
➤ Turpentine
➤ Any other combustibles

Why the fuss over deodorant cans? Pressurized cans include propellants that can change state if left in a hot trailer for a few days. Combustibles such as kerosene can leak out and not only damage other things but potentially start a fire in your moving vehicle.

So what can you do about it?

The pros say: Paints, fuels, matches, and aerosols should NOT be moved by you or your mover.

Take paints, aerosols, and other flammables to recycling locations in your area where they can be disposed of properly. If you're moving refillable propane tanks, have them purged and sealed by a propane gas dealer. Discard any non-refillable tanks.

Taking these precautions is better than later saying, "Gosh, I wish I'd…"

For your safety, the safety of your possessions, and that of the movers, get rid of these items before moving day. Plan to replace them as needed at your new home.

What would you do at your new home with three quarts of lemon-yellow paint anyway?

Plants: Move It and Lose It

"Any plants or produce to declare?"

Moving Words
Flammable or *inflammable*: easily ignited.

Nonflammable or *uninflammable*: <u>not</u> easily ignited.

In some interstate moves, you'll hear this question as you attempt to cross a state line—especially Arizona and California. I'm sure there's probably a prison full of people who have attempted to sneak an orange or a favorite rose bush into these states without declaring them. It's a major crime problem!

Actually, the concern is that moving plants and bugs in from a quarantined area can impact agricultural crops in the new area. Kinda makes sense.

Support your local Produce Police!

In addition, many house plants just won't survive the harshness of being packed in a vehicle for a three-day cross-country trip through a variety of climates. So be kind to your plants and don't take them far away from the place of their birth. Donate them to friends or enemies.

Chapter 20 has lots more info on this topic.

Goldfish and Other Recyclables

If you have an aquarium or a goldfish pond, how can you get your favorite fish from here to there? That depends.

If you're only moving a few hours away, transportation in plastic bags or half-full fish bowls is relatively easy. The problem can be trying to move tropical fish very far. They like their moderately warm water and will swim on their sides if they don't always get it.

Aquarium magazines have ads for products to help you ship fish via overnight carriers to the destination of your choice. But what happens at the other end? Some movers with expensive tropical fish contract with an aquarium shop in the area where they're moving to to receive and hold the fish for arrival of the owners.

Otherwise, they make excellent hors d'oeuvres!

How to Move Vehicles You Wouldn't or Couldn't Sell

In a time not long ago, a family move meant packing everyone and everything into the car and driving to wherever. Today, we have two or more vehicles involved: dad's commuter car, mom's taxi, junior's clunker, sis' status symbol, the travel trailer or motor home, the RV, the boat, and maybe that 1936 Packard dad has in the garage.

So how are you going to get all these wheels from here to there? If your boss is paying for the entire move: no problem! But if you're doing some or all of it yourself: problem!

Fortunately, some solutions are available.

Wanna Drive?

You might be lucky enough to find that the number of vehicles exactly matches the number of qualified drivers. If not, auto transport services will relocate your vehicle for a fee. Find them advertised in the phone book or classified ads, but make sure they are fully licensed and bonded. You would be pretty sad to arrive in Cleveland and find out your car was dismantled in Peoria.

If some of your vehicle(s) aren't drivable (dad's dismantled DeSoto?), consider either selling it or having an auto transport service take it to point B sans driver. Check the phone book for Automotive Transport services.

Dealing with Tow Bars and Other Fears

Another option is to tow one or more vehicles to your new home. If you are moving with a rental truck, you can rent a tow bar or a car dolly to attach to the truck.

Renting or buying a tow bar is (obviously) for vehicles that are towable. Even if the car is in running condition, some cars should not be towed because the automatic transmission or four-wheel drive unit will be damaged. Which cars? Check your vehicle's owner's manual for information on how — or whether—to tow it.

Fortunately, most cars that can't be towed by using a tow bar can be moved by using a car dolly or flatbed trailer. A car dolly lets you set the car's front wheels on the dolly's axle. A flatbed trailer lets you set the entire car on the trailer.

Either way, don't forget to use tiedowns to lash the car to the dolly or trailer.

"Say, hon, isn't that our car that just passed us?!"

Move That Trailer!

Moving a travel trailer can be easy as long as your towing vehicle isn't previously occupied towing a moving trailer or otherwise indisposed.

If your moving vehicle isn't available, you might be able to get a friend to tow your travel trailer for a short move, or you can hire a transport service to relocate it for you.

Or you can sell it here and buy another one there.

"Moving. Must sell..."

Not Available without a Prescription: Your Moving Survival Box

"Say, where'd we put the sedatives for the kids?"

"I gotta have coffee when we get to the new place!"

One of the best tips for amateur movers is to make sure you have packed a Smart Moving Survival Box. It's the box of things you take with you as you travel from here to there no matter what the distance or mode. It helps you be more relaxed and more comfortable with your move. It makes sure you're ready for your new adventure.

Sedatives are optional, but recommended.

Your Box of Goodies

A Smart Moving Survival Box may actually be more than one box. It could be one for the trip and one for your new house. It will include whatever you need to survive this ghastly ordeal!

Your Departure Survival Box should include things to help you enjoy the relocation. For longer moves, that means games and books to keep the kids from bickering (good luck!), snacks for the road, important telephone numbers, postcards and stamps, a cheap novel or two, a cellular telephone and coverage map…anything that will make the trip more comfortable.

Making Your Move
Save on your food bill during a trip by carrying an ice chest and stopping at grocery stores rather than eating in restaurants three times a day. Buy fruit, granola bars, juice, even sandwich makings. You will eat more healthfully, feel better, and save money.

Your Arrival Survival Box can include the things you and your family members consider necessary when you get where you're going, for example:

➤ Toilet paper

➤ Hand soap

➤ Coffee maker and coffee

➤ Flashlight

➤ Matches

➤ Paper towels

➤ Linens

➤ Household tool kit

➤ Phone numbers

✓ Suggest to everyone in your moving party that each pack a small survival box that includes a few things such as toothbrush, toothpaste, cosmetics, or other personal items.

One more good idea: Pack some familiar items such as framed photos, decorations, and other things that will help everyone feel more at home when they arrive.

Making Your Move

Send a postcard! Take paper, envelopes, stamps, and addresses of friends left behind and send them cards as you travel from here to there. It's cheaper than calling them!

The Least You Need to Know

➤ Professional movers suggest investing in good packing materials and planning well.

➤ Don't pack flammables, combustibles, or living things.

➤ Make sure you pack one or more Smart Moving Survival Boxes with things you'll need for the trip and on arrival at your new home.

Chapter 13

Stuff It: Loading and Driving Your Moving Vehicle

It's show time!

You've planned this move to within an inch of its life. You've stuffed everything you own into a variety of containers. Now it's time to shove all those containers into a rented or borrowed truck or moving trailer. Then you're going to have to move the moving vehicle(s) from here to there—without police escort!

Lucky you!

Actually, loading and driving a moving vehicle is a relatively easy process. You can learn the basic rules to vehicle loading, and controlling the vehicle down the road isn't as tough as it may seem. I'll give you some techniques based on my dozen-plus years of driving commercial vehicles.

Buckle up!

You're Gonna Drive That Big Thing to Where?

The first fact you need to know about your moving vehicle is its size: how big it is. Sure, you need to know its length, but more important, how much cargo room is in it?

Your rental agent can tell you the cubic feet of space available in the unit you've selected. Or you can estimate it yourself. Small trailers may have only 100 cubic feet of interior space, while a large moving truck will have 1,600 cubic feet or more. As you learned in Chapter 8, a cubic foot is simply a square foot (width times length) times the height. So an area 1'×1'×1' is 1 cubic foot.

Making Your Move

The best way to move family pets is in the car or truck cab with you. And avoid fines and other added costs by making sure you know the animal regulations of the city and state where you are moving.

So a 4'×8' trailer that's 4' tall inside is 128 (4×8×4) cubic feet. A 20'×8' truck with an 8' ceiling has 1,280 cubic feet. Add in the overhead or attic of 3'×3'×8' (72 cu. ft.) and you have about 1,350 cubic feet of loading space.

You selected the appropriate vehicle with guidelines in Chapter 9. Whether this vehicle is a moving truck, a moving trailer, or a friend's pickup, you need to know how to efficiently pack and relocate it.

Packing Tightly without a Chain Saw

After you've matched the available space (1,800 cubic feet, for example) to the space you need for your stuff (fewer than 1,800 cubic feet, I hope!), it's now just a matter of using the space efficiently.

Smart loading of your truck will make the drive easier and safer. A loosely packed load can shift and cause the truck or towing vehicle to sway, which can lead to loss of control. A poorly balanced load can make driving harder and even damage the towing vehicle. And a poorly packed truck might lead to damage of your furniture and other possessions. It's well worth the time to plan how your truck should be loaded—and to follow your plan. Jot the plan down in your Smart Moving Notebook. While you are taking your time loading, remember that unloading will be much quicker because of smart loading.

First, wrap all of your furniture and appliances in moving pads (see Chapter 11). It may seem expensive to rent so many pads, but otherwise you take a chance on having things arrive at your new home with new scratches or gouges. These wraps come in assorted sizes, thicknesses, and names (furniture blanket, furniture wrap, furniture pad, moving quilt). You also can use old blankets, pillows, sleeping bags, and similar soft, thick, padded items as furniture wraps.

Next, mentally divide your truck's cargo area into quarters. You will load it one quarter at a time, working from floor to ceiling and packing it as solidly as possible. Think square. Try to create heavy squares as the first level of your load, and build up from there.

How to tie a "trucker's" or cinching knot to keep loads from moving.

For example, you can fit two, three, or four pieces together to make a rectangle or square, and then wrap them all together with a furniture wrap. Once a quarter of the space is packed, tie it off with rope. Fill any small spaces with boxes or other small items.

The key to efficient loading is to pack tightly. Don't waste space. Put boxes under chair legs. Place long, flat pieces under sofas and other furniture with legs. Leave lightweight items in furniture drawers. You get the idea. Take your time and load well.

Now, let's get more specific.

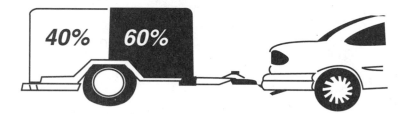

Remember to load the front end of your trailer with slightly more weight.

Insider's Tips on Loading the Truck

Now that you know the basics of loading a moving truck, here are some tips and techniques used by professional movers to make the job easier and safer:

➤ If you have a sufficient loading crew, have one person stay in the truck's loading area and two people carry things to him or her for tight packing.

➤ Back the truck as close as possible to the door of your home, and then extend the loading ramp to the top step of your house.

➤ Pack fragile items, such as electronics, in the space over the cab, called the *attic*.

➤ Load large, heavy items first. Working from the wall behind the cab (the front of the storage area), put the refrigerator across from the washer and dryer, for good weight distribution.

Moving Words
The *attic* is the overhead space over the cab in most moving trucks.

➤ Load other heavy items toward the front of the truck.

➤ Place mattresses, box springs, table tops, and other long, flat items along the sides of the truck.

➤ Pack any large mirror or framed and glazed pictures between a mattress and box spring.

➤ Tie down whatever goes along the walls.

➤ Put heavy boxes on the bottom. You can stack boxes of about the same size, strength, and weight.

➤ Put lighter boxes on top of heavy ones, but don't put heavy boxes on top of light ones.

➤ Load dressers and desks so that their drawers face the wall, keeping them from opening.

➤ Place lightweight or oddly shaped items on top of the load.

➤ Load a box of items you will need at the new house at the back of the truck—where it will come off the truck first.

➤ Lock the truck after it is all loaded.

Careful planning and packing can safely get an entire household of furniture in your moving van.

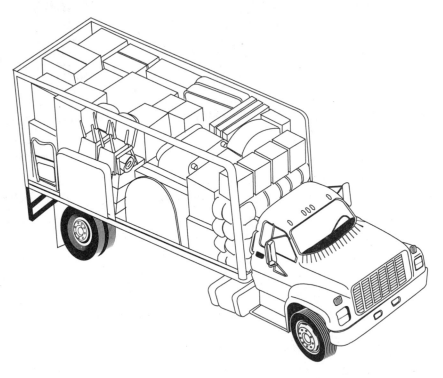

Six Days on the Road: Professional Truck Driving Tips

Today's rental trucks drive like big cars. They have automatic transmission, a comfortable cab, a radio, and lots of mirrors for seeing things.

Of course, you may have no inclination or desire to drive your truck. You've done enough work already. Hire to have the driving done if you want. Or delegate it to a trusted family member, relative, or friend. Or hire a professional driver.

I wasn't able to fly back to Iowa for our move to Oregon a few years ago, so we paid airfare and a few bucks to a nephew with truck driving experience. He was glad for the cash and the vacation.

If you do decide to borrow or rent a truck and drive it yourself, talk to the owner or read any literature from the rental company. Ask if there are any special quirks you should know about. One family learned the hard way that the parking brakes on the truck they borrowed held only if a foot was on the brake pedal when the parking brake was applied. Take a test drive. Practice backing up. Learn to use the side mirrors. Find the spare tire.

Stayin' Alive: Professional Tips for Safe Driving

Professional drivers may log a million miles or more between tickets and may drive five million miles or more without an accident. That's safe driving. Here are some of the tips they pass on to you:

➤ Never, never, never drink and drive.

➤ Use your seat belt and require that all passengers use them.

➤ Set the side mirrors before you pull out; and use them often.

➤ Start out slowly and get the feel of the truck.

➤ Watch your mirrors during turns to learn how much extra space you need.

➤ Allow extra time when merging into traffic because it takes longer for a truck to accelerate than it does for a car.

➤ Allow extra time and distance for stopping because it also takes longer to stop a truck than it does a car.

➤ Observe special truck speed limits as posted on highways.

➤ Plan a route that allows truck traffic.

➤ Expect that your trip will take longer than it would in a car.

➤ Don't be in a hurry. If you must pass, allow plenty of time and space.

➤ If you are not used to driving a truck, avoid backing up, if possible.

➤ If you must back up, let your assistant spot you as you back into the driveway or other location.

➤ Know what your overhead clearance is and watch for low bridges or tunnels, service station canopies, motel entrances, drive-up windows, and other obstacles.

➤ When in doubt, hog the far-right lane, slow down, and drive with your flashers on.

Fold, Spindle, Mutilate: Professional Tips on Loading a Trailer

Making Your Move

Don't have a vehicle to tow your trailer? Then rent one! Most larger moving rental lots have pickup trucks and utility vans for rent, and all set up to tow one of their trailers. It's cheaper than buying a big car because your teeny car won't pull a trailer!

Loading a trailer is not really much different from loading a truck. Professionals suggest that you place at least 60 percent of the weight of the load in the front half of the trailer. The weight should be evenly distributed from side to side to prevent swaying.

Of course, if you have a refrigerator or other appliance or furniture taller than 4 feet, make sure you rent a trailer with a door that's taller than 4 feet. Don't lay a refrigerator on its side to move it.

Otherwise, follow the guidelines given earlier in the section "Insider's Tips on Loading the Truck."

One more tip: Make sure the air pressure in the trailer's tires is correct for its gross weight. Low air pressure can make the trailer sway, which will, in turn, make your towing vehicle sway. Not fun!

Is It Still Back There?: Professional Tips on Pulling a Trailer

As with driving a truck, before you tow a trailer of any kind, evaluate your driving experience and knowledge of towing. If you do decide to tow a trailer, again ask for and read any advice from an experienced driver or your rental company. The following tips will also help:

➤ Use your seat belt and require that passengers use theirs.

➤ Set your mirrors and use them often.

➤ Test your brakes. It will take longer to stop with the added weight.

➤ Your tires may need extra inflation to carry the load. Check your manual or ask at your tire store.

➤ Watch your radiator indicator. Your car could overheat with the extra weight to pull.

➤ Check the hitch before you start driving after a rest stop to be sure safety chains and latches are secure.

➤ Avoid backing up, if possible. Think ahead and plan your stops so that you don't have to back out, even if it means walking farther.

➤ If you must back up, place your hands on the bottom of the wheel at approximately 4 and 8 o'clock instead of 2 and 10 o'clock, gripping the wheel from the inside, and go slowly. This technique lets you steer the trailer and your car as if you were steering just your car.

➤ Rely on a spotter to back up. Agree on signals.

➤ Remind the spotter that if he or she can't see the driver in the mirror, the driver can't see the spotter.

➤ Most folks get nervous and agitated when backing a trailer or helping someone back it. Be gentle with each other.

Moving Violations
Once, when driving from NY to Delaware, we stopped for lunch and checked the hitch. All was okay. Well, we ate, then got back in the car, backed out, straightened out, and headed for the parking lot exit—*sans* trailer. "Pranksters" had disengaged the hitch. We were not amused.

Get Out Your Teamster Card: Using a Truck to Pull a Trailer

If you need to tow your car or another object, such as a boat, or if your possessions require a truckload plus a trailer, your driving task will be more difficult—especially if you are not an experienced truck driver. When deciding how to get everything from here to there, calculate the total length of the combination you may be piloting down the freeway. The number may be intimidating! If you do need to take such a combination, allow extra time for your trip and consider the following tips:

➤ Use seat belts, and insist that anyone in the vehicle also use them.

➤ Set your mirrors and use them often.

➤ Remember, the more weight, the longer it will take to stop your rolling vehicle.

➤ Plan ahead. It may not be easy to find a place to park your car and trailer.

➤ If you can't see the sides of the vehicle being towed, you can attach a horizontal flag that will extend to where you can see it in your side mirror.

➤ Follow the backing techniques covered in the previous section, "Is It Still Back There?: Professional Tips on Pulling a Trailer."

➤ If you get into a tight spot and cannot seem to maneuver out of it, relax, admit the problem, and try to find an experienced truck driver to lend a hand.

The Least You Need to Know

➤ Make sure you've selected the correct size of moving vehicle before you begin packing it.

➤ Place heavier appliances in the front of the unit.

➤ Wrap furniture and appliances with rented moving pads or heavy blankets.

➤ Take your time and get some help when backing a truck or trailer.

➤ You don't have to be a professional trucker to drive a truck or pull a trailer. You just have to think like one.

Part 4
Getting Moved

"Hakuna Matada! No worries! The boss is taking care of the move!"

"Hey, I think we can save a few bucks by hiring Two-Dopes-and-a-Dolly Moving Company!"

"Sure, buddy. Jus' sign here and we'll take care of everything! Right, Louie?"

"Uh, the moving van was supposed to be here last Wednesday. You say it hasn't left yet?!"

"So, how much more will it cost me to have everything in the house rather than here on the sidewalk?"

"Daughter, if you ever marry a mover, we'll disown you!"

Contrary to popular opinion, most professional movers are really nice folks with spouses and 2.4 children. They're a lot like you and me—or maybe just me.

Anyway, Part 4 of this book offers Smart Moving tips on hiring a professional moving service, choosing alternate moving services, what you need to know about moving service contracts, and what to do if you get into a bad one.

So, get ready to be moved!

Chapter 14

Hiring a Mover Who Moves You

In This Chapter

➤ Good and bad sides of hiring a mover

➤ Knowing what your mover can do

➤ Picking a Smart Mover

➤ Storing your stuff

Official Warning Signs of Dumb Movers:

"Where's this place you want to move, again?"

"Yea, I think we can move ya for, uh, two thousand bucks…or thereabouts."

"Nah, we don't need to sign no papers. And we only take cash. Up front."

"We'll load the truck starting at midnight 'cause we have to get the truck back by dawn."

"Experience? Sure, we moved my Aunt Ethel's stuff when Uncle Charlie went into the pen."

There are some real Dumb Movers out there—folks who have a truck they can borrow and 60 minutes' experience moving furniture (or maybe they were on *60 Minutes*!). But they're pretty easy to spot.

And there are some really great professional movers who have the knowledge, experience, equipment, and attitude to do a good job for you. They're pretty easy to spot, too—if you know what to look for.

And that's what this chapter's all about: finding and hiring a qualified mover who won't move you to tears.

Hiring the Pros

Most folks who decide *not* to hire a mover do so because of the costs. They believe they can move themselves cheaper than hiring someone else to do it. Maybe. Maybe not.

But, as I mentioned earlier in this book, you should at least find out what hiring a professional will cost before making a decision. Call a few moving counselors out to your abode and let them give you an estimate of costs. Accept their packets of information. Learn what you can about the moving process and how they will handle it for you.

Let's take a look at some of the advantages and disadvantages of hiring a mover—and how to overcome the disadvantages.

> **Moving Words**
>
> A *moving counselor* is the moving company representative who estimates the cost of your shipment and who will answer your questions about the estimate, services, or moving.

So, Why Should I Hire You?

Obviously, hiring a professional mover makes the moving task much easier for you. It's a no-brainer decision if your employer is footing the bill. Even if you're paying, there are many times when it makes sense to hire to have the job done rather than do it yourself.

A professional mover can offer peace of mind and ensure that your belongings arrive at your new home in good condition. He or she has the knowledge, experience, equipment, and materials to do the job in the least time, with the least mess, and the least damage, loss, or breakage.

A professional mover can minimize the chaos. Your family routine will be interrupted less if you can have a moving company pack and load your belongings efficiently and quickly.

A professional mover can do all the grunt work. If you don't have the good health and strength to pack, lift, carry, load, and unload a hundred or more boxes—plus all that furniture and appliances—a professional moving service may be your best choice.

A professional mover can better manage longer moves, especially those that require crossing national boundary lines.

A professional mover can pack your stuff like a, well, pro. In fact, the packing crew is typically well trained and experienced. They've probably gone to school to learn how to pack efficiently. And, as most packing crews are employed by the local agent; they are local people—not gypsies. They are a part of your community.

Hiring a professional moving company also frees you to focus on aspects of the move that can get neglected if you're distracted by packing and loading. If you hire a mover, you can better help the kids get through moving day. You'll have more time to make sure the old house and new house are clean. And you can be better prepared for your first day at the new job.

Here's another advantage to hiring a moving company: After you decide on a mover, you will have a representative of the company to call on for advice and information. That person can explain what services are provided, what tasks you will be expected to perform yourself, how your house full of belongings will be handled, what you can anticipate on moving day, and when your possessions will be delivered to your new home.

Downsides

Yes, hiring a professional mover does have a downside: the cost. Having a professional mover do the work can cost you double that of a do-it-yourself move—or half as much, depending on how things go.

Another potential downside: The professional mover might bet really be a professional, in which case you would have been better off moving everything yourself!

Choices

How can you reduce the cost of using a professional mover? You can do what you would do in a restaurant if you didn't like the dinner menu: Select from the à la carte menu.

Moving services can be offered in the same way as dinners: soup-to-nuts or one-from-column-A-and-two-from-column-B.

Hey, What Kinda Mover Are You, Anyway?!

Moving businesses often offer several levels of service that you can select and use to fit your moving needs and budget. Here they are:

➤ **Relocation services** take care of everything from selecting the best moving company to helping you get an interim place to stay at the other end. In addition, these businesses may be able to provide the names of recommended doctors and other services.

➤ **Interstate moving companies** move you and your entire household from here to there—packing, transporting, and unpacking your goods.

➤ **Local movers** pack, transport, and unpack your goods for shorter moves.

➤ **Pack-and-stack services** prepare everything for you to load in a rental vehicle or for a household shipper.

➤ **Household shippers** are transportation services that move your packed stuff from here to there; you're responsible for packing and unpacking it.

➤ **Trucking services** are bare-bones transportation services that transport most things if you pack and crate them to survive abusive treatment.

Factoid: Many moving companies offer more than one service to customers, depending on need. So an interstate mover can pack and stack or be your household shipper or help only with relocation services. This is à la carte moving!

We'll get more specific about these other moving options in Chapter 15.

Pick a Peck of Pickled Packers

Lots of moving companies are willing to move your things and take your check, but not all companies are all equal. Some are big with well-known names. Their trucks have passed you on the highway. Some are small and lesser-known. How do you know whom to trust with all your worldly goods? To get the answer, you will have to do some digging.

On the downside: some movers will arrive in crisp uniforms, offer friendly advice, carefully transport your cherished furnishings, arrive on time, and in all other ways exhibit courtesy and pride in their work. Others will put your precious belongings in a filthy truck, take twice as long to move you as estimated and hold your things in ransom until you cough up the extra cash, and then expect a hefty tip. And they're gone before you realize they've broken your Limoges china, scratched your Duncan Phyfe table, and left your carefully boxed work wardrobe on the curb at your old house!

Who's the Boss?

So how can you tell whether or not you're getting a professional mover? And what about the quality of a moving service?

First, make sure the business is licensed and regulated. Movers who transport goods across state lines must be licensed and follow the rules of the Interstate Commerce Commission (ICC). The ICC regulations protect you and define your rights and responsibilities and those of your mover. In addition, states have agencies that regulate transportation services. These agencies are typically listed in the phone book under a public utility commission (PUC) or department of transportation (DOT).

Second, verify whether your mover is a member of a trade organization such as the American Movers Conference (1611 Duke St., Alexandria, VA 22314-3482; telephone: 703/683-7410; e-mail: AMC1@erols.com; Web site: **http://www.amconf.org**). Membership not only means they take their industry seriously, but also gives you a higher power to contact if you have a dispute.

Third, check with area Better Business Bureaus to find out whether any bad claims have been filed against the company. Check out the Better Business Bureau Web site to find an office near you (**http://www.bbb.org**).

Finally, ask among your friends, neighbors, employers, acquaintances, real estate agents, and people on the street to learn about their moving experiences and the companies they would and wouldn't recommend.

Calling the Mover

As you call moving services in the telephone book, ask these questions:

Moving Words
A *carrier* is the company actually providing transportation for your shipment.

> ➤ How long have they been in business?
>
> ➤ How much experience do their packers and drivers have?
>
> ➤ Do they offer storage?
>
> ➤ Are they licensed for interstate transport?

How they answer questions is nearly as important as the answers. Eliminate any company that is unhelpful and unwilling to answer all your questions.

Now you can ask the three or four companies that impressed you the most for specific estimates. Because you are moving all your possessions, they should be willing, even eager, to send a company representative to your home to ask lots of questions, evaluate your household, and provide a free estimate of the cost of moving from here to there. To get an accurate estimate, you will have to tell them exactly what is to be moved, to where, when, and how. You should now ask them lots of specific questions such as the following:

> ➤ What services do you offer?
>
> ➤ What insurance coverage do you offer?
>
> ➤ Are you and your crew bonded?
>
> ➤ Can I save money by packing some or all of my own possessions?
>
> ➤ What guarantee do you offer that my goods will arrive in good condition?
>
> ➤ What is covered if I pack some of it myself?
>
> ➤ Do you supply packing materials? At what cost?
>
> ➤ Can you move my second car? My boat?
>
> ➤ Will you arrive on time to begin my packing and/or loading?
>
> ➤ Do you guarantee my things will arrive at my new home on the day we agree upon?
>
> ➤ Do you offer any discounts for senior citizens, employees of my firm, or off-season moves?
>
> ➤ Can I visit your office and see your equipment and local storage facility?
>
> ➤ Can I call you during the move and learn just where my things are at any given time?

Sounds Kinda High to Me!

We've talked about getting bids from moving services. Let's now get more specific.

First, one bid by itself isn't competitive. You don't really know if the bid is high, low, unreasonable, or a bargain without comparing companies, so get more than one bid on your moving services. But remember to provide the same moving information to each moving counselor so you're comparing costs for the same services. Compare apples with apples.

So-called bids are really estimates. There are two kinds of estimates of moving costs: binding and nonbinding.

Binding Estimates

A binding estimate holds the shipper to the figure given to you, the consumer. You cannot be required to pay more than the amount of the estimate.

A mover may charge you for giving a binding estimate, which describes the goods to be shipped and the services to be provided.

A binding estimate must be in writing and you must have a copy before you move. If you receive a binding estimate, you must pay by cash, certified check, or money order at the time of delivery unless the shipper agrees to other arrangements. If the charges are not paid at the time of delivery, the mover may hold your goods, *with storage charges*, until the bill is paid in full. Got that?

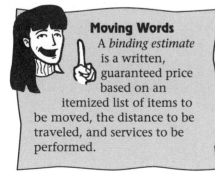

Moving Words
A *binding estimate* is a written, guaranteed price based on an itemized list of items to be moved, the distance to be traveled, and services to be performed.

Nonbinding Estimates: Kinda like No-Fault Insurance

A nonbinding estimate does not bind the fees and services. When you receive a nonbinding estimate, you have no guarantee that the final cost will not exceed the estimate.

The mover is not permitted to charge for nonbinding estimates. However, these also must be in writing and describe the shipment and all services provided. The estimate must be entered on the order for service and bill of lading relating to your shipment.

If you accept a nonbinding estimate, the mover cannot charge more than the amount of the original estimate plus ten percent at the time of delivery. You will then have at least 30 days after delivery to pay any remaining charges.

If, however, you ask the mover to provide more services than those included in the estimate, the mover may charge for those added services and demand full payment on delivery.

Price Isn't Everything!

You will probably have to wait until the moving company representative returns to the office and computes all the information before getting a final estimate. After you have received three or four estimates, you can decide on a mover.

You need to consider some other things when reviewing moving estimates:

➤ Which company offers the services you need?

➤ Which company made you feel that your belongings would be cared for properly?

If one estimate is significantly lower than the others, ask yourself why. Did they forget to include something in the estimate? Unless you have a binding estimate, you might be unpleasantly surprised at the discrepancy between their estimate and your final bill. If it sounds like a lot of work to select the best mover, just remember that you are selecting the people who will be in charge of moving all the things you cherish either across town or across the country.

Of course, make sure that you understand the kind of estimate you have as well as what's included—and not included.

Moving Words
The *bill of lading* is the contract between you and the moving company. It also serves as your receipt for your belongings. See Chapter 16 for more on this legal document.

Making Your Move
If you are given a nonbinding estimate, don't sign or accept the order for service or bill of lading unless the same estimate is entered on each form.

Moving Words
A *non-binding estimate* is a price given to you before the move that does not guarantee the final bill. The final bill will be calculated on the weight of the shipment, the distance to be traveled, and the services to be performed.

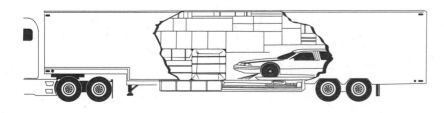

Professional movers know exactly how to pack a household for safe transit.

➤ Does the estimate include packing?

➤ Does the estimate include preparing appliances?

➤ Does it include disassembly of beds and similar pieces of furniture?

➤ Will the movers take things off the walls, or will you need to do this step yourself?

➤ Is storage or other services included?

Also, there are a few items that moving companies cannot or will not transport. Your mover will most likely ask that you keep your valuable jewelry, furs, convertible documents (checks, stocks, and so on), insurance policies, and cash with you. And they will give you a complete list of other items they cannot carry.

Making a smart decision about your mover means not only saving money, but also saving worry.

Goof-Proofing Your Move

Here are some mistakes others have made that you can avoid:

➤ Assuming that you cannot afford a mover without gathering any estimates

➤ Getting an estimate from just one moving company

➤ Considering only price

➤ Not understanding the different types of estimates offered by movers

➤ Not checking out the mover's reputation

➤ Not getting adequate answers to questions on the mover's liability and insurance

➤ Not understanding the inventory, order of service, or the bill of lading—the contract between you and the mover

Stow It!

Sometimes, going from here to there means your stuff needs to be parked somewhere temporarily.

If the timing of your move is not just right, you may need to store your household goods for a few weeks while you find a new home in your new city, or while you wait for the one you have chosen to become available. Or you may want to remodel the house you just purchased, or even to build a new home on your new lot.

While many places are available in which you can store your goods, including self-service storage units in many areas, you might be better off storing your things with your moving company. If you think you will need storage, be sure to determine whether or not it is one of the services potential movers offer.

An advantage of storing with your mover is that the company will then deliver your furniture and other possessions when you are ready for them. And you will probably be able to go to the warehouse and find things if necessary.

What's in Store?

When you cannot move straight from the old house to the new house, you have to put all your belongings somewhere. This situation can occur when you have to move quickly and have not located a permanent home in the new town. Or it can happen when you find a new home but cannot take possession (either rental or purchase) for a few days or even weeks after you have to be out of the old house. It can also happen when you purchase a house that needs remodeling. Sometimes the work cannot be completed or completed enough for you to move in before you have to vacate your old home. If you are building a home, you can also experience unexpected delays.

So, what do you do with all your things while you are staying in a motel, hotel, campground, or with friends?

If you need to store your possessions for only a short time, you may be able to use the truck for storage for a few days if it is not needed elsewhere. Of course, the company will charge you a storage fee for those days. You might find, however, that keeping a rental truck a couple days extra is cheaper than unloading your things and renting another truck. If you must leave your belonging stored in the truck, back it up to a wall if possible so that the back cannot be broken into. Of course, make sure you park it in a safe area.

What Else Is in Store?

For short-term storage (fewer than 30 days) check with your mover; many offer short-term storage. Then compare their rates with local self-storage units.

Here's an idea: If you are remodeling but the work does not affect the garage or basement, you might be able to store all, or at least most of your belongings in one of these areas. If you are waiting for someone to move out of the house, you might work a deal with them to store your things in the garage or basement if they have already cleared out those areas.

Putting your stuff on hold until you can get situated isn't always the best option, but it can be the best decision for a Smart Mover.

The Least You Need to Know

➤ If moving costs are an important factor, consider à la carte moving and storage services.

➤ Make sure the mover you select is regulated in some way or is accountable to an organization in case you need to settle a dispute.

➤ Make sure you know whether the estimate for moving services is binding or non-binding, and which is best for you.

➤ If you will need to store your stuff between here and there, start planning for it now.

Chapter 15

So What Else Is New: Moving Company Options

"Do I have any options here—or should I just hand over my wallet to the movers and let them notify me when it's empty?!"

Even if you've decided to hire someone to move you, you have lots of options left. And each option can help you make a smarter move—and maybe save some money.

It covers some of the à la carte moving options on your moving menu in more depth. You don't have to sign up for the one-size-fits-all move; instead, you can

➤ Pack your possessions yourself and let a professional mover transport them.

➤ Hire professional packers to get your possessions ready for you to move them yourself.

➤ Separately hire and collectively supervise packers and movers.

I Want to Do It Myself!

Moving Words
Carrier packed (CP) refers to articles packed into boxes and crates by the moving company. Excelsior!

Okay. First option: You pack, they drive, and you unpack. If this is your idea of fun (or saving money) read Chapters 10, 11, and 12. They were written for the do-it-yourselfer who plans to take on the whole moving job. But they can be valuable to anyone considering doing only the front or back end of the move.

Sure, it's great to have some burly guys come into your home and gently pack and move everything without a chip or scratch. However, and that's a big however, many of us can't afford to have a mover take on all the responsibility. And some of us just don't want to entrust our "things" to strangers.

So, yes, you can save money by packing some or all of your possessions yourself. If you choose to do so, you can purchase from your mover standard moving boxes, as well as all the specialty cartons necessary. Such boxes and cartons will protect your goods much more effectively than liquor store or grocery store boxes.

Second option: Pack most of your things yourself, but leave the most valuable and most breakable for the professional packers. You will then both save money and be assured that everything will arrive at the new house in the same condition in which it left the old one. And if it doesn't, the mover is responsible—not you.

Before you decide to do your own packing, find out from your mover how doing it yourself will affect your insurance coverage. It may be that your mover will only guarantee safe arrival of items their professional packers handle.

Remember, if you run into trouble or run out of time, you can probably call your mover at the last minute and arrange for packers to come to your home and pack those final items.

It's Not My Job!

Who does what? It's entirely up to you. The movers will do as much as you will pay them to do. Well, almost. Tempting as it may be to try, they probably won't agree to clean your oven before they move it or your carpets after they move all the furniture out. But, if you want them to, they will pack anything and everything in your house, garage, and yard. They will pick up, pack up, and load onto the truck anything that is on the premises at the time they arrive to move you. They don't care whether or not you have de-cluttered first.

If it's there and they are contracted to pack and move, it goes. In other words, make sure all your sorting is done well before the movers arrive. Anything headed to the dump, the Salvation Army, or Aunt Flo's should already be there. If it's not, make sure it's clearly marked to stay, or you may end up paying to move it and then unpacking it at your new home. And paying for the privilege.

It's All Your Fault!

Who's responsible for what? That depends on who does what. Your mover is responsible for the safe arrival of your possessions only if its employees have packed them and only to the extent of the insurance covered in the contract.

Make sure that you and all others involved in the move clearly understand not only who will do what, but also who is responsible if something doesn't get done—or gets damaged.

If you choose to do most or all of the packing yourself, you can start weeks or even months early sorting, collecting boxes, and even packing boxes of things you want to keep but won't need or use until after the move. Mark boxes for their eventual destination room. Do be wary of packing too much too far in advance. Otherwise, you might end up unpacking boxes to find that special item you use just once in a blue moon. Blue moons are more common than they used to be!

Some movers are more helpful than others—similar to the way some restaurants say "Have it *your* way" and others say "No substitutions." If you want to do all the packing yourself, a mover may assist you in determining your packing material needs and can offer the materials to you at a fair price.

Even if you want to do the majority of your packing yourself, you may want to call on your mover to pack fragile and valuable items such as mirrors, paintings, collections, electronics, and art objects. And if you plan to pack it all yourself, but run out of time, give your mover a call. You can probably get last-minute help to make sure you meet your deadline.

You also can turn to your mover for help during many last-minute crises. A representative of your moving company can probably recommend specialists for crating your most delicate, valuable items and for safely preparing your appliances.

Even if you don't have a mover and you get into trouble at the eleventh hour, you may be able to get help from professionals. If moving day is approaching rapidly and you realize you will not complete all the work, call a few movers. If they are not booked solid, they can probably send a crew to your house to help with the final packing and loading. You may pay a higher hourly rate than if you had scheduled in advance, but it may make the difference in meeting your deadlines and getting to your new hometown in time for your first day at the new job.

Hiring a professional moving company for some or all of the job can greatly reduce the stress and the work that you invest in your move. Even if you expect to do all the work yourself, you will be able to make a more informed decision if you get estimates from some moving companies. Then, if you completely handle the move, you will know just how much money you saved. Or you may even decide that the extra expense is justified by saving time and by simplifying your family's life during a hectic period.

Pack-and-Stack or Pack-and-Crack?

This is an age of specialists. You can, for example, find podiatrists who work only on *left* feet. Likewise, a variety of specialists are available in the moving industry. One is called the pack-and-stack service.

The name pretty clearly explains the service provided. If you plan to load and transport your goods yourself, but you hate packing, fear packing, or your time is limited, check around. A local pack-and-stack service will be happy to help out.

A pack-and-stack service can come into your home and safely pack all your belongings into the proper boxes and cartons, thus greatly increasing the odds that your things will arrive at your new home unscratched and unbroken.

We're in the Book!

So where will you find these folks who want to help you get out of town? In the telephone book. You'll find them under headings such as "Movers," "Moving Services—Labor & Materials," and "Packing Services." Makes sense.

You also can find packing services by asking around. Ask friends and acquaintances who've recently moved. Ask your employer—or your former employer, if you're still on speaking terms.

When you call a company, ask about its experience and the materials it will use, as well as how much it will charge. Typically, a pack-and-stack service will charge by the box or carton packed.

As with any other moving services, get an estimate of costs. Most packing services will quote you prices by the size of the box or other container. They may also have a per-hour rate for disassembly of beds, preparation of appliances, or other related services.

Just as with a full-service moving company, get a written estimate from several pack-and-stack services. And make sure you base your final decision on value as much as price. Paying a little more for a more professional packing service may be less costly than replacing damaged goods. Of course, make sure the movers are bonded and insured.

And don't forget to let other moving services whom you've hired know how to contact each other.

Who's in Charge Here?

Whether you hire a pack-and-stack service to pack everything or do it yourself, you can still get ready for the movers' arrival on moving day.

Be a Good Scout

If you opt to pack all your boxes and cartons yourself, the moving crew will expect to find everything sealed and ready for loading upon their arrival on moving day. If possible, plan to spend your last night at a motel or hotel or with friends or family. That way, you can finish everything up the day before the movers arrive. If all boxes and cartons are sealed and clearly marked, the movers can quickly and efficiently load the truck and be on their way to your new home.

Depending on how your moving contract reads, you may save money if you dismantle beds, prepare appliances, and gather outdoor items in an easily accessible location.

Be sure to clearly mark any items that should not get loaded on the truck. For example, you may have a car survival kit, suitcases for travel, or coats that go with you rather than the movers. Gather all such items into one location and mark them boldly so that they aren't packed on the truck. If Uncle Mort plans to pick up the chain saw and lawn mower, mark them clearly so that he doesn't have to drive to your new house three states away to get them—unless you want him to have a reason for visiting soon.

Watch Those Options

On the other side of the proverbial coin lies danger: too many options. Just as à la carte pricing can help you cut unnecessary costs, it can also inflate your total bill. A burger combo is more expensive if you buy the burger, fries, and drink separately. The combo is a better deal.

Moving services can add up as well if you buy each piece separately—or if you order more services than you need.

In addition, you may wind up paying for other services. Make sure they are necessary before you purchase them.

Remember, the total cost of your move may be increased if you want additional or special services. Before you agree to special services, make sure you clearly understand what the additional cost will be. Always consider that you may find other movers who can provide the service you need without additional charges.

One service option is a space reservation. If you agree to have your shipment transported under a space reservation agreement, you'll pay for a minimum space in the moving van regardless of how much your shipment actually uses.

Another service option is exclusive use of a vehicle. If your shipment needs to be moved by itself on the mover's truck or trailer, most movers will provide such service. Translation: mo' money. Do you need the extra service?

Still another service option is guaranteed service on or between agreed-upon dates. If you take this service option, the mover guarantees that your shipment will be picked up, transported to destination, and delivered on specific dates. If the mover fails to provide the service as agreed, you should receive from the company a penalty fee or refund.

Before agreeing to any service options, ask the mover about the final costs. Consider all possible alternatives if you feel that the charges will be more than you are willing to pay.

Helping the Movers Help You

How can you help the movers move you?

First, be at the house before the movers arrive and plan to be there until after they leave. They'll need someone at the house who knows exactly what goes and what stays, who has keys to any locked areas, who knows the trick to opening that sticky attic cubbyhole, and who can make a final check to see that everything (from the attic, basement, garage, and even that extra lawn mower stored at the neighbor's) gets loaded onto the truck.

Think about other things that can help:

➤ Park your car down the block.

➤ Clear sidewalks and driveways of toys and tools.

➤ Prop doors open.

➤ Keep the kids and pets out of the way.

Moving Words
A *flight charge* is an extra fee for carrying large, bulky items (such as your mother-in-law) up or down stairs.

If you're paying anyone by the hour, minutes repeatedly walking around Johnny's bike on the sidewalk do add up.

Probably your most important task on moving day will be checking inventory. Your mover will make a thorough inventory as everything goes out the door and into the truck. You are responsible to see that the inventory is accurate and complete. The mover may indicate on the inventory whether items being loaded have damage already. Again, your job is to check his or her accuracy.

Stay out of the way of the packers and movers so they can do their jobs efficiently. You don't have to be out of sight; you have every right to watch how they handle your things. Just give them room to do it well.

Keep children and pets out of the way, too. Lots of bulky items are being moved and it's difficult to see, let alone avoid stepping on, small children or small animals. Not only will children and pets wandering around get in the way and slow down progress, but they could get injured. And with doors open for loading, curious tots or pets could wander out the door into the street or even out of the neighborhood.

Long before the movers arrive, talk to the company's representative to learn how you can best help the movers to ensure the safe loading, transport, and delivery of your goods to your new home.

The Least You Need to Know

➤ You can save money by packing everything—or at least some things—yourself and letting the movers transport it from here to there.

➤ You can hire a professional packing service to prepare some or all of your things for the move. You don't have to hire the moving company's packers.

➤ More options can mean more headaches—or fewer.

➤ Stay involved in the moving process regardless of how much of it you'll be doing yourself.

Chapter 16

"I Am Da Law!": The Legal Side of Moving

In This Chapter

➤ All about bills of lading

➤ Weighing your shipment

➤ Setting your moving dates

➤ Knowing what you're signing

➤ How and when to pay for moving services

Hiring a moving company will require a magnifying glass to read all the fine print.

That fine print will read something like this:

> The party of the first part agrees to be moved without obvious recourse by the party of the second part. Should the party of the first part complain in any way when asked to sign and pay, the party of the second part has full legal right to hold all belongings owned by the party of the first part until said party pays through the nose or other orifice. If the party of the first part can actually read and understand this paragraph, written by the party of the second part's attorney, said attorney is not doing his/her/its job.

The moving process involves a bunch of laws and documents. These include estimates, bills of lading, orders of service, and other contracts.

How can you get through this maze of paperwork without losing both your household goods and your mind?

Actually, most of the papers you sign make sense. And most are pretty fair documents. You won't have to run to your attorney's office with every scrap of paper the mover hands you for signature. But you should know what each one is and what you're getting yourself into.

The function of this chapter is to help you understand the legal side of moving.

The bill of lading you sign is your contract with the mover.

Hey, Read the Bill of Lading!

Bill who?

You'll be hearing a lot about this guy called Bill of Lading. He holds a tremendous amount of power.

Actually, the bill of lading is the contract between you and the mover. The law requires that the mover prepares a "bill of lading" for every shipment it transports. The driver who loads your shipment must give you a copy of the bill of lading before loading your furniture. You must also sign it.

So who's supposed to read that bill thing? You are. It's your responsibility to read the bill of lading before you sign it. And, if you don't understand or agree with something on the bill of lading, don't sign it until you do.

Where's the Magnifying Glass?

So what's on this bill of lading?

Your bill of lading will include:

➤ Names and office address of the shipper and carrier

➤ Where the goods are picked up and when

➤ Where the goods are to be delivered and an estimate of when

➤ An attachment of an inventory of goods

➤ The number of boxes/pieces and the total weight

➤ Special instructions for the shipper

➤ The total cost of the shipment, plus how and when it is to be paid

➤ Legal fine print (see Chapter 17)

Moving Words
Bill of Lading: A Knight of the Round Table. Also the formal contract between you and the moving company. This document serves as both your contract and your receipt for your belongings. Make sure you've read and understand the fine print on the bill before signing.

The bill of lading requires the mover to provide the service you have requested, and it requires you to pay the mover the charges for the service.

Be careful not to lose or misplace your copy of the bill of lading in the confusion of moving. Have it available until your shipment is delivered, all charges are paid, and all claims, if any, are settled.

Back & Back Savers

Read the bill of lading and inventory sheets carefully. The bill of lading is your contract. The inventory is your record of your possessions and their condition. You will need these papers if any questions arise about your shipment after delivery.

Guess the Weight and Win a Kewpie Doll

Chances are, your moving charges are based on the weight of the shipment. The shipment must be weighed before you leave, a process called *origin weighing*, or when you arrive, called *destination weighing*.

What Did It Weigh When It Left?: Origin Weighing

Moving Words
The *tare weight* is the weight of the truck and its contents before your belongings are loaded onto it. The *gross weight* is the weight of the truck after your belongings are loaded.

If your shipment will be weighed in the city you're leaving, the driver must weigh the truck and its contents before coming to your residence. This "before" weight is called the *tare weight*.

So are you paying to move the moving truck, too?

Nope. When the truck is first weighed, the truck may already be partially loaded with someone else's stuff. The truck should also contain pads, dollies, hand trucks, ramps, and other equipment. These items will not be counted in the weight of your shipment.

After loading, the truck will be weighed again to obtain the loaded weight, called the *gross weight*. The *net weight* of your shipment is the difference between the gross weight and the tare weight. As a formula, it looks like this:

gross weight	-	tare weight	=	net weight
(truck + load)		(empty truck)		(your load)

Movers usually have a minimum weight for transporting a shipment—typically at least 500 pounds. Even if your shipment weighs less, you'll be charged for the minimum.

What Did It Weigh When It Arrived?: Destination Weighing

Moving Words
Net weight is the weight of your goods, found by subtracting the tare weight from the gross weight. Broken pieces are excluded.

Destination weighing is done in reverse to origin weighing. On arriving in the area to which you are moving, the driver weighs the truck to get the gross weight. After unloading you shipment, the driver again weighs the truck to get the tare weight. The difference is the net weight of your stuff.

Obviously, where the truck is weighed will make no difference in the net weight. The only difference is that the mover will not be able to figure the exact charges on your shipment after the truck is unloaded.

Who says what it weighs?

The folks running the certified scales say. Each time the truck is weighed, the driver gets a weight ticket showing the date and place of weighing and the certified weight. The ticket will also have your name and shipment number as well as the truck's identification numbers. The ticket is signed by the scale operator.

If both the origin and destination weighings are made on the same scale, they will probably both be entered on one weight ticket. A copy of every weight ticket made for your shipment will be with your freight bill when you're asked to pay.

Don't trust the trucker? You have the right to watch every weighing of your shipment. The mover must inform you where and when each weighing will me made. Let the mover know in advance if you want to watch it being done.

Looks like You've Lost a Few Pounds!

If your shipment is weighed at origin and you've agreed to pay charges on delivery, the mover must give you written notice of the weight and charges before unloading. If you believe that the weight is not accurate, you have the right to request that the shipment be reweighed *before* letting the movers unload.

The mover can't charge you for the reweighing. And, if the new weight is different from the origin weight, the mover must refigure the charges based on the new weight. You might wind up paying less — or more!

Before you ask for your shipment to be reweighed, use this easy formula to calculate an approximate weight.

Making Your Move
Ask to have your shipment reweighed if you have *any* question about the mover's numbers. Your bill is prepared based on the weight of your shipment.

1. Count the number of items in your shipment. Usually there will be either 30 or 40 items listed on each page of the inventory. For example, if each page contains 30 items and your inventory consists of three complete pages and a fourth page with 10 items listed, the total number of items is 100.

2. If an automobile is listed on the inventory, don't include it in the count of the total items. Subtract the weight of any automobile in your shipment from the total weight of the shipment. If the automobile was not weighed separately, its weight can be found on its title or license receipt.

3. Divide the number of items in your shipment into the weight. If the average weight is 35 and 45 pounds per article, chances are a reweigh isn't needed. For example, if your 4,000-pound shipment (excluding cars) includes 100 items, the average weight per item is 40 pounds and is within the normal range.

It's Tuesday! Where's Our Stuff?

When will your stuff arrive at your new home?

Arrival date partially depends on weather and other problems en route. But most movers have enough experience to give you a pretty good estimate.

Agree with your mover on set times for pickup and delivery. You may have to negotiate a date that fits your needs and conditions, but make sure you both agree on the dates.

Don't agree to have your shipment picked up or delivered "as soon as possible." Make the dates both reasonable (based on distance, terrain, and road and weather conditions) and specific.

The agreed dates of service must be entered on the order for service. Don't sign or accept an order for service if the agreed dates for service are not entered on the form—or if the dates don't match the agreed upon dates. Those dates will then be put on the bill of lading as part of your contract with the mover.

After your goods are loaded, the mover is legally bound to provide the service written in the bill of lading.

Fine Print Alert: If unforeseen circumstances pop up (weather, earthquake, sonic boom) to prevent pickup or delivery as contracted, the mover can climb to a church steeple and cry "defense of *force majeure*." It's the mover's only defense for not doing what is agreed in the bill of lading.

What if, after your stuff is picked up, you ask the mover to change the delivery date? Depends. Most movers will agree to do so if it won't cause unreasonable delay to their equipment or interfere with another customer's move. But the mover doesn't have to agree to a change in delivery dates any more than you do.

What if the mover doesn't arrive with your shipment on the agreed date? If that means you have to hang out in a motel for a night or more, you may be able to recover those expenses from the mover—your basic "delay claim." You can present the claim to the mover and, if the company doesn't honor it, you can try suing. Or you can send over your pit bull!

Chances are, your shipment will be picked up and delivered on time. If you really have to get nasty with the mover, see Chapter 17 before you let loose your pit bull.

Sign Your Life Away

It's time to start signing stuff. The most important document you'll sign is the bill of lading. It says who will do what, when, and for how much. It includes an inventory of your stuff. And the fine print tells what you or the mover can do if things don't happen as written.

Remember, although the contract is supposed to be balanced between both parties, the mover's attorneys wrote it. So it's moderately biased. But aren't we all?

Sign Here, Mac!

Let's back up to loading time.

The mover's driver usually inventories your shipment as it is loaded, listing any damage or unusual wear. This serves as a record of the condition of each item.

The driver usually places a small numbered tag on each item as the inventory is prepared. The number should correspond to that on the inventory form.

Once done loading, the driver will probably sign each page and ask you to do likewise. Before you sign, make sure that every item in your shipment is listed and that the entries of condition are correct.

Don't let anyone rush you through this task; you have the right to note any disagreement. If an item is missing or damaged when your shipment is delivered, your ability to receive compensation from the mover for any loss or damage may depend on the notations made on the inventory.

The driver will give you a copy of the full inventory. Attach it to your copy of the bill of lading as your receipt for the goods.

When your stuff is delivered, you'll need to sign the mover's receipt for your shipment. This usually means signing each page of the mover's copy of the inventory.

When your shipment is delivered, it's up to you to check the items delivered against the items on your inventory. Check each item for new damage. If you discover damage, make a record of it on the inventory form. And be sure to show the damage to the driver and request that it be noted on the driver's copy of the inventory.

If you don't understand something on the inventory, such as codes, don't hesitate to ask. Your right to make a damage claim later depends on this inventory, so check it thoroughly.

After everything is unloaded, the driver will ask you to sign the driver's copy of the inventory. Don't sign it until you're satisfied that it is accurate. Make sure it notes any missing or damaged items. When you sign the inventory at the time of unloading, you are giving the driver a receipt for your goods and an assurance that they were all delivered in acceptable condition.

Remember, movers are not allowed to have you sign a receipt relieving them from all liability for loss or damage to the shipment. Just make sure you're signing for your shipment "in apparent good condition except as noted." These notations on your receipt will be vital if you need to make a damage claim against the mover.

Get Out Your Wallet!

Time to pay the driver.

As the mover presents you with the bill for payment, the representative will give you a freight bill. The bill of lading indicates what services were provided and the charge for each service. Most movers use a copy of the bill of lading as a freight bill. Some use a separate document.

If your shipment was agreed as collect on delivery (COD), you'll be expected to pay the total charges at the time of delivery. An exception is if the total charges exceed 110 percent of a nonbinding estimate. If more, you can pay the excess later, as agreed.

How can you pay? Most movers will accept payment in cash, by certified check, or by money order. Most will not accept a personal check unless arrangements were made earlier to do so. Have the money ready when the movers arrive; you will quickly max out your ATM limit trying to get your stuff out of hock.

Some movers will let you pay by credit card. But make sure before you flash your Gold.

What if you don't pay as agreed? The fine print on the bill of lading says the mover can refuse to give you your stuff. Until you work it out, the mover can put it in storage at your expense.

What if, before payment, you find an error in the charges? Try correcting the error with the driver, with the mover's local agent, or by contacting the mover's main office. If you find the error after making payment, write to the mover explaining the error and request a refund.

Chapter 17 will cover moving disputes in greater detail.

It Ain't All Here!

With most moves, all your stuff will fit in one moving truck or part of a truck. Sometimes, however, shipment size or scheduling will necessitate splitting the shipment among two or more trucks. (This situation is more typical when a car is part of the shipment.)

So how do you receive and pay for a split shipment?

You're not required to pay the total charges until all portions of the shipment have been delivered, but the mover can require payment for each portion as it is delivered. Or the mover can choose to not require payment until everything is delivered. So, if you suspect or are notified that your stuff will be in a split shipment, work out payment details now.

Worse Than Losing Your Luggage!

So what if something—or everything—gets lost?

Not only are you entitled to compensation for whatever was lost, you can also get a refund on the moving charges for lost items.

However, you may have to pay for everything on delivery—even if it wasn't delivered—noting on the bill of lading what didn't arrive. You can then file a claim. Most movers will be helpful with this process.

Fortunately, most shipments move on time, in good condition, and at agreed rates. Otherwise, there'd be more lawyers than there already are!

Making Your Move

Be prepared to pay for your shipment as agreed, often upon delivery. If you do not pay as agreed, the shipper can hold your shipment and charge storage.

The Least You Need to Know

➤ The bill of lading is your contract with the mover, so make sure you understand what you're signing.

➤ If you dispute the weight of the shipment, you have the right to ask that it be reweighed and to be present at the weigh-in.

➤ Check your shipment upon arrival against the inventory sheets to make sure all items have arrived and are in good condition.

➤ Know when, how, and how much you have to pay for your shipment.

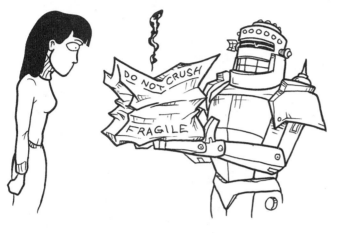

Moved to Tears: Winning Disputes with Your Mover

In This Chapter

➤ Avoiding disputes with your mover

➤ Ensuring that you're satisfied with service

➤ Getting a fair referee to arbitrate disputes

➤ When to go to court

"They broke my antique vase and won't pay for it!"

"The truck was a week late and we had to stay in a motel until it finally arrived!"

"The bill was twice the estimate!"

"They packed the cream cheese in with my stereo!"

Most moves go smoothly, with no problems, because most moving companies have years of experience and want to have many years more. They handle things professionally—most of the time.

Actually, most moving disputes are with Gypsy Jim and His Fly-By-Night Moving Service or other less-than-professional movers. These companies are more likely to lose or damage stuff.

This chapter offers proven tips on avoiding as well as winning disputes with your mover.

I hope this is one chapter you won't need to use!

Who's Lie-able?!

First, let's talk about liability.

All moving companies are required to assume liability for the value of goods they transport. However, there are different levels of liability. As a Smart Mover, you need to know what's covered and what isn't.

Minimal Value at Minimal Cost

Da law she say: The mover is required to assume liability for the entire shipment at $1.25 per pound times the weight of your shipment. So, if your shipment weights 4,000 pounds, the mover is liable to you for loss or damage up to $5,000 (4,000 × $1.25 = $5,000).

The mover can charge you $7 for each $1,000 of liability, however. Under this arrangement, if you shipped a 10-pound painting valued at $1,000 in your 4,000-pound shipment, you could collect for the full value of the painting if it was lost or damaged. Under this plan, your valuables are somewhat protected, but you pay for the protection. Of course, if your painting is valued at $10,000, you'll get no more than the coverage limit for the entire shipment: $5,000.

What if the value of your shipment is more than $1.25 per pound? You can buy additional liability protection from the mover. You do this by declaring a specific dollar value for your shipment.

If you declare that your 4,000-pound shipment is worth $10,000, the mover will charge you $7 for each $1,000 of declared value, which in this case would result in a charge of $70.

If you ship articles that are unusually expensive, such as art or antiques, be sure to declare their full value in the declaration. You must do this in writing.

Movers can legally limit their liability for loss or damage of valuable things unless you specifically list them on the shipping papers. Valuable things are those worth more than $100 a pound.

Release Value at No Extra Cost

The least liability a mover can assume for your stuff is called the *released value*. This value is not more than 60 cents per pound, *per article*. So if that 10-pound painting mentioned earlier was lost or damaged and you had agreed to a released-value shipment, the mover would have to pay you a whole six bucks!

So you'll automatically get—and pay extra for—mimimal value coverage unless you sign the bill-of-lading clause that says you want the no-extra-cost "release value."

Any other options? Yes!

Pay More, Get More

Most movers offer another plan: added-value protection. It simply means more coverage—and more cost. If you think you'll need it, be sure to ask your mover about it. Each mover will have a different program and costs.

How About Homeowner's Insurance?

There's one more option: Get a moving insurance policy from your household insurance agent. In fact, you should check with the agent before you move as your stuff may be covered in transit.

Thoroughly confused yet? Let's summarize your options:

➤ Your load automatically gets minimal-value insurance ($1.25 a pound) and you get charged for the extra coverage...

➤ Unless you sign a waiver and get release-value coverage ($.50 a pound) at no extra cost...

➤ Or you purchase additional insurance from your mover...

➤ Or you have or buy additional coverage from your homeowner insurance agent.

Insurance is always expensive—until you have a claim. Then it's cheap!

> **Making Your Move**
> Check your inventory very carefully when the movers unload your possessions from the van. If anything is missing or appears damaged, note this condition on the inventory. This extra documentation will expedite any complaint procedure. See Chapter 16 for more details.

Your Bill of Rights against Wrongs

So, as a movee, what rights do you have?

Should your move result in the loss of or damage to any of your property, you have the right to file a claim with the mover to recover money for the loss or damage.

Moving Words
A *claim* is your statement of loss of or damage to any part of your shipment.

But what if you don't discover the problem for a few weeks after the move?

You have nine months from the delivery date to file a claim with the mover. However, you should file a claim as soon as possible. The mover must acknowledge receiving your claim within 30 days, and the company must make an offer or deny your claim within 120 days.

If any of your household goods are damaged or lost, note the problem on the driver's copy of the inventory sheet before signing it. If you find damage while unpacking, file a claim as soon as possible, but within nine months of delivery. The mover must respond to your claim within 30 days and offer a resolution within 120 days of the claim.

The Government's Role in Your Move

Moving Words
The *Interstate Commerce Commission (ICC)* is a federal agency in charge of the regulation of interstate transportation. They're the good guys—usually.

The Interstate Commerce Commission (ICC) sets the rules for movers and other trucking services, but it doesn't resolve claims. If you cannot settle a claim with the mover, the next step is to file a civil action to recover in court. You'll probably need an attorney.

Any other options?

Yes. Most major movers participate in a dispute resolution program. This means you can have a neutral arbitrator review the claims of both you and the mover, and then offer a resolution. For most disputes, this is the best step after trying to work directly with the mover.

We'll look at arbitration in a moment.

To avoid problems in the first place, remember these facts about Smart Moving:

➤ Movers may give binding estimates.

➤ Non-binding estimates may not be accurate; actual charges often exceed the estimates.

➤ Specify pickup and delivery dates in the order for service.

➤ The bill of lading is your contact with the mover. Read it carefully. If you have any questions, ask your mover or call the ICC.

➤ Be sure that you understand the extent of your mover's liability for loss and damage.

➤ You have the right to be present each time your shipment is weighed.

➤ You may request a re-weigh of your shipment.

➤ If you have moved on the basis of a non-binding estimate, you should have enough cash or a certified check to pay the estimated cost of your move plus ten percent at time of delivery.

Complain! Complain!

Da law she say: All interstate moving companies are required to maintain a complaint and inquiry procedure. In fact, your moving packet probably includes a booklet that explains what to do in case of a problem with your mover. This booklet is a good place to start when determining what steps to take.

Let's say you've got a gripe with your mover. Something is broken or missing, or you were overcharged. What can you do about it?

Lots!

First, complain to the mover. If you know of the problem as the mover is relocating you, mention it to the mover's representative. If you don't find out until later, contact the mover's rep as soon as you know. Be polite and professional in your first approach. Bring or send copies of your documents concerning the shipment.

Then what?

All movers are supposed to respond promptly to complaints or inquiries from their customers. If you don't get a response from the driver or the mover's local agent within 30 days, start working your way up the ladder. Contact the mover's principal office.

And?

When you talk with the agent or the main office, make sure you have copies of all the documents relating to the move. The most crucial document will be the bill of lading; the bill number will be important in this procedure.

Then?

If you don't get satisfaction from the mover's office, contact the nearest ICC office. Same rule: Make sure you have the paperwork and a clear explanation of the problem.

I Can't Get No Satisfaction

The Department of Transportation requires that moving companies cooperate in the Dispute Settlement Program for Household Goods Shippers, which is managed by the American Arbitration Association. This organization is independent and non-profit, and it isn't affiliated with any mover, the American Movers Conference, or the government. The American Arbitration Association's Web site is **http://www.adr.org**.

So if you can't get results with your mover or the ICC, you can still get heard by some impartial folks. It beats going to court!

Here Come Da Judge!

Okay, your mover has made you a settlement offer or has denied your claim—and you're still not satisfied. Now what?

Within 60 days, you can write and request arbitration from:

> American Movers Conference
> Dispute Settlement Program
> 1622 Duke Street
> Alexandria, VA 22314
> tel: 703/683-7410
> fax: 703/683-7527
> e-mail: AMC1@erols.com
> Web site: **http://www.amconf.org**

Here's what you must include in your request:

➤ Name of the mover

➤ Identification number of the shipment

➤ Dates and location of pickup and delivery

➤ Description of the loss

➤ Estimated value of the loss

If your dispute meets its arbitration guidelines, the AMC will notify the mover. It will also send you a description of the program and forms to fill out.

No Job's Complete Until the Paperwork Is Done

To start arbitration, you'll need to fill out and return the forms along with $150. That's your half of the cost of the arbitration proceedings. The mover also submits information about the dispute and $150. The arbitrator will then examine all the evidence and reach a decision within about 60 days.

"The judge's decision is final."

The arbitrator's decision is legally binding on you and the mover. However, the arbitrator has jurisdiction only over claims for loss or damage to the household goods and their transport. The arbitrator can't rule on claims such as loss of wages, punitive damages, or violations of law.

In addition, the amount of any award probably won't exceed the carrier's liability noted in the bill of lading.

For other claims, see your lawyer.

The Least You Need to Know

➤ Avoid moving problems by reading and understanding everything you sign.

➤ Know what insurance coverage you have as well as what's available to you.

➤ Once you see a problem, let someone know—and keep letting folks know until something is done about it.

➤ Arbitration is available, but won't necessarily resolve all legal problems between you and the mover. You also may need an attorney.

Part 5
Moving Day

Hey, it's Moving Day!

You've been dreading this day since Day One. And it's finally here!

So how the heck can you get through it without prescription drugs and other medical intervention?

By being a Smart Mover!

And this part of the book you hold in your nervous hands offers some clues:

> ➤ *How to survive moving out*

> ➤ *How to move children without losing your mind*

> ➤ *How to move those critters that have infested and now rule your life: your pets*

> ➤ *How to move in without being committed*

So grab your Smart Moving Notebook and your favorite sedative.

We're moving out!

Chapter 18

Get Out Of Town by Sundown; or, How to Survive Moving Out

In This Chapter

➤ Handling the inevitable crisis

➤ Helping the mover without getting in the way

➤ Cleaning up the place before moving on

➤ Getting from here to there smoothly

It's Moving Day!

Lucky you!

You've somehow survived the last few weeks or months since making the decision to move.

You've selected a mover—or decided to move everything yourself—and moving day has arrived. It's too late to back out now!

So what can go wrong? Everything! And what can you do about it?

That's what this chapter is about: surviving moving day by being ready for any and every pitfall.

The Sky Is Falling!

You've been following the sound advice in this book, minimizing the stress of your move, right?

Still, there's this lingering feeling that you've forgotten something—or someone. And you're saying, "This is too easy. Something's *gotta* go wrong!"

Well, maybe it will or maybe it won't. In either case, you're ready to deal with it. Really, you are. Trust me.

You're a Certified Smart Mover!

Murphy's Moving and Storage Company

So what can go wrong on the day you move out?

Here's an abbreviated list for those of you who haven't already played every scenario over and over in your imagination:

➤ Your helpers don't show up to get you loaded.

➤ The moving truck doesn't show up.

➤ Your rent-a-truck has a dead battery.

➤ Your babysitter is a no-show.

➤ It's 110° and humid, there's three feet of snow on the ground, or rain is bucketing out of the sky.

➤ You or someone breaks a leg/arm/shoulder/hip/foot/hand.

➤ Grandma stops by for a surprise visit.

Avoiding Catastrophes

"Okay, hon, the truck is loaded, the house is cleaned up, and it's getting late. Where's Junior?"

"I thought he was with *you!*"

The best way to avoid moving catastrophes is to plan smart. You've been using your Smart Moving Notebook to make good plans and track your move, so you're already very organized.

Here are some additional planning ideas that can help you avoid moving-day catastrophes:

➤ Make a confirmation call to your mover the day before moving day.

➤ Inspect the vehicle a few days in advance, making sure that all maintenance service has been done.

➤ Confirm with your volunteers the day, time, and location that you need them.

➤ Make sure everyone is safety conscious.

➤ Make sure Grandma boarded that plane for Hawaii.

Even if a crisis occurs that, in all your advance planning, you failed to anticipate, don't panic. Calm, reason, and this book will get you through it.

It's Show Time!

By the time you get up on the morning of moving day, all your boxes should be packed (unless your mover will be doing it) and nearly everything should be ready to carry out of the house and load onto the truck. You've arranged for utilities to be shut off. You've cleaned and defrosted the refrigerator. You've arranged for a friend (if any) to watch the dog (if any) or the baby (if any).

Here are some good tips:

➤ Eat a good breakfast and make sure that everyone else does, too. Better yet, take the family out to eat. A good breakfast will energize everyone for the tasks to come. (And no one will have to clean up.)

➤ Strip all your beds of linen.

➤ Send the dog and young children off with a hug and a kiss and reassurance that you will pick them up by dinner time or by bedtime.

➤ Older children can help, whether you are moving yourselves or having a moving company do the job.

Who's in Charge Here?

If you have a moving company doing the loading, your job for the day is supervising and answering questions from the movers. They will do all the heavy work, unless you have made an arrangement with the moving company to help load to keep costs down.

Also, be sure anything that does not go to the new house is either already out of the way or clearly marked.

> **Moving Words**
> The agent who accepts your order for shipping and registers it with the van line is called the *booking agent*. He or she can also help you "make book" on whether it will arrive in one piece.

Beware: Moving company packers will move everything. They have even been known to carefully package up trash, since their job is to pack, not to sort or decide what goes and what stays. Make sure anything not to be moved is clearly marked and separated from items to be moved.

Sidewalk Supervising

Twiddling thumbs will get you through the day, but it won't keep you from fretting. Keep yourself busy as a sidewalk supervisor.

Stay with the moving van driver as he makes an inventory of your possessions. Make notes on the inventory about the condition of any items (in the event some of them arrive in less-than-perfect condition). Be sure to read the bill of lading carefully before you sign it; it is the contract between you and the moving company. Put the bill of lading with your other valuable papers. You need to keep it until your possessions are delivered and the bill paid. If there is any dispute, the annotated bill of lading will be needed for settlement.

Be sure the driver has correct and complete directions to your new home. He or she should also have a telephone number to contact you, should there be any problem en route. If you will be on the road, give a number where someone will have your travel itinerary and be able to reach you. The moving company office should have this information also. Confirm with the driver the date and time of delivery of your goods to your new house.

Let 'Em Do Their Job!

If you are paying a moving company to do the job, stand back and let the workers do the hard work. They have the tools and the know-how to make quick work of disassembling beds and loading appliances.

Your biggest job is to stand by to answer questions from the movers and to make sure they pack and load everything carefully.

Before the truck leaves, take a last walk through the house to make sure they loaded everything that should go with them. You probably won't have room in your car or suitcase for any overlooked items.

Also, be careful not to let them pack the things that go with you in the car, or that kitchen table and chairs that Aunt Sally is coming by to pick up later. Set them aside, all together, clearly marked (can I say this too often?).

Sane Self-Moving for the Insane

Moving day is more work if you're moving yourself with a borrowed or rented vehicle. Make sure your helpers are early risers. An early start to the day will help things go more smoothly. Entice them with coffee and donuts.

Pick up the moving vehicle early (if not the night before). Know beforehand who will do what.

If there is last-minute packing (and there will be!), assign one or two people to handle that task. Another team can disassemble and prepare beds. Have a set of basic tools handy: hammer, screwdrivers, pliers, adjustable wrench.

The children can run errands, carry light boxes, help load the car, serve refreshments, and help in many other ways. Make sure they have assigned tasks. Just telling them to stay out of the way will not work!

One or two people with a dolly can move lots of boxes out quickly. Let the strong young folks do the heaviest work, such as moving appliances and lifting heavy boxes.

Have someone who has experience moving, or at least who has read the information in Chapter 6 on packing a truck or trailer, supervise the actual loading. Avoid the temptation to just load whatever happens to come out of the house next. Careful loading will ensure safe arrival of your belongings. You may want to read Chapter 6 again yourself.

Keep the crew working, but allow occasional breaks and keep snacks handy to keep the energy flowing.

Stop for a satisfying lunch. Healthy sandwiches, fruit, and vegetables will restore energy better than fat-laden hamburgers and French fries.

Offer a continuous supply of nonalcoholic beverages. Save the beer (if any) for when the job is finished.

Clean It Up or Burn It Down?

If you dread the cleanup part of moving out, consider hiring to have it done. If you're renting and have paid a nonrefundable cleaning fee, however, don't bother cleaning. You've already paid for it.

If you have a quick move out, clear out each room and put the contents either in the main room or directly on the moving vehicle. Then have someone clean that room. Tackling the job this way means that the place will be clean soon after the last box is loaded.

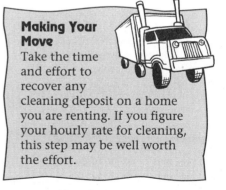

Making Your Move
Take the time and effort to recover any cleaning deposit on a home you are renting. If you figure your hourly rate for cleaning, this step may be well worth the effort.

Let's do a walk-through before cleaning up.

The Walk-Through

The first purpose of the walk-through is to make sure nothing has been left behind. This should be done before the moving van or rental truck leaves just in case you do find something.

Beyond that, in a slow tour of the entire house, including the attic, basement, closets, cupboards, garage, any outbuildings, and the yard, make a list of things that need to be done to leave the old homestead clean and ready for the next occupant. If you've been diligent about planning and working ahead, much of the cleaning may already be completed. Let's hope that after Mr. Fix-It packed up his shop, he took a few minutes to sweep the floor and clean the windows. If he didn't, make sure he's on the cleanup crew.

From your list of what needs to be cleaned, make a list of cleaning supplies that were kept off the truck. Ideally, you'll be able to gather this stuff and get a fresh start on the day after the truck leaves.

Grab a Mop

If you have been renting your old home, you may have a cleaning deposit to recover upon moving out. While some of the cleaning may have been done during the moving process, cleaning is easiest once everything is moved out.

You may want your vacuum, mop, broom, rags, bleach, all-purpose cleaner, and any specialized cleaning products that help with your particular house. One or two good friends may volunteer to help. Let them! The work will go quickly.

Many areas of the house, such as bedrooms and living room, may not need more than vacuuming. Or, they may need walls washed, carpets cleaned and paint touched up. Allow time for these extra tasks. Wash down kitchens and bathrooms with bleach or other disinfectant. Two people, working inside and out, can make short work of a houseful of windows.

Even if you do not have a cleaning deposit on your home, it is courteous to the new owners or renters to leave the house clean. The new occupants would also appreciate a folder containing the owners' manuals and any other information you have on appliances and other stuff that stay with the house. You can include a list of local repairmen, and information on utilities if you wish. Just think how helpful it will be if someone moving out of your new home leaves the same kind of information!

Now, you're ready to lock up, head for the motel or a friend's house, and get a good night's rest before hitting the road to your new home. Or, if your move is local, you're ready to head to the new neighborhood and your new house.

The Charwoman

With all of the work that you have to do to move from here to there, consider treating yourself to a house cleaner once the house is empty. A professional cleaning company, with all the right tools and products, can efficiently clean your house. Check into it. The price just might pleasantly surprise you. A cleaning crew can come in and vacuum drapes, clean windows, scrub bathrooms, wash down walls, clean appliances, and steam-clean carpets throughout the entire house faster than you alone can thoroughly clean one room. You deserve a break!

You Can Take It with You

Even if your move is a short distance, you'll take a few items in the car or make them readily accessible on the truck. Naturally, the longer the trip to your new home, the more items you will need with you.

Make sure you have keys for your new home, extra car or truck keys, and other stuff you'll need when you arrive.

And if you're moving to Lower Slobovia, make sure you take passports, visas, and other needed documents. Don't pack them!

Anything of Value?

You will want to carry your valuable jewelry, stocks, and other items with you. Be sure to take your credit cards, checkbook and cash or travelers' checks. Also hand-carry any valuables that you'd rather not ship: coin collections, silver, jewelry, crystal, or fine china.

If a moving company is transporting your belongings, make sure you carry all the paperwork on your shipment.

And make sure you have some cash, your checkbook(s), and ATM and credit cards.

Prescriptions and Other Necessities of Life

Anyone in your group on medication? Or should be? Gather all prescribed medications and their prescriptions.

Also, make sure you carry an ample supply of any over-the-counter medications you may need along the way.

Depending on where you're moving, you may need health certificates, immunization information, and other documents for yourself, your family, and your pets and plants. So keep them handy.

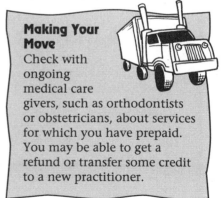

Making Your Move
Check with ongoing medical care givers, such as orthodontists or obstetricians, about services for which you have prepaid. You may be able to get a refund or transfer some credit to a new practitioner.

Are We Having Fun Yet?

If you are driving more than a couple of hours with children, take games, books, personal radios or tape or CD players. Also take writing paper, stamps, and envelopes so children can write notes to friends they are leaving.

Give each child a small box or bag and let them take whatever they want in the container. For an overnight or longer trip, pack all toiletries and clothing you will need, plus a little extra just to be safe. Include a notebook that your child can use to write about the trip, or just scribble.

Traveler's Aids

If you're driving a long distance to your new home, you might want to take along these items:

➤ Maps
➤ First-aid kit
➤ Emergency road kit
➤ Car tools
➤ Sunglasses
➤ Camera and film
➤ Clothing
➤ Snacks
➤ Water and/or pop
➤ Paper plates, cups, and plastic dinnerware
➤ Pet supplies
➤ Address book
➤ Paper towels and moist towelettes
➤ Trash bags

What a Mess!!!!

If you are moving to a new place that will need to be cleaned when you arrive, pack these things where they will be handy:

➤ Broom
➤ Mop
➤ Bucket
➤ All-purpose cleaner
➤ Rags or sturdy paper towels
➤ Vacuum cleaner
➤ Window cleaner

Need My Coffee!

What will you need for the first few hours at the new house? Pack it up now and keep it handy:

➤ Coffee maker and coffee

➤ Teapot and tea

➤ Toaster

➤ Toilet paper

➤ Cleaning supplies

➤ Linens

➤ Alarm clock

➤ Hand soap

➤ Towels

➤ Trash bags

➤ Telephone

Frivolity for Movers

Moving can be fun.

No, really!

But it can also be drudgery, so take your fun where you can. If you're going from here to there, put some fun in your trip—even if your moving budget is limited.

Look for free and low-cost natural wonders and man-made attractions; they're located throughout the entire United States. If you did your research early, as suggested in previous chapters, you know what is between here and there, what route you will be taking, and how long you have to get there. Even if you are driving a rental truck with your car on a trailer behind, you can find a few fun things to do.

If your drive is more than a couple hours, break it into manageable segments, remembering that adults, as well as children, travel more comfortably with frequent stops for stretching and exercising.

When you reach your new city, take the time to do at least a short sightseeing expedition before tackling the move into the house. Again, as with a move within a city, give the kids time to explore the house, yard, and neighborhood.

Break Time

You have to stop anyway, so why not do so at scenic overlooks and historic markers? Most are right on the highway and offer adequate parking for trucks. Many rest areas have maps and information about local attractions.

Also, check out visitor centers. Usually, they are located on a main route through town. You can learn about local sights, lodging, and restaurants—and you might find discount certificates for some. On one move, for example, we found a wonderful clock museum in Spillville, Iowa.

Don't pass up small museums. They can be some of the most interesting, offering a vivid look at local history.

No matter where you are traveling, you can find something interesting, fun, and educational. It can be free, low-cost, or expensive. To find these fun spots, you just need a sense of adventure and a little time to investigate.

If your trip is lengthy, stop often. This tactic might add an extra hour or even a day to the trip, but you will be more rested. Stop at a local market and pick up picnic items, and then stop at a rest area or city park for lunch or dinner. Carry a cooler with fruits, cut-up vegetables, granola bars, juice, pretzels and other easy, nutritious foods for breakfast and lunch. Then stop for dinner at a restaurant.

Whenever you stop, stretch, walk, do a few exercises, and change drivers if possible. Make sure the kids (if any) get out, too. Urge them to run and play for a few minutes. Take the dog or cat (if any) out for a walk.

Moving Memories

You can enhance a long trip and the resulting memories by using a section of your Smart Moving Notebook as a travel journal. Each evening record what you did during the day: what you saw, how far you traveled, where you ate. Keep a record of all your expenses (remember, some are tax deductible) and save the receipts.

Also, write down your feelings about what you did during the day, how you feel about leaving the old home, and how you feel about approaching the new home. One family member can serve as scribe for the entire trip; you can take turns each day, or everyone can write a brief account each day.

Depending on your children's ages, they might like to have diaries of their own. In a few years it will be fun to re-read your journals and remember the trip and your feelings about moving.

Lock It or Lose It

If you're pulling a trailer or driving a moving truck, be sure the cargo door is always locked with your own padlock.

Also, lock the car or truck when you leave for even a brief time. Close windows all the way unless you have pets inside.

✓ Whenever you stop at night, back your truck or trailer up to a wall so that the cargo door is not accessible. Also, remember to check the cargo inside the truck or trailer periodically to make sure nothing has shifted. Shifting cargo means unsafe driving as well as damaged goods.

✓ Also check oil and water levels in your vehicle(s), make sure any hitches are secure, and check tire pressure.

Reach Out and Touch Someone from Your Moving Vehicle

If you're on the road for very long, keep in touch with the folks and/or the movers. How? By phone.

If you have a cell phone, make sure folks have your number in case of emergency. You may be able to track your moving truck along its route. Or you can use the cell phone to make reservations at motels in upcoming towns. Or you can help other travelers handle emergencies.

Even if you don't have a cell phone, you can stay in touch. Long-distance phone carriers will gladly offer you a calling card. Calls charged to such cards are typically cheaper than calling collect. Also, you can purchase prepaid calling cards almost anywhere.

Stay in touch!

The Least You Need to Know

➤ Dealing with last-minute crises is easier if you've used your Smart Moving Notebook to plan ahead.

➤ Moving out is easier if one person serves as supervisor, overseer, and straw boss.

➤ Plan now how you will clean up the old place as you leave.

➤ Plan for a smooth transition of people and stuff, making sure you have what you need as you go from here to there.

Chapter 19

Moving Children Without Losing Your Mind

In This Chapter

➤ Telling kids about the move

➤ Understanding the move from a child's perspective

➤ Helping kids cope with the move

➤ Keeping kids out of the way during the move

Moving is atop the stress list for adults. It's off the charts for kids!

"After $4,000 in orthodontics, Sally finally has a boyfriend—and we're moving!"

"Roger just made the football team—and we're moving!"

"Bobbie is supposed to start kindergarten next month—and we're moving!"

"Junior just made the Ten Most Wanted list—so we're moving!"

This chapter can help you with one of the most difficult parts of moving: helping your children accept the move.

Hey, Kids! Guess What?

About eight million kids move with their families each year. And, unbeknownst to them, 99.7 percent actually survive the move. And an astonishing number even benefit from the move—whether or not they like it.

Moving upsets everyone. Routines change. Emotions boil. Fears emerge. Confusion reigns. Especially in children.

How can you break the news? A family meeting is an excellent way to tell your children about a move. Home is the best place for the meeting, especially around the dinner table. If you don't have frequent (or any) family meetings, take everyone to dinner and broach the subject. But, if you're expecting fireworks, have dinner in a neighboring town where no one knows you.

Sound tough? It can be. Here are some tips.

Buck & Back Savers

Mobility magazine, published by the Employee Relocation Council, includes articles about relocation and children. You can reach the publisher at 800/372-5952, e-mail them at mobility@erc.org, or visit their Web site at **http://www.erc.org**.

We're Moving Where?

Break it to them gently.

Tell your children the reason for the move. Tailor your explanation to their age. The youngest children only need to know that mommy or daddy has to work at a new office in a new town—or that the family needs to be closer to grandma and grandpa to help them.

Older teens will want and deserve to know more. They can understand that the family needs the increased income of a better job—or whatever the reason for the move. They may not like the move, but they will probably understand the reasons behind it.

Here are some useful tips:

➤ Tell them the advantages of moving (new sports, entertainment, a better school, a big MALL!).

➤ Be prepared for negative reactions; children seldom like change.

➤ Let the children ask any questions they want and answer them as fully as you can with language and examples they can understand.

➤ Maintain a positive attitude yourself, but don't sugarcoat the subject.

➤ Let them know you understand their wariness and will help them make the transition in any way you can.

➤ Give them some influence and control over some aspects of the move. A toddler can "pack for a teddy bear" or "help" you do serious packing.

➤ Be a good listener! Be patient.

Make sure your kids get to make up a box of things to help them get from here to there.

I Wanna Help!

As the move moves along, make sure everyone knows how things are going. Keep everyone up to date on plans and tasks. Maybe you can have a weekly moving meeting at a favorite restaurant.

Also, keep everyone involved. Let the children help make some decisions. If possible, take them house hunting with you, or at least take them to visit the new house after you have found it. Ask them what they would like in a new house and point out those features when they ask. If they cannot visit, try to get photos of the new house so that everyone can begin to get to know it.

If the move is to another city, get information about your new hometown to share with the kids. If it isn't too far away, make a visit. Tour the neighborhood and the city. Find some city parks. Visit a museum. Tour the children's new school. Drive by where mom or dad will be working. Find an attraction that you can promise to visit as soon as you are settled in the new house. And keep your promise!

Visit the local church or synagogue, introduce your family to the minister, priest, or rabbi, and find out about youth-oriented activities the church sponsors. Walk around the nearest shopping streets or mall. Kids (especially teenagers) love to shop or at least hang out in shopping areas. Knowing what they can expect should lessen the stress of moving.

Visit places especially geared to children (to keep them off the streets and out of trouble), such as a YMCA or Boys' and Girls' Club or teen center. Check out public sports facilities, such as tennis courts, basketball courts, baseball fields, ice rinks, swimming pools or beaches.

After the move, your children may need help adjusting to all the changes in their lives. So, rebuild family routines as quickly as possible.

Make the routines similar to those at the old house. Have meals at about the same time, and keep curfews, bedtimes, and other familiar activities.

Remember that the adjustment will probably take longer than you think it should. Unless serious problems occur, allow your children up to a year to become fully adjusted.

If a year goes by and your children are still unsettled, seek professional help to address any residual problems brought on by the move.

If you're moving the family because of a divorce or death, your children could benefit from counseling even before the move.

What's the Move Look like from There?

Your boss walks in and says, "Clean out your office. We're moving you to Timbuktu for awhile. Don't quite know what's there or what you'll be doing, but, uh, good luck!"

Of course, you can always refuse and go find another job.

But what can your kids do when you announce that the family is moving—find another family?

Add this bombshell to the frustration of not knowing how to express what you're feeling: "What about...What can I...How will I...Now what will I...?"

Best advice: Before you announce the move, empathize with each child, considering how he or she will handle the emotions of the move. Then look for ways to make the situation easier.

Daddy, What's a Move?

Very young children may not need to know about your upcoming move as soon as you make a decision. In fact, telling them too far in advance can expand their fear of the unknown.

If possible, put off telling very young children until the last few weeks—or until packing begins.

Home is the young child's entire world. A particular house is not their world; the family and things in it is. As long as the family remains intact, most preschoolers will focus on the loss of their familiar home rather than friends or other outside influences.

So, if you can, bring children to your new home in advance of the move—or at least as soon as you arrive—and help them get acquainted. Help them pick out their room.

Remember that some children seem to handle moving well, but are really in turmoil about the change. Consider each child's uniqueness and needs as you help them move.

Can Bobby Next Door Move with Us?

Young school-age children usually have strong friendship bonds and also take a while to make new friends.

Check the new neighborhood for children near their ages. Find out if their new school has an orientation program for new students. Get them involved in after-school activities.

Also, check out your favorite church, synagogue or spiritual meeting place for activities that can help your kids cope and socialize.

Ain't No Way I'm Movin'!

"I'll live on the streets!"

As appealing as this proposition may seem to you, resist the urge to let them!

Teenagers find moving more difficult than younger children. And they will typically make it more difficult. Their life probably revolves around friends and activities outside the home. You're now threatening to disrupt their entire social structure.

And teens know what fun *they* have with "the new kid."

Actually, teens can benefit from a move, but they have to realize the benefits themselves rather than be told.

So the approach for helping a teen move is different from that for younger family members.

Some tips:

➤ Don't be too busy for your teen. No matter how stressful and time-consuming the move is for you, take time out to talk to your teen. Express sympathy for his concerns and offer suggestions to help him make the transition.

➤ If you have a choice, move during the late summer so that your teen begins the school year with other "new" students.

➤ Encourage your teen to get involved with others her own age who share the same interests. If your teen belonged to a Stamp Club or a Bible Study Group in your old neighborhood, chances are there's one associated with the school or church in your new neighborhood.

➤ If your teen is involved in sports, find out about schools, teams, and facilities in the new area. Find out where the tennis courts, basketball courts, ball fields, or ice rinks are in your new neighborhood and send your teen to check them out. She may get a chance to play for a better team than she would in your old neighborhood.

➤ Expect outrageous behavior. Teens often can't communicate their real feelings—or even understand them. You may want to overlook the green hair, odd body piercing, or appalling clothes and concentrate instead on communicating your support and understanding.

It goes like this:

➤ Young children focus on the loss of their room and home.

➤ Teenagers focus on the emotions that moving brings.

➤ Adults focus on the physical move.

Moving Violations

Our oldest son was eight when we moved 2,000 miles to a new job and, seemingly, a new world. Quiet by nature, he expressed his displeasure by running away from our new home. Fortunately, we found him and helped him cope with his fears.

Many teens will be shocked and angry when told of the move. These feelings can lead to depression and panic. Such feelings are helping your teenager to disconnect from the old life and prepare for the new. You can help by knowing what to expect, explaining to your teen that the emotions they are feeling are normal, if uncomfortable, and allowing them to talk about their feelings.

But, guess what. After the move to your new home, your teenager will probably get used to the new home, school, neighborhood, and town. Expect the acclimation to take six to eighteen months from the move until your teen really feels at home. And understand that they may have roller-coaster emotions after the move: loving the new place one day and hating it the next. Ride it out.

Helping Young Children Cope

What can you do to help younger children cope with the move?

Playact the move. Use dolls, a few boxes, and a toy truck to help children visualize the moving process.

Reassure very young children that they *will* be moving with you.

Three-year-old Amy watched as her family gave away their dog when they moved to a new home. She feared that because she too was a small member of the family, she might also be given away. It took lots of reassurance from mom, dad, and her big brother that her stay with Aunt Sandra on moving day wasn't a trick to leave her behind.

If your young child is in day care, find a new day-care situation as soon as possible. Young children make friends quickly.

I Can't Deal with This and Zits, Too!

The older the child, the more he needs to remain in control of his own life. Help children keep in control through knowledge, understanding, and respect.

Moving Kids 5 to 12 Years Old without Getting Bitten

Younger school-age children can be helped through support and space to explore and adjust to feelings. As much as possible, let your child be involved—or at least feel involvement—in the move.

➤ Ask the child to be in charge of helping a pet or stuffed animal make the move safely.

➤ Give the child a disposable camera (under $10) that can be used for taking pictures of the old home, the trip, and the new home.

Talk to school counselors and teachers at your child's new school. Curricula vary, so find out where your child is in comparison to new classmates and arrange for help in any areas where your child is behind. Make sure the school knows of any medical conditions that may need attention during school.

Moving Teenagers without Getting the Police Involved

Some teens have difficulty coping with the stress of a move because they don't take good care of their bodies. Encourage your teen to eat well, get plenty of rest, and exercise. Help your teenager get involved in your new neighborhood or town. These steps will help them cope with the inevitable stress of moving. In addition, here are some other tips to ease the challenge of moving a teen:

➤ Go to church as a family and find out about teen groups.

➤ Suggest that she volunteers to help coach a young baseball team, help out at a nursing home, or get involved in some other activity that gives them responsibility and makes them feel needed. Sometimes teens are more open to responsibilities outside the home than in the home.

➤ Encourage her to try the sports that are most popular in your new area as well as getting into old favorites.

➤ Build on shared interests with your teen and discover together what makes your new hometown or state unique. It doesn't matter whether the event is a sporting event, a science or natural history museum, or shopping. What matters is that you and your teen are doing something together.

➤ If your teen is Internet-savvy, make sure she gets her friend's e-mail addresses. E-mailing is quick, easy, and a lot cheaper than a phone call.

➤ Budget to let your teen make a few phone calls to old friends.

➤ Letters from old friends help. Leave paper, envelopes, and stamps in his room. And remind your teenager that he will probably not receive many letters if he doesn't write any.

➤ Start planning to bring a friend to visit or to send your teen back to visit after a few months.

I'm Not Leaving My Friends!

When you announce your plans to move, your teen may flatly refuse to move. Most, however, reluctantly come around after awhile.

But what if an older teenager remains serious about staying?

Here are some suggestions.

First, discover why your child wants to stay behind. Some reasons are valid. Some are not. Your teen may simply want to stay with her friends. Or she may want to remain on an athletic team. Or assert independence and punish you for moving. Or gain more freedom. Or finish a special program at the school. Or graduate with her class.

Listen!

If your teen is a high-school senior and feels strongly that he has valid reasons for wanting to stay at his old school, discuss them. Don't say no immediately; say you'll listen. Along with your teenager, list all the options available. He can:

➤ Move now.

➤ Finish the term and then join the family.

➤ Finish the school year at the old school.

➤ Complete high school before joining the family.

Ask:

➤ Where would he live? With a relative or friend? In an apartment? In a residential hotel or YMCA?

➤ Is the teen really mature enough to be emancipated?

➤ What will it cost? Is your teen ready to support himself or herself? Will your teen take a part-time job to help pay the extra bills?

As all the factors are considered, your teen may decide that moving on with the family is the best option—or not. In either case, the teen has participated in a major decision.

I Can Do It Myself!

If you and your teen decide that staying behind is the best solution, set some ground rules. Make sure they're clearly understood and agreed upon beforehand by you, your teen, and anyone who will be responsible for her.

Such as what?

➤ Who will pay for what?

➤ What household chores will she be expected to perform?

➤ When is curfew?

➤ Will she go to church or attend other functions?

➤ How will routine medical needs as well as emergencies be handled?

Write out a contract that everyone signs.

Remember: In order to encourage your teen to begin thinking like an adult, treat her like one. After all, she soon will be—ready or not!

And the moving decision can help bring you closer together.

Out of Harm's Way—or Thereabouts

Gangway! Coming through!

When moving, your first thought may be to send the kids off to play while you get the work done. This solution may be easier in the short term, but can lose the opportunity to do something together as a family, and your children may feel left out of the event. Make them feel it's their move, too, and not just yours.

Helping prepare for the move can help your kids adjust more quickly. They will definitely feel more involved if they help.

Yes, even toddlers can help with some tasks. They can help pack some of their sturdy toys. They can help decide what toys to take along for the trip to the new house. And some will love the task of handing you wrapping paper as you pack other items. In fact, the younger the child, the more willing he will be to help.

Let your children pack their own things—even if you secretly repack them for safety reasons later.

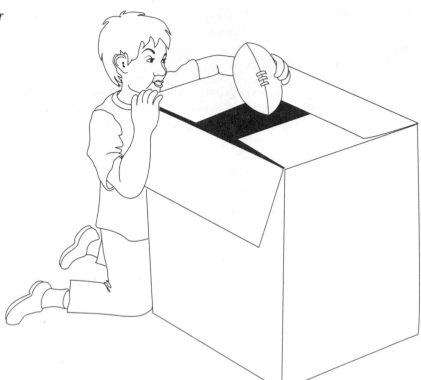

No, You Can't Pack the Kitty!

If you aren't using a packing service, put your teenagers in charge of packing their possessions. Give them the packing materials they need and let them go. Show them what can happen to things that aren't packed well, and then let them make the decisions. They're the ones who will have to live with the consequences of poor packing.

A teen with a driver's license will probably willingly run errands, such as picking up more boxes and packing tape.

With a few instructions, children between age 5 and 12 can also handle a lot of their own packing. After you supervise the first few boxes, leave them to do the job. Of course, you can ask them not to seal any boxes until you survey the contents. Remind them to mark each box clearly. (Use press-on dots in different colors for each child.)

Moving is for everyone!

Kids on Moving-Out Day

No, it's too late for birth control!

If you've hired a moving company, plan to have most family members away from the house on moving day. The movers can then work most efficiently.

If you're doing it yourself, however, consider your children's temperaments and abilities. Let them help as much as possible. Whether onsite or off, babies and toddlers will be better off with a babysitter.

Older children can carry not-too-heavy boxes and other smaller items, serve as gofers, and run errands. Cooperative teens can do as much work as an adult. Maybe more!

Kids on Moving-In Day

You've arrived!

Figure Moving-In Day the same as for Moving-Out Day: Let kids who can help, help. Better yet: Help kids get excited about new rooms, a new house, a new yard, and a new neighborhood.

Most kids can be in charge of arranging their own new rooms. After some help to place furniture, they can start unpacking the boxes marked for their rooms.

In a safe new neighborhood, children who are old enough can take a walk through the 'hood.

Keep 'Em Busy!

So what else can young beings do to participate and even help with the move?

Glad you asked!

➤ Teens can watch younger children.

➤ Children can be in charge of animals.

➤ Children can fix and serve snacks to the moving crew.

➤ Each child can be assigned to a willing adult as a special helper for the day.

The Least You Need to Know

➤ Help kids understand the reasons for and the benefits of the move from their perspective.

➤ Encourage your kids (especially older ones) to talk to you about how the move affects them.

➤ Keep kids busy with jobs that keep them from injury and give them some control over the move.

213

Moving Critters and Other Living Things

> **In This Chapter**
>
> ➤ Preparing pets for moving
>
> ➤ Transporting pets safely
>
> ➤ Leaving pets behind
>
> ➤ Moving plants

The movie, *Homeward Bound,* is cute—but it isn't reality.

If your two dogs and a cat somehow get lost in the move, they probably won't mysteriously show up at your new home, tired and speaking with human voices.

Our real fear concerning animals is that we'll lose them somewhere along the way, and we don't want to do that. Teenagers, maybe, but not our pets.

By now you've guessed what we're going to cover in this chapter. No? Need another hint? Moving pets! And plants!

He Followed Me Home!

Taking your dog?

For many people there's no question. When they move, their pets move.

If your move is short, relocating a pet is relatively simple. If your move is across the country, it will be more difficult to take the dogs and cats, but it can still be done comfortably.

The issues concerned are emotions, health, and comfort.

Mice Have Feelings, Too!

Should you move your pets?

Our pets are just like the rest of us—some are easygoing and some are easily upset.

You know your furred and feathered friends best. Consider their temperaments as you make moving plans. Will Felix the cat curl up on Sissy's lap and happily sleep away the trip? Or will he turn into a frothing, hair-on-end mad cat ready to claw and bite anyone unfortunate enough to be within striking distance?

And will you worry every minute if Penelope the pampered pooch flies while you drive? Or would you consider it a nuisance having to find motels or hotels that will accept your animal companions?

I Hate Shots!

Your pets will travel more happily if they are in good health. Schedule a vet appointment for at least a couple weeks before moving day to make sure everyone is in top condition.

If vaccinations are nearly due, get them even if it's a little early. Then you won't have to worry about finding a vet so quickly in your new town. You can also ask your vet for recommendations of new doctors.

Remember to ask for a copy of your pet's medical and inoculation records to take with you to your new vet.

Say, Can I Have One of Those Shots?

If you have a Nervous Nelly cat or dog, ask your vet about mild tranquilizers for the trip. While not recommended unless absolutely necessary, they can help relieve the stress for both your animal and you.

It's no fun traveling with a jittery hound.

Okay, Who Packed the Parakeet?

Moving day is hectic for everyone, including pets who are in the house when the truck arrives.

If you do keep your pets at home, they will need to be confined somewhere out of the way of the movers, whether the movers are family and friends or professionals.

While most pets are happiest at home, moving day might be a good day to send them to a friend, pet sitter, or kennel for safekeeping.

Is There Anything Tabby Can Watch on Cable?

If they are kept at home for moving day, find your pets a safe, comfortable, confined space out of the inevitable confusion. Best, of course, is a familiar, well-liked space, such as the crate of a crate-trained dog.

Make sure they are fed their regular foods on their regular schedule, walked on time, and that plenty of fresh water is easily available. Stop and talk with them often to reassure them. If you have children, assign one to check on the pets often and exercise them if they are confined to a small space.

Beware of the Pet Police

Most U.S. communities have ordinances regulating pet control and licenses. Call the city clerk in your new city and ask about the local animal ordinances.

If your move is interstate, you might want to contact the Department of Agriculture or the State Veterinarian's Office in your new state and ask about animal entry laws. A few states (Arizona and California, for example) have border inspection stations, but most rely on your compliance with the law.

If you're moving internationally, taking your pets may be out of the question. Check with the country's embassy for more info. For example, you may have to leave Bowser in quarantine for six months or more in the new country (England, Australia, and New Zealand, to name a few). Is it worth it to Bowser?

Depending upon your destination, you will need to carry health certificates, permits, rabies tags, and identification.

Halt! Who Goes There?

To enter many states, you'll need an entry permit for your pet. Either you or your veterinarian can apply for this permit, which may require a fee. You also might need a health certificate in order to apply for the entry permit.

Most states require a health certificate for entering dogs and horses. About half the states require certificates for cats, birds, and other household pets.

If you have questions about your pet's health, take him to the vet early so that any problems can be cleared up in time to issue a health certificate for the time of the move. Some states require that the health certificate be less than 10 days old.

Don't Get Rabid!

Nearly all states require dogs and cats to wear valid rabies tags on their collars. These dated tags are issued when your pet is inoculated against rabies. Requirements such as length of time between vaccinations vary, however, so be sure to check with your new veterinarian.

Some cities have even stricter requirements. Check with your veterinarian before moving.

I Need to See Some ID

When traveling, a cat or dog should have identification attached to its collar. Birds should have identification on leg bands. Include your animal's name, your name, and your new address on this tag.

Ask your veterinarian about the computer chip system of identifying pets. The tiny chips are inserted with a syringe, causing no more pain to the animal than an inoculation. The information on the chip is registered with an identification service, offering a permanent record of ownership of your pet.

Many veterinarians will also tattoo information on your pet. This simple procedure can be performed easily when the pet is under anesthetic for another procedure, such as spaying or neutering.

The owner's Social Security number is often used as the identifier, but a telephone number or other information can also be used.

Of course, if you move frequently, your pet's going to get pretty sore!

Cat Taxi, Please

Yes, there are special transportation services for pets. Check the phone book in larger metro areas.

A pet transportation service will make all the arrangements and handle all the details of moving your pet from one home to another.

Check with several animal transporters if more than one is available in your area. Services may vary from basic to full-service. Some will schedule all arrangements, pick up your pet at your home, provide whatever travel container is necessary, and deliver your friend to your new address after you arrive. Others will meet you at the airport, with your crate or other shipping container, and hand your pet over to you when it deplanes.

Your mover can probably recommend a reputable service. You may want to visit the service's facility and talk with several members of the staff before turning over responsibility for a family member.

Here are some Smart Mover questions to ask a pet transportation service:

➤ How will my pet be restrained?

➤ How long will the trip take?

➤ Where will they be while traveling?

➤ What food and water will be available?

➤ Who will handle my pet?

➤ How much experience do you have?

➤ Will my pet be around other animals?

➤ Do you require health certificates for every animal?

➤ How much do you charge?

After all your questions are answered and you feel reassured that your pet will receive VIP service, you can attend to other details of your move.

Ever Seen a Horse Fly?

Animals can be moved by air. If possible, ship animals only during moderate weather. In fact, some airlines will refuse to ship animals if it is cooler than about 45 degrees Fahrenheit or hotter than 85 degrees Fahrenheit.

If your pet must be flown to your new home, first have the pet checked by your veterinarian. Get any needed inoculations, a health certificate, and any necessary medications.

My Pet Wants a One-Way Ticket to Hawaii

Make flight arrangements early and ask about special requirements. You will need an FAA-approved animal crate. Whether your animal travels with you or as air freight, clearly mark the words "LIVE ANIMAL" on the outside of the carrier.

Make arrangements for shipping your pet as early as possible. You'll probably need to prepay the shipment fees. On the day of the flight, feed the animal lightly at least five hours before the flight and water at least two hours before the flight.

If possible, let your pet get some exercise (and any needed medication) at the airport just prior to the flight. Be sure to have the animal's health certificate, permits, rabies tag, and identification tag available.

Mini-Condos for Your Pet

Making Your Move
The Animal Welfare Act prohibits any air transport of kittens and puppies under eight weeks old. Check with the airline for regulations and for details concerning other pets.

If your pet is small, an FAA-approved carrier no larger than 21"×18"×8" can usually be taken with you into the passenger compartment. Please, for the safety of the flight, make sure your skunk has been descented. Arrive early, because most airlines operate on a first-come, first-served basis when allowing animals in the passenger cabin and only allow a certain number to be carried on.

The only exception to animals being crated in the passenger compartment of an airplane is for Seeing Eye dogs. Usually a Seeing Eye dog is allowed to sit in the aisle of the cabin at the owner's feet. The airline must be notified in advance that the dog will be on the flight.

If your animal is too large to go into the passenger compartment or if you're traveling separately, pets can be sent air freight.

Tropical fish should be shipped only after packing by a professional who specializes in tropical fish. Most airlines will not ship snakes, thank God.

How to ship? Place your pet in the approved shipping container clearly marked "LIVE ANIMAL." Include your name, address, and telephone number, as well as those of the person who will meet the pet at the end of the flight. Attach the animal's leash to the outside of the carrier.

Room Service? Two Milk Bones!

If your pet is going in the passenger cabin with you, your goal will be to keep the animal calm and quiet. If it has been fed, watered, and walked prior to the flight, everything should go well until you reach your destination.

If the flight is long, offer your pet a few sips of water. If you must change airplanes, try to schedule a long enough delay to take the animal out of the airport for a hydrant stop.

If your animal is in cargo, you will not be able to check on it during flight, and the pilot will probably refuse to land the plane so you can snuggle Cuddles.

Are We There Yet?

Of course, unless you accompany your pet on the flight, you will need to make arrangements for a good friend to send the animal off or pick it up at the destination. Be sure that you or your friend picks your pet up on time at the destination. Any animals not picked up after about 24 hours can, at owner's expense, either be shipped back to the point of origin or placed in a kennel.

Whether the animal flies with you or as air cargo, take it out of the airport and out of the crate as soon as possible. Allow the animal to stretch its legs and relieve itself before climbing in the car to go to its new home.

Even horses can be shipped as air cargo, but it is expensive and requires that someone travel with the animal. The horse will need a shipping stall approved by the airline and maybe even a loading ramp. Shipping charges must be paid in advance and tack must be handled separately.

Home, Bowser?

If your pet could talk, it would probably say, "Chauffeur me!"

Your animal will usually be more comfortable riding in the car with you, and this option is far less expensive than sending it by air.

Be sure your animal is in good health and carry any required health certificates, permits, identification, and rabies tags.

In addition, take a test ride, use proven pet travel techniques, make frequent stops, and consider medication.

Take your pets on a short test drive before trying to move them cross-country in your car.

The Test Ride

If your dog is not used to riding in a car, take it on several short trips and work on its travel manners. This step is easier if your dog has been obedience trained. To safely travel in a car, your dog should be trained to sit or lie down quietly.

An alternative is to keep the dog in a crate. If your move includes overnight stops, take a crate anyway so that the dog has a familiar space in unfamiliar surroundings such as motel rooms.

Cats usually hate to ride in a car, but they will settle in eventually. They are safest, and usually happiest, crated. They like having a cozy, close place to nap.

Whether a dog or cat, if it's in the crate, it's comfortable and it's not going to jump out of the car and run away when you open the door. Nor will it have the opportunity to plunge its teeth or claws into your right arm just as you're executing that hairpin turn down a steep hill. Or cower under the brake pedal.

If your pet gets carsick easily, ask your veterinarian about options. Medication is one. It also helps to feed very lightly or withhold food until the day's drive is completed. And some pets will get sick the first few miles of the trip, and then adjust to the motion and be fine for the day or the entire trip.

Even if your animal has never been prone to motion sickness, it's good insurance to carry paper towels, trash bags, and cleaner in case of sickness or accidents. Confining your pet to a crate will also confine any mess to that crate, and you can clean the crate much more easily than you can clean the car's carpeting or upholstery.

Travel like a Pro

Make sure your pet has its collar and tags, and never let it loose while traveling. Even a well-behaved dog may bolt when let loose in a strange place.

Cats can be taught, at an early age, to walk on a leash and will not be lost if they are only taken out when on one.

As when traveling with small children, plan plenty of rest stops to let your pet exercise and relieve itself.

Keep your pet under control at all times and don't let it annoy others.

Remember your pet when you make motel, hotel, or campground reservations. Many places accept pets, but some do not, and those that do may have certain restrictions. Cuddly kitty may be welcome, but your three mastiffs might cause alarm. Ask ahead of time.

Believe it or not, some motels welcome pets. Most motel chains offer directories of locations of their motels along with information, usually including whether or not they accept pets.

Never leave your pets in a completely closed car. Even in cool weather, on a sunny day the temperature inside your car can reach killing degrees. If you must leave your pet alone in the car for a few minutes, park in the shade and open each window an inch or so. Never leave an animal alone in a car in hot weather.

Do You Want to Check It as Carrion?

Make a list of things you need to take for your pet:

➤ Food (and, depending on the food, a can opener)

➤ Prescribed medication

➤ Water

➤ Feeding dishes

➤ Leash

➤ Paper towels (for accidents)

➤ Litter and disposable box for litter-trained pets

➤ Scoop and plastic bags (for intentionals)

➤ One or two toys

➤ Treats

➤ Brush

➤ Flea spray

➤ Pet crate

If you are to stay in a motel, take your animal's regular bed or a carrier.

Some of you fine readers will be moving non-furred pets. How can you get them from here to there without losing them somewhere else?

Most small pets (guinea pigs, hamsters) and birds travel best in the cages they live in at home.

Make sure they have plenty of water. Those tiny bodies dehydrate quickly.

Keep your bird calm by covering its cage. Take care to keep birds out of drafts and extreme temperatures. Feed it as usual.

Buck & Back Savers

For one job, I stayed in a city apartment for a couple of weeks, and then commuted back home to the country for a week. I decided to move my pet parakeet to keep me company in the big city. With ample food and water, his cage was placed on the front seat, seat belted, and covered with a dark cloth. The radio played all the way (George *loves* oldies!). He traveled just fine.

Yes, even tropical fish can be moved by car. The shorter the trip the better.

Unless your aquarium is five or fewer gallons in capacity, your fish will travel more safely in another carrier. Use a clean plastic bag or an unbreakable container such as a bucket with a lid, and fill this carrier half full with water from the aquarium.

Remember, your fish are delicate and need a fairly constant water temperature, so a Styrofoam or insulated cooler will make a good holder. Carefully transfer the fish (being cautious not to overcrowd) and close the container. Fish need air, so open the container every few hours to renew the air supply.

Horsing Around

Need to move a horse? If your equine is an experienced trailer traveler, no problem. If not, start now to get some practice in before the move. You can rent horse trailers.

If your trip requires motel stops, check beforehand to be sure you can park a trailer with a horse in the parking lot overnight. The horse will be fine in the trailer overnight. If you are camping, be sure horses are permitted in the campground. Another alternative is to board the horse at stables along the way.

Time to Lift a Leg

With the exception of maybe fish and birds, most animals, including the driver, will benefit from frequent stops. If you travel with dogs who need to be exercised, rest areas, when available, offer the best breaks because most include areas for walking dogs.

If your cat needs to be walked, find a quiet area away from rest areas and the dogs that frequent them. Offer only small amounts of water at each break.

Pets can travel well together.

No, Fido, I Didn't Mean That Kind of "Go"!

When you simply can't take one or more of your pets with you, start early to find them a new home.

Please don't just give your animals away to someone you don't know. Too many animals end up as research subjects or in animal shelters. The following sections offer some alternative options and opportunities.

...to a Good Home

Advertise your pet in the local media. Post a notice on your veterinarian's bulletin board. Make it clear that you will only place your animal in a good home.

Spend some time with any prospective new owners. If you don't feel confident they will treat your pet well, wait. Someone else will come along who will love your pet as much as you do.

Friends and Family

Give friends and family members the first chance to offer a happy new home to Ben the Boa. Don't force the issue, however, or your beloved pet may end up in a reluctant home. Instead, expend a little more effort and find a new family ready to welcome your pet with open arms.

Pet Adoptions

If you have trouble finding a home, research whether your city has a local adoption agency for pets. Some communities have a society that will even find foster homes for animals while they search out top-notch adoptive homes.

Ask your breeder, veterinarian, animal groomer, obedience teacher, and others to find out if there is such a group in your area.

Moving Flowering Pets

Of course, not all of the living things in our life have feet or slither. Some are living plants.

The best advice about moving house plants: don't.

Either give them away or sell them. You can always take cuttings with you to start new plants.

Most moving companies will not transport plants more than 150 miles, and they will not guarantee their condition upon arrival. Plants can be difficult to move and take up a lot of space in your vehicle.

Check with the U.S. Department of Agriculture for regulations about moving plants into your new home state. If you decide you must move some of your house plants, follow these guidelines:

➤ Three weeks before moving, repot the plants into unbreakable plastic pots. Use commercial potting soil. (Many plant diseases are soil-borne.)

➤ Two weeks before moving, prune as appropriate. Your plants will take up less space and be healthier.

➤ One week before moving, check for and eliminate insects and parasites. Either carefully use a commercial insecticide, or better, place each plant in a black plastic bag for five or six hours along with a flea collar or pest strip.

➤ A couple of days before moving, water all plants normally.

➤ One day before moving, wrap the base of the plant and loosely wrap the top of the plant with damp newspaper; then wrap the whole plant with plastic. For trips longer than a couple of days, use dry newspaper around the bottom of the plant and soft, dry paper to cushion the branches. Place the plant in a moving carton and use more packing material as necessary to cushion the plant and hold it upright in a box. Cut holes in the sides of the box to provide air, and then fasten the lid loosely. Label the carton.

Hanging plants can also be hung on the metal rack in a wardrobe carton.

Care During the Move (I Can't Ride in the Trunk)

If possible, pack your plants in the interior of the car. They may get too hot or too cold in the trunk.

If you must load your plants into the back of a truck, load them last and unload them first. During the summer, park in the shade and open windows a crack; in the winter, park in the sun and keep windows closed. If you stop overnight, take the plants inside.

Unless your trip is more than four days, you do not need to open the cartons. If your trip is longer, after about four days open the cartons and check to see whether your plants need water.

Try to quickly make your pet at home in his new home.

SPOT

THERE'S
NO PLACE
LIKE HOME

Home, Sweet Home

Once you've arrived, unpack plants as soon as you can. Open boxes from the bottom and lift the carton off the plant to avoid damage. Place your plants for the light they need, and try not to move them soon after their initial placement; they need to rest and acclimate. Don't you wish you could do the same?

The Least You Need to Know

➤ The issues involved in deciding whether and how to move pets are health, comfort, and emotions (yours and your pet's).

➤ On moving day, consider boarding your pet or sending it to a neighbor for a sleepover.

➤ It may be easier to hire a pet transportation service to help you move your pet safely and comfortably.

➤ Move living plants with care, keeping them adequately watered and appropriately warm or cool.

Moving In: Where Da Ya Want Dis, Lady?

In This Chapter

➤ Getting acquainted with your new home

➤ Preparing for the move-in

➤ Unloading your stuff or directing the movers

➤ Helping everyone feel at home

Home, sweet home!

Well, not quite yet. You still have to move your stuff in and put it away somewhere. But your new place will soon be a home.

This chapter offers tips on how to get acquainted with your new living quarters, how to unload your stuff or direct the movers, and how to make your house/apartment/condo/trailer a home.

Hello, House! How's Your Door Hanging?

✓ **Making Your Move**
Unload your rental truck promptly and return it on time, avoiding any extra charges.

At last. You're home. At your new home.

Of course, it doesn't have any furniture yet. Maybe even no window coverings. But if you stuck to your organizational plan for moving, the electricity and water are on. It's time to say hello.

Exercising Your Feet

Whether you are renting or buying the house or apartment, whether or not you have seen it before, wander through and get acquainted. Get each family member to do the same. This may be the first time you have seen it without furniture. Imagine it furnished with your belongings. See the living room with your oak and glass. Or the master bedroom with your antique brass bed. Take your time. Examine all the nooks and corners, all the cupboards and closets.

On this first exploration, look at the positives and the possibilities. Soon enough, you will take another look to see what needs to be cleaned, repaired, painted, or remodeled.

Exercising Your Imagination

Your new residence is a fresh canvas ready for your ideas. Spend time in each room, looking and imagining.

➤ How do the windows open? (Open them to air out the house.)

➤ Where is the thermostat that controls the furnace?

➤ Where does the laundry chute come out?

➤ What's behind that door?

➤ What might you store in those cupboards?

➤ Is there room over the mantel for your favorite painting?

➤ Where's the best place for your couch?

➤ What's the best way to bring in the china cabinet?

➤ Can you safely store your treasures in the attic or basement?

➤ Could you some day add a bedroom or a personal retreat?

➤ What's in the garage?

➤ Is there a workbench?

➤ Is there room for cars as well as bicycles?

➤ Where can the lawn mower go?

Once you have become acquainted with the interior of the house and garage, tour the yard.

➤ Where will the swing set go?

➤ Is there room for lawn games?

➤ Is there a sunny garden space?

➤ Can you hook up the hose to an exterior faucet?

➤ Is the yard fenced for pets and small children?

➤ Is the fence in good repair?

➤ Are stairs, railings, banisters, and decking in good repair?

➤ Will the barbecue fit on the patio?

Take the time to walk around and read the neighborhood. Toys in the yard indicate children who might be around your own youngsters' ages. A boat or classic car in the driveway lets you know someone nearby shares your interests. Introduce yourself to anyone you meet.

You might just stumble upon a park where you can picnic and where the kids can play. Or you might discover an old-fashioned neighborhood grocery store where you can pick up last-minute items for dinner.

If you still have some time and energy left, get in the car and drive around town. Show the kids their school. Find the nearest supermarket and pharmacy. Beginning to know your way around will help you feel comfortable quickly in your new home and town.

Your pets also need to get to know the new house, the yard, and the neighborhood, but it may be easier to wait until after the truck is unloaded and the extra people gone. A frightened cat or dog could bolt out an open door and get lost or trampled upon.

Before you take your pet in the house, give it a chance to take care of personal business. Then, be sure all doors and unscreened windows are closed. Bring the animal in and let it explore its new home.

Decide where the animal will eat and set out fresh water in this place. If feeding time is near, go ahead and feed it. Otherwise, offer a treat.

If the yard is safely fenced, let your dog explore there too. If the yard is not fenced, take the dog out on a leash. Even cats that normally spend lots of time outside should be kept inside for a few days. They need to learn that the new house is home and to stay close—at least at mealtime. If you can, take your dog for a walk—on a leash, of course.

We're Not Ready Yet!

Whether you moved yourself in a truck or trailer, or you're waiting for the moving van to arrive, start planning the best way to unload and move in.

You'll need to figure where to park your personal vehicles and moving vehicles. Also, prepare the house for moving in. And be a good host/hostess to your moving crew: paid or volunteer.

Park It!

Where should you park your car and any moving vehicles? You have two choices, depending on function:

➤ Out of the way

➤ In the way

If your personal vehicle has stuff in it that needs to be out of the way (critters) or stuff for moving in (cleaning supplies), park near the door. The same goes for your trailer or rental truck: Park as near the main door as possible. Once empty, park it out of the way—even down the block—where it won't obstruct larger moving vehicles.

If you have helpers, ask them to park out of the way so that the moving vehicle has lots of room to maneuver.

Moving Words
A *destination agent* is the agent at the destination who will assist you or the van operator.

If you're using a rental truck or trailer, decide which door will be used to bring in most of your stuff. Then take your time to figure the best place to park the vehicle for unloading.

If a moving van is doing the work, make sure your vehicles are parked out of the way. The movers will take care of the rest.

Do I Really Have to Clean Another House?

Moving Words
An extra charge that is added if a shipment must be either picked up or delivered with the use of an elevator or stairs is called an *elevator carry*. Or would you rather lug it up 21 flights yourself?

Maybe you drove the truck and everything is now sitting out in the driveway. Or maybe the moving company van will arrive tomorrow. In either case, you might as well do some cleaning before anything is moved in.

If you find out that the house needs more than just light cleaning, consider making arrangements to store your belongings temporarily and stay in a motel while you clean, or hire someone to clean. With some luck, your good planning will make this measure unnecessary.

Get everyone involved in the cleaning chores. Even small children can sweep decks and sidewalks and perform other simple tasks. They'll be busy, and out of the way, and feel more like it's their home if they help.

Because the house is empty, cleaning it should go quickly.

If you have the budget, consider hiring a local cleaning firm in advance. They can come in before you arrive and wash walls and other surfaces, scour bathrooms and kitchen, vacuum and shampoo carpets, and scrub other floor surfaces. Get an estimate. It might not be as costly as you think, and it certainly will simplify your move.

Take Your Shoes off!

Don't track in the mud!

You and your cleaning helpers have spent an hour or a day cleaning the new house; don't let your moving crew track up your clean floor or carpet with dirty footprints. Put down clear carpet or paper runners in areas where there will be lots of foot traffic.

If you're using a professional moving service, the workers will probably roll out paper runners before starting.

Moving Words
Temporary storage of your shipment at the moving company's warehouse is called *Storage in Transit,* which is not to be confused with Storage in Limbo.

Got Sumptin ta Drink?

Be a good host/hostess in your new home. Offer your workers light refreshments—at least beverages. Even moving company employees might appreciate a drink of cold water, soda, or lemonade, and a cookie or doughnut.

The Van's Here! The Van's Here!

It's exciting to see your belongings arrive in a moving van, fully aware that you won't have to unload them.

So what can you do make yourself useful?

Here are some ideas:

➤ Keep out of the way, but be available to answer questions.

➤ Find something for the kids to do: Visit the library, the mall, or the video store.

➤ Turn all the lights on in the house for better visibility. Replace any burned-out or missing bulbs.

➤ Prop doors open.

➤ Open garage and storage-building doors.

Making Your Move

Watch out for unloaders who want to slip by you at the door as they may be concealing damaged furniture or boxes. If you suspect a problem, ask the mover to set the piece down so you can inspect it.

➤ Clear sidewalks and driveways.

➤ Turn on a radio or stereo, if possible.

➤ Make sure no children or pets can escape or get in the way and be hurt.

➤ Turn on fans and open windows if it will be a warm day.

➤ Make sure that the bathroom is equipped with soap, paper towels, and toilet paper.

➤ Mark rooms with a paper sign on the door: master bedroom, girls' bedroom, den, baby's room.

➤ Draw a map of your new house, marking the rooms on the map.

➤ Get out your wallet to pay for your shipment when it arrives.

➤ Use your copy of the inventory to check boxes into the house.

➤ Stand by the main door to inspect any obvious damage to items coming in.

Identify each room and the job of placing marked boxes will be easier for the crew.

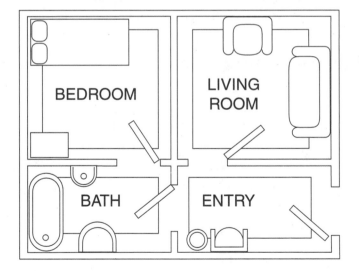

Maybe We Should Have Rented a Dump Truck!

And what if you have to do the unloading? How can you make the process go smoothly and efficiently?

Organization is the key.

> ➤ Know what everyone does well and assign tasks accordingly.

> ➤ Label each room with the same designations and in the same colors that you used when marking all your boxes.

> ➤ Appoint one person to supervise the move.

> ➤ Keep an eye out for people who may try to "borrow" things from your moving truck before you're fully moved in.

> ➤ Place incoming furniture and boxes in the appropriate room and, if possible, the preferred location in the room to save moving things twice.

> ➤ Use the proper moving tools: utility dolly, appliance dolly, box knife.

> ➤ Set up beds early and make them before you do any other unpacking. You'll be glad later!

> ➤ Don't carry too much or work too hard and exhaust yourself halfway through the unloading.

> ➤ Make sure everyone takes a break at least every couple of hours.

> ➤ Eat something.

We'll cover unpacking in more detail in Chapter 22. Thanks for asking.

Moving Words
Taking your things out of boxes and cartons and disposing of the cartons and packing materials is called *unpacking*. It's a moving euphemism for "dumping in the middle of the floor."

Moving Words
Shipments that require payment upon delivery are known as *C.O.D. (Cash On Delivery)*. Payment can usually be made in cash, traveler's checks, money order, cashier's check, credit card, or blood.

Truck's Empty. House's Full!

Once the truck is unloaded—by you or someone else—take a break. Make some coffee or get a soft drink. Congratulate yourselves on your safe arrival. The mountain of stuff may look insurmountable, but it's not. (And don't forget to make the beds.)

Next, and arguably more important, make sure each bathroom is equipped with toilet paper, soap, and towels. Put paper cups, soap, and paper or real towels in the kitchen.

Hang a shower curtain, if needed. A hot shower before bed or upon rising will feel wonderful.

Don't try to do everything in one day. It will probably take several weeks before all the boxes are unpacked and you feel really settled and "at home" in the new house. If you unpack just a few boxes each day, the mountain will quickly become a livable home.

Make sure you eat well so you'll have energy to face all those unpacked boxes tomorrow.

Home, Home on the Range

"Honey, I'm home—aren't I?"

It's time to begin making the new house feel like your home. And maybe making the town your new hometown.

So, get your stuff out of boxes and around the house. Get to know the neighbors. Go to the unofficial city center, the neighborhood shopping mall.

Here are a few ideas for making everyone feel at home in your new home:

➤ Hook up your stereo and speakers and put on some favorite music.

➤ Hook up your TV and VCR and watch a familiar "feel-good" movie.

➤ Hook up your computer and get some fun games going.

➤ Hang your favorite picture.

➤ Buy a couple house plants or plant a tree or bush in the yard.

➤ Put your name on the mailbox.

➤ Pick up any mail held at the post office and start home delivery.

➤ Register to vote.

➤ Get a new driver's license, if you changed states.

➤ Change the registration on your car, if you changed states.

➤ Post telephone numbers of the hospital, police, and fire station.

➤ Find out about trash pickup and recycling.

➤ Bake your favorite cookies, cake, or pie.

➤ Prepare your favorite meal.

➤ Host a neighborhood barbecue.

➤ Knock on your neighbors' doors and introduce yourself and your family.

➤ Call the local Welcome Wagon. They will bring you gifts, as well as gift and discount certificates.

Buck & Back Savers

Need something to spruce up the new place? Make a trip to the library. Some have framed art that you can borrow just like a library book. It can help to make your home more complete until you can choose and purchase your own art.

To make kids more comfortable:

➤ Unpack some favorite toys immediately.

➤ Maintain a daily schedule similar to the one the children were used to at the old house.

➤ Learn about local activities for children:

     Swimming

     Little League

     Story Hour at the library

     Day camps

     Bible school

     Park and recreation department programs

     After-school activities

➤ Make sure your kids meet local children.

➤ Find out which neighbors or co-workers have children close to your children's ages and invite them to your home.

➤ Encourage your children to call, write, or even e-mail friends from your old neighborhood.

Making Your Move

First thing: Call the Welcome Wagon or Newcomers' Club in your new location. They often offer discounts and gifts from merchants wanting your business. These groups can be found through the local Chamber of Commerce.

Enjoy your new home!

The Least You Need to Know

➤ Get acquainted with your new home by walking through before everything's moved in so that you can picture where everything will go.

➤ Prepare for the move-in by parking cars out of the way, making room for the moving van or rental vehicle, turning on lights, and propping doors open—weather permitting.

➤ Unload your stuff or direct the movers by making a map of your place and marking rooms the same way as your incoming boxes.

➤ Help everyone feel at home using familiar routines (favorite foods) and new ones (visiting neighbors and the mall).

Part 6
Moving On

The infernal question:

Is there life after moving?

The guru, Swami Movingandstorage, replies:

Definitely, yes! (Twenty dollars, please.)

So here's your chance to get a life of your very own! Here's how you can remold the threads of your life into a new tapestry. Here's how to efficiently get back to whatever you were doing before you were so rudely interrupted by the move.

This final part of your book guides you in feathering your new nest and—yes, folks— actually restarting a life. (Offer void if you didn't already have one when you walked in.)

It offers final tips on how to become a Certified Smart Mover—or at least certifiable.

Feathering Your New Nest

In This Chapter

➤ Unpacking your new home

➤ Cleaning up the mess

➤ Getting things turned on

➤ Getting rid of junk

➤ Making quick repairs

Everything you own is now somewhere within your new living space.

The hard part—getting from here to there—is done. The important tasks now involve unpacking, getting acquainted, getting utilities turned on, and getting rid of the boxes and trash.

You're ready to feather your nest.

Let's get started.

Unpacking and Other Anguishes

Moving Words
Pickup and delivery charges are transportation charges for moving your shipment between a temporary storage warehouse and your residence.

Moving Words
Warehouse handling is an extra charge for placing or removing items from temporary storage.

Where to start?

There are stacks of boxes, scads of stuff, and loads of unrecognizable containers. What can you do to start making your house/apartment/condo/duplex into a home?

Begin unpacking and placing the familiar things from your former life.

If you've planned ahead, furniture and boxes are now in the appropriate rooms. If not, they may be scattered helter-skelter throughout your abode. Walk through your home and familiarize yourself with where things are—or should be. As needed, make notes or sketches in your Smart Moving Notebook.

If you have room, start placing your furniture in the best location within the room. Yes, you may move it again next month but, for now, place it as best you can.

Next, set up any appliances you'll be needing. That means the microwave (open me first!), stove, refrigerator, and small kitchen and bathroom appliances. You're probably tired of take-out food by now and a good home-cooked meal may sound appetizing—or not. Even if you're not going to do any cooking, you'll soon need the hair dryer.

Then, before you really start unpacking, put away any boxes that you don't need to unpack in the next week. These can be placed in an empty corner of the room, a spare room, the garage, or a basement or outbuilding, depending on available space and energy.

Okay, now you're ready to tackle the unpacking job. Where to start?

There are no firm rules. So much depends on how many folks in your moving group, whether they are a help or hindrance to unpacking, and how much time is available. Here are some suggestions.

Where to Start?!

"What if we just call a freelance arsonist, and then the insurance adjuster?!"

No! I know you're frustrated at all the boxes stacked to the ceiling. But burning the place down isn't the answer.

Unpacking smart is the answer!

What should you unpack first? Unless you want to sleep on the couch for a while, unpack bedding and make beds first. Or, if you'd prefer, at least get all the beds set up and some sleeping bags out. You're better off starting tomorrow morning with a good night's rest, and you'll be grateful the beds are already made when you're ready to collapse into them.

Making Your Move
Set up and make beds as soon as you move into the new house to save a night's motel bill.

Next, unpack bathroom items and other personal things. Even putting an overnight case with your bathroom things in the throne room will help make your place a temporary home.

Now What?

"Okay, I'm ready for a good night's rest and I know where my toothbrush is. Now what?"

Next, unpack your kitchen. For some folks, this step simply means unboxing and plugging in the microwave and coffee pot. For others, it means installing or connecting the stove, refrigerator, or other major kitchen appliances.

Unpacking the kitchen also means making sure the cabinets and drawers are clean and filling them with dishes, pots and pans, utensils, and whatever foodstuffs and cooking supplies you brought.

Now aren't you glad you marked those boxes well when you packed them up?

TV or Not TV

"We're busy right now, Junior. Go watch *The Lion King* again."

"Ashley, do you want to watch *The Lion King* again? First, unpack the three boxes in your room."

Next probably comes the living room or family room. If you have young children, place the couch and set up the TV and VCR. Make a deal with the kids: After they unpack a certain number of boxes or help for a set amount of time, you'll let them loose on the home theatre. You won't have to wonder what they're getting into while you do more unpacking.

You're on Your Own

After the common stuff that everyone uses (kitchen, bath, laundry room, living room) is unpacked, move on to unpacking bedrooms. Depending on their ages, physical capabilities, and endurance levels, each family member can unpack and arrange his or her own room.

For procrastinators: We're taking all the boxes to the moving company on Monday—with or without your stuff in them!

And for My Last Trick...

Making Your Move
Some folks start unpacking room by room. They work on the room until it is just like they want it, and then they move on to the next. Consider this method for your move-in.

Tomorrow, this weekend, or next month, unpack the decorative dust-catchers and arrange them as the final touches on your new home.

Unpack the pictures, collections, wall decorations, mantle clutter, and other things.

Then? Head for the garage or storage building if you have one. There are probably lots of boxes left that were un-identified or considered less-necessary. Unpack them or store them as appropriate. And here's a bonus: Any packed boxes that you store in the attic or basement will be ready for your next move!

Cleaning the House: Vacuum or Shovel?

Making Your Move
If your new home needs a thorough cleaning and you want to hire out the job, schedule the cleaning before you move anything into the house. A professional cleaning crew can zip through very quickly if no furniture or boxes are in the way.

In the ideal world of moving, you've probably arranged to have your new home cleaned—or did it yourself before the moving vehicle arrived. But, if you don't live in an ideal world, here are some suggestions for cleaning your house once the unpacking's done.

What to Do After the Bomb Squad Leaves

First, take a break!

Have a cup of coffee or a cold drink. Eat a piece of fruit. Sit down and remember why you are doing all this. Now that you're finally in your new home with your possessions around you, evaluate again the potential of the house.

Remember that you are in the middle of a big job. A messy job. Don't expect your home to be spotless for a while. Get rid of as much of the moving mess as possible.

Next, break down moving boxes as soon as they are empty and store them in the family room, garage, attic, or elsewhere, depending on whether you plan to keep them for the next move, use them for out-of-season storage, recycle them, or sell them back to the movers.

If you used a rental truck, hand truck, and furniture pads, return them as soon as possible. You want to avoid extra charges and get your deposit back!

Clean Up That Mess!

If you did a basic cleaning when it was easiest—when the house was empty—you're ahead of the game now. Now you just have to maintain the place.

Once the kitchen and bathroom are furnished with your belongings, keep them wiped up and tidy while working at putting away things throughout the rest of the house. Besides being less work in the long run, it'll give you a clean, neat haven to escape to when the unpacking becomes overwhelming.

Make every member of the family understand that moving is not an excuse to become a slob, dropping clothing or other items on any handy surface, including the floor, with the promise, "I'll find a spot for it later." Now is better.

Start a List

You probably got rid of lots of stuff as you moved smart. In fact, you may have thrown away some aerosol products and other essentials, knowing that they shouldn't be transported across state lines. On the other hand, you may be sure you packed that screwdriver, but in which box?

So you're going to have to make a trip—or many trips—to the store(s). Make the fewest trips possible by starting your lists now. In fact, you probably have some blank pages left in your Smart Moving Notebook. Use them. Start separate lists for these essentials:

➤ Groceries

➤ Hardware store (for that elusive screwdriver)

➤ Doctors and vet

➤ Pharmacy

➤ Garden Center

➤ Mover (questions and problems)

➤ Jobs that need to be done soon

➤ Repairs that should be made

➤ Other (take trailer back by Tuesday, start newspaper delivery, never move again!)

Hi. I'm Your New Neighbor

We were pleasantly surprised when moving into a small town neighborhood in the Midwest as neighbors began showing up and introducing themselves once the moving van pulled away. Some brought edibles.

But moving to a big city, we may never see the folks on the other side of the fence. It's a different world.

If the neighbors knock on your door, take advantage of the opportunity to take another break. It's worth the time spent to start good neighborly relationships.

If the neighbors don't knock on your door, knock on theirs and introduce yourself and your family. Invite them over for coffee. They'll understand about the moving mess. Ask them for advice about the neighborhood and town:

➤ What plumber do they recommend?

➤ Where is the nearest pharmacy?

➤ What grocery store sells the freshest produce?

➤ Is there a farmers' market?

➤ When is trash picked up?

➤ Who has young kids on the block? Or budding rock musicians?

Friendly Neighbors and Other Oddities

Most people want to be friends with their neighbors—or at least friendly. Unless you prefer to maintain complete privacy from your neighbors, accept and return their friendly overtures. Chat in the driveway. Accept their offer of giving your child a ride to school along with theirs. Wave to those cutting lawns.

Crowded cities can seem decidedly unfriendly. In an apartment building, smile and say hello to your neighbors in the hallways, at the mailboxes, or in the laundry room. When you recognize them in the local grocery or delicatessen, say hello and introduce yourself. Your neighbors will look at you less suspiciously when they know you belong in the building.

That's Mighty Neighborly

Being a friendly neighbor isn't just social, however. If you want to be a good neighbor, be as considerate as you would like your neighbors to be to you:

➤ Don't block their driveway or the sidewalk.

➤ Keep your pets at home and quiet.

➤ Make sure you and your kids keep their music at a reasonable level.

➤ Don't make noisy exits and entrances when working people need to sleep.

➤ Let them know when you're having a party. Invite them to it.

➤ If your tree sheds, try to keep the leaves raked so they don't blow onto the neighbors' lawns.

Being a good neighbor also means being a good member of the community. As time and interests allow, join the PTA, find a church or synagogue, become a Moose or other fraternal animal, visit a civic group meeting, join the Neighborhood Watch, or learn about the Newcomers' Club.

Many small and large communities have Newcomers' Clubs that are intended to offer help for people new to the area. They can offer a variety of information and resources.

Any Ambidextrous Chiropractors around Here?

Lost in your new neighborhood? Don't know where to get groceries, send the kids to school, or catch a bus?

Besides the Newcomers' Club mentioned in the previous section, also make friends with the local librarians. In addition to recommending books and periodicals, they can be a wealth of information about the area and its resources. They can also direct you to local groups that share your interests. As quickly as possible, get a new library card: your key to a world of knowledge and escape. Take the kids and get them library cards, too.

Utilities: Cable and Other Necessities

If you haven't already done so, make sure you get all the utilities turned on or at least transferred into your name.

You may need a deposit to get service started. Some utilities will accept a letter of credit from your prior utility service.

If you're moving internationally, ask your mover, employer, or local resource to help you with the logistics of utilities. In addition, you may need electrical adapters for appliances.

Bats, Birds, Bugs, Slithery Things, and Plants That Bite

The first time we heard katydids singing in the evening at our new home, we thought the Venusians had landed. It's an unusual sound that folks in some regions take for granted and those in other areas never hear.

Wherever you move, there will be critters: bugs, birds, reptiles, politicians. And maybe they will be new to you. Chances are, the literature about your new home's region won't mention that King snakes grow to eight feet in length—but aren't poisonous. Or that local water bugs are as big as Volkswagen bugs.

Moving Violations
One rustic home into which we moved had critters in the attic that the prior owners accepted as part of the ambiance. We begged to differ, not being particularly fond of bats. Eventually, the bats won and we moved somewhere else—with no forwarding address.

So, if you have an aversion to specific critters (or plants: stinging nettles, poison ivy, and so on), specifically ask about them *before* you move to your new area. It may be a deterrent. And if you must go where the wild things are, find out how the locals cope.

If you're moving into a managed residence (apartment, condo), ask if the owners regularly fumigate or treat for pests.

Entomology and Moving

How can you find out if the area to which you're moving will have unwanted residents?

Ask anyone and everyone. Ask those who have lived in the area to which you're moving. Ask moving agents (who are often well-traveled or at least regionally knowledgeable). Ask real estate agents who are supposed to (but don't always) answer truthfully.

And common sense will give you some clues:

➤ Snakes prefer warmer and dryer climates.

➤ Bugs prefer warmer and wetter climates.

➤ Bats prefer places that mosquitoes like.

➤ Birds prefer places that worms and bugs like.

➤ Politicians are everywhere and breed frequently.

Name That Bug

You can also learn more about bugs and other pests by asking at the city or county health department. Its workers will know all about local critters and whether they pose any health hazard.

You can also contact a local natural history or science museum, library, community college, or university agriculture department. People in these areas can tell you more than you will ever want to know about that pest.

Raid!!!!!!!???????

What can you do about the pests? In some cases, not much. It may be a case of live and let live. If they are health hazards, such as cockroaches, talk with an exterminator. Or check out the pest control section of a major hardware store in the area. If the pests can be treated by consumers, you'll find appropriate products to do so.

Keep in mind that certain animals may be protected locally. Check with local authorities before you take action against what you feel are pests. We found that our brown bat houseguests were on an endangered species list. That meant we weren't supposed to disturb them. As we weren't on an endangered list, we could either live with them or move.

Bye-bye!

Getting Rid of Boxes and Trash

Your stuff is now unpacked and placed in relative proximity to its intended location. But what about all those boxes, the packing material, the pieces of tape, and the other trash from your unpacking exercise?

Most of it is bulky, not big. The boxes can be cleaned out of packing material and disassembled. The packing can be scrunched down and stuffed into heavy-duty trash bags for disposal. The boxes can be recycled or sold back to the mover or rental company.

Here are some smart moving suggestions.

Recycling

Recycling makes sense. Unfortunately, the way it's mandated in some areas doesn't always seem to make sense. One container is for cans, another for glass, another for paper—and a separate truck burns excessive hydrocarbons to pick up these expensive recycling containers at your curb.

Even so, recycling or reusing moving materials makes good sense. Most moving materials can be reused in their present state without the assistance of a remanufacturer. Moving boxes are still boxes. Packing peanuts are still packing. Wrapping materials are still useful for something.

So check with local powers-that-be regarding recycling regulations and schedules for picking up or dropping off. And, if at all possible, reuse rather than recycle.

Reselling Packing Boxes

If you purchased standard moving boxes (1.5, 3, 4.5, 6 cubic feet, wardrobe and dishpacks), you can probably resell them.

Who wants them? Moving companies, moving vehicle rental stores, other movees.

How much will you get for them? Typically about one-third to one-half of their new price. For example, a 3-cubic-foot box that sells new for $3 to $4 may get you $1 to $2 as a used box—if in good shape.

Your moving agent may buy them back. Or you may have only rented the boxes from the agent.

Back & Buck Savers

If your employer is paying for the move, you can't ethically sell the boxes unless you then give the resulting money to your employer. But you can give the empty boxes to the moving crew who can sell them to the moving company as your employer's gratuity to them. Get a receipt.

Just Plain Junk and What to Do with It

An then there's all the other packing stuff: styrofoam peanuts, packing paper, cardboard. What to do with it?

Some can and should be recycled. Other materials can be used for packing gifts for mailing. Still others are just plain trash and should be discarded or recycled as appropriate.

Consider donating packing materials to a worthwhile local charity. For example, a rescue mission may use the materials in their work shelter's shipping department.

Be creative—even with plain junk.

Quick Repairs

You're in the home now. But you've discovered a leaky faucet, a broken window, or a stopped-up toilet or sink drain. What to do? First reach for your copy of *The Complete Idiot's Guide to Trouble-Free Home Repair* or its more portable cousin, *The Pocket Idiot's Guide to Home Repair*. If neither of these resources is available, read on for some quick fixes.

Fix a Leaking Faucet

To fix a leaky faucet:

1. Shut off the water supply and remove the faucet handle.
2. Loosen the packing nut and slip both the nut and the old packing off the stem.
3. Take the packing to a local hardware store and ask for a replacement packing set for your faucet.
4. Install the new packing, following instructions on the packing kit container.

Fix a Broken Window

To replace broken glass in a single-glazed window:

1. Spread out a heavy cloth to protect the floor from falling pieces of glass. Put on some heavy gloves to protect your hands from the shards. Place a container nearby to receive the broken pieces. (Banish kids and pets from the area.)

2. Remove the broken glass from the window frame.

3. Remove any old putty or rubber seal from the frame.

4. Look for and remove any small metal parts (called *glazier's points*) that hold the glass in place in the frame.

5. Clean out the frame with a putty knife.

6. Measure the thickness of the glass and the area that needs replaced, and then go get a new piece of glass that is the same size and thickness. Some larger hardware stores will have common sizes in stock. Otherwise an associate will cut the glass to the size you need. (Be sure to cover the empty frame with plastic to keep bugs and weather out while you go to the store.)

7. Carefully install the glass, the glaziers' points, and the putty or seal.

Double-glazed windows should be replaced by the manufacturer.

Unplug a Stopped Toilet

Now here's a job no one likes—not even plumbers! But, with the right tools, it can be relatively easy.

Avoid using chemical solvents. To unplug a stopped toilet:

1. Use a suction plunger, or "plumber's helper," to attempt to unplug the drain hole. Moving the plunger up and down applies suction pressure to dislodge anything stuck in the drain.

2. If this doesn't work, use a closet auger, or "snake," to dislodge whatever's stuck in the drain. The thick metal wire is pushed or "snaked" down the drain until it hits an obstruction. The auger's handle is then turned to dislodge the blockage.

3. If the drain is still clogged, call your plumber and look for a co-signer.

Clearing a Drain

Other drains in the home (kitchen, bathroom sink, fish cleaning tub) can also become clogged. Kitchen drains may get food lodged in them. Bathroom sinks and tubs can become clogged with hair. You don't want to know what clogs a fish-cleaning tub!

To clear a sink drain (without a disposal):

1. Use a suction plunger, or "plumber's helper," over the drain to dislodge the blockage. Plungers typically work better if there is water standing in the sink.

2. If the plunger doesn't unblock the drain, use one of the liquid drain-opener products. Be careful as some contain lye or other caustic products that can splash on your skin and burn you. Do not plunge after using a chemical solvent!

3. If it still isn't happening, consider removing the U-shaped trap underneath the sink. To do so:

   a) Place a container under it to catch water in the trap.

   b) Wear thick rubber gloves and a face and eye mask to avoid lye burns.

   c) Turn the connections at each end of the trap until it comes free. Pour water from the trap into the bucket.

   d) If you don't find an obstruction in the trap, use an auger (see preceding) to clean out the drain line below the trap.

   e) Clean out or replace the trap unit, making sure you get new seals for each end.

   f) Reassemble and test.

The Least You Need to Know

➤ Unpack your new home in stages starting with the most important stuff: beds, bathrooms, and kitchen things.

➤ Clean up as you go by breaking down and stacking boxes, and putting packing materials in bags to recycle or resell.

➤ Get utilities turned on even before you move in, if possible: electric, gas, and, most important, cable.

➤ Get rid of junk by reselling moving boxes, recycling grocery boxes, and finding out how, where, and when to recycle other things used in moving.

➤ Make quick repairs to faucets, windows, toilets, sink drains, and other necessities.

Chapter 23

After the Move: Get Your CSM T-Shirt Here!

In This Chapter

➤ Making a better life after your move

➤ Getting involved in your new town

➤ Picking up new resources and habits

➤ Putting excess baggage in the basement

➤ Remembering the old place

Whew!

What a move! We'll never do *that* again!

Maybe yes and maybe no. The average American (if there is such a creature) moves, on average, every 4.7 years. And that figure factors in all those folks who stay put for a lifetime. So you and I must be moving even more frequently.

How do we survive these moves? How do we keep from overdosing on sleeping pills when the boss or spouse says, "It's time to move!"?

Actually, moving can be a good thing. It can force us to clean out the garbage in our lives, unpack the attic of our existence, and discard the superfluousness.

Moving can give us a fresh start at a new life.

Get a Life

Moving means moving forward. On our endless quest for the meaning of life and chewing gum, we can move horizontally as well as vertically.

Horizontal moving is physically moving from here to there. From Pacoima to Napa, from Burney to Ft. Morgan, from Vancouver to Marshalltown.

Vertical moving is one to a better or worse life. Relationships are enhanced, put on hold, found, and revised. Wisdom is built, tested, shared, and modified.

And the physical move is a good opportunity to make a concurrent philosophical or spiritual move.

Hey, I can change my hair color and no one will know!

So What Do You Want from Life—Besides a Million Bucks?

Does making other changes make sense for you?

Some folks use a move as an excuse to review and rebuild dreams that often get tucked away in the process of living.

"I think I'll take horseback riding lessons like I've always wanted."

"Well, my last employer clearly showed me who I *don't* want to work for. Now I think I can find one who will treat me like an adult with skills."

"There's a small airport nearby. I think I'll renew a dream and take some flying lessons."

"Dear John: I know exactly what I want from my life—and it *isn't* you! Bye!"

So What's New with You?

Sometimes, all a person needs to start a new and better life is simply an opportunity for a new beginning.

"My new employer has a no-smoking policy at work, so I'm going to take this opportunity to quit the habit right now."

"Hon, our smaller home gives us a better chance to know each other."

"We'll never forget Byron's life. But we need to leave his death behind us and move on."

"Daughter, here's your chance to start over with new friends, new goals, and a new image."

I Had a New Life Plan, but My Dog Ate It

A move can also offer a good opportunity to file away old excuses. If you've ever said, "Someday I'll _____" (fill in the blank), consider that "someday" can be "today."

"I never did like to go out to eat because we couldn't find good Thai food."

"I didn't finish my degree because I didn't like the local college."

"If I could just find a new gym I'd try to lose a few pounds."

You Mean We Have to Go to School Here, Too?

Kids can have an especially difficult time with moves. Most young people, whether they recognize it or not, are really pretty insecure. And now you've taken them from the familiar to the unfamiliar.

Remind them that they, too, can build a new and better life. They can retain old friends while making new.

Help youngsters in your entourage handle the unspoken fear of the unknown. Remind them of what hasn't changed: your love for them. Take time out from your hectic schedule to do things together as a family. This will give the kids a real sense of belonging and help them feel secure in their new environment.

To make the transition easier, many parents try to keep the family routines intact, and they consider adding new ones. Routines are anchors in a changing world.

Stranger in These Parts?

Every community has its own personality. Some are schizophrenic. And the personality of one neighborhood is typically different from another just a few blocks away.

It's the people and the homes that give a neighborhood and community its personality. And you have just changed its personality by moving into it.

Change your community for the better by offering your good qualities—and those of your living group—to the new place. Encourage other members of your household to do the same.

The Eternal Newbie

Of course, being a newcomer isn't a bad thing. It just makes you "different." In fact, being a newcomer in some areas can give you opportunities that being an old-timer doesn't. You can ask for directions: "Say, I'm new here, so can you tell me how to get to the mall?" You can take advantage of Newcomer discounts offered by the Welcome Wagon and other ventures. Of course, if you move to a small town, they already *know* that you're a newcomer.

Been Here Long?

Someday you're going to have to give up your newcomer status and become an old-timer. Some prefer the term *veteran resident*. No, there's typically no ceremony or dues involved. You just wake up one day and everyone treats you like you attended school locally.

How can you ultimately attain status as a veteran resident?

➤ Find a church, synagogue, mosque, temple, ashram, or meeting for sharing your spiritual side.

➤ Look for clubs that share your interests in gardening, classic cars, classical music, or whatever you enjoy when you're not caught up in moving.

➤ Do some volunteer work.

➤ Write letters to the editor of your local newspaper. (But be careful not to trash your new neighborhood, or you may find yourself moving again sooner than you think.)

➤ Join the PTA—even if you don't have kids, because it will get you acquainted with your community.

Are You Registered?

You'll soon find yourself forming an opinion regarding local politics. Remember that you have no voice to comment on said politics until you're registered to vote. In some communities, you must also vote a certain party or in at least 30 elections to graduate from the newcomer's club.

In any case, call your local Board of Elections and find out about registering to vote.

May I See Your License, Please?

Making Your Move

The mail carrier can be your best new friend. Watch your new mailbox for coupons and discounts from nearby supermarkets and other businesses welcoming you to the area.

No matter where you move to, you're probably going to have to change your driver's license and vehicle registration. Even if you move across town, you'll need to let the folks at BMV know where to send those speeding tickets.

If you're using the services of a welcoming group, they can supply you with the specifics of new licenses and registration. In some areas, it's simply a matter of sending in a check. In others, you'll have to appear in their office and act inordinately humble as you wait in line.

Where's the Library?

Now that all those boxes are unpacked and you haven't quite yet found the shopping mall, start your search of the new place.

Maps are available at chambers of commerce or real estate offices, from welcoming groups, and even at the library—if you can just find the darn place.

Today, libraries are popping up in the strangest places: shopping malls, strip malls, and residential areas. Look in the phone book or ask a neighbor. Once found, you'll have a treasure trove of local resources.

TIP: To get the flavor of a community and come up to speed on local issues and politics, ask a local librarian if the library throws out area newspapers older than, say, a week. If so, ask for them. Also check the back files of the newspaper at the paper's office.

New Habits for New Habitats

The sign near the old dirt road correctly declared "Choose your rut as you'll be in it for the next ten miles." Sometimes we can really get into ruts.

"Well, I've always done it this way."

And a move is an intersection in your road of life. It's a good time to choose a new rut.

Looking for ideas?

I Know It's a Bad Habit, But...

Got some habits you'd just as soon not have?

Trade them in!

Maybe it's smoking, overeating, biting your nails, or watching six hours of soaps every day.

Whatever the habit, if you identify it as unwanted, consider leaving it behind with no forwarding address. There may even be support groups for breaking bad habits in your new community. Ask at the library, your church, school, or civic center.

Hey, maybe you can use your Smart Moving Notebook to jot down some unwanted habits.

Nice Habit! What'd Ya Pay for It?

Conversely, you may want to add some habits to your repertoire. Maybe you want to give a smile to folks who seem to need one. Maybe you'd like to say "no" and hang up on those folks who call for "the person in charge of your long-distance telephone account."

Finding New Doctors, Lawyers, and Psychotherapists

How are you ever going to find a dentist like Dr. Soper who doesn't mind your sobbing in the waiting room?

Well, ask Dr. Soper for a referral before you move! He may know of a kind dentist in your new location. Or he can look it up in the Directory of Sissy Dentistry.

And what about lawyers and other professionals? Same thing: Ask for referrals before you leave. Or call local legal, dental, medical, or veterinary referral services. Look them up in the Yellow Pages under "Lawyer Referral Services," "Dentists' Information Bureaus," "Physicians' and Surgeons' Information Bureaus," "Veterinarian Information & Referral Services," or similar headings. Check with your local library if you're still having a problem finding the professional you need.

If you're not moving far away, you may even elect to return to your old providers as needed.

Developing Patterns of Efficiency and Bliss

The point here being: Your move is a good chance to trade in your old, tired, habits for some fresh, new ones. There may be a transfer fee, but it will be small compared to the value of your enhanced life.

Satisfaction guaranteed or double your bad habits back.

Get It On

You've heard the expression: When you're up to your neck in alligators, it's hard to remember that your initial intent was to drain the pool.

So it is with the process of moving. Why was it that we decided to move? Oh, yeah. To get a fresh start.

Give yourself a breathing period after your move. Maybe a week or a month or more. Then get on with your new and improved life.

Keeping the Good Stuff for Yourself

And do so with the same rule you used in deciding what to move: Keep what's worth keeping and get rid of the rest.

"Sorry Aunt Betty, those shell sculptures from Cancun you gave us last year sure are pretty, but there just isn't room for them in our new home."

Dumping the Bad Stuff

"The fire just about wiped us out. But at least we won't have to make lots of moving decisions!"

It doesn't take a fire to clean house. Plan to leave bad memories, experiences, and tragedies behind you. Don't move them. And don't go back for them.

Fresh Starts for Smart Movers

If your move is intended to give you a fresh start at life, make it happen. Redesign your new life. Make the needed changes. Leave what you don't need. Move on.

You don't have to change your surname, but you can take this opportunity to pick up a new first name—or nickname.

"My given name is Jarod, but please call me J.R."

"I'm now Donna...so you can quit calling me John."

"The Old Place"

Have you ever, after many years, gone back to a place that was once home?

It's true: You can't go home. That pretty yellow house with the white picket fence is now painted purple with a ten-foot chain-link fence and a cannon in the front yard.

So forget the old place. It will never be the same again. Just take along the memories.

Can you ever go back and visit the old neighborhood? Sure! Just don't expect it to be as you left it. It may or it may not remain as you remember it. But your memories of it will probably be different than the reality.

Stay in touch with those you choose to be your friends. Use the holidays or a friend's birthday for an opportunity to call or write and renew friendships.

Being Glad You Moved Smart

No regrets. Even if your move was a forced one, don't spend lots of time looking back and wishing things were different. Make them different for the future.

Be glad that you're a Certified Smart Mover.

And welcome to your new home.

The Least You Need to Know

➤ Make a better life for yourself by deciding what you want from your life and trashing excuses that keep you from it.

➤ Get involved in your new town and become a veteran resident who enjoys the best it has to offer.

➤ Pick up new resources and develope habits that improve the quality of your life.

➤ Get rid of things you don't want in your life; don't move them with you.

➤ Remember that you can't go home, but you can build a nice new home of memories in your mind.

Glossary of Smart Moving Words

agent A local moving company with a franchise from a national moving company. Some are also known as road agents.

attic The overhead space over the cab in most moving trucks.

bill of lading The formal contract between you and the moving company. It also serves as your receipt for your belongings.

binding estimate A written, guaranteed price based on an itemized list of items to be moved, the distance to be traveled, and services to be performed.

booking agent The agent who accepts your order for shipping and registers it with the van line. He or she can also help you "make book" on whether it will arrive in one piece.

C.O.D. (Cash On Delivery) Shipments that require payment upon delivery. Payment can usually be made in cash, traveler's checks, money order, cashier's check, or credit card.

carrier The company actually providing transportation for your shipment.

carrier packed (CP) Articles packed into boxes and crates by the moving company.

claim Your statement of loss or damage to any part of your shipment.

destination agent The agent at the destination who will assist you or the van operator.

elevator carry An extra charge that is added if a shipment must be either picked up or delivered with the use of an elevator or stairs.

estimate A moving agent's assessment of the cost of moving your goods based on weight, mileage, and service requirements (up a flight of stairs, and so on).

flammable Easily ignited.

flight charge An extra fee for carrying large, bulky items up or down stairs.

fragiles Glassware and other breakables.

gross weight The weight of the truck and contents after your goods have been loaded.

inflammable Easily ignited; not to be confused with *nonflammable*.

Interstate Commerce Commission (ICC) A federal agency in charge of the regulation of interstate transportation. They're the good guys—usually.

long haul A move that is more than 450 miles—a safe distance beyond the reach of most visiting relatives.

moving counselor The moving company representative who estimates the cost of your shipment and who will answer your questions about the estimate, services, or moving.

net weight The weight of your goods, found by subtracting the tare weight from the gross weight. Broken pieces are excluded.

non-binding estimate A price given to you before the move that does not guarantee the final bill. The final bill will be calculated on the weight of the shipment, the distance to be traveled, and the services to be performed.

nonflammable Not easily ignited.

noninflammable Not easily ignited.

PBO Trade euphemism for items packed by the owner. Stands for "pile of broken objects."

pickup and delivery charges Transportation charges for moving your shipment between a temporary storage warehouse and your residence.

slider A dolly with two small wheels with a rubber track around them.

stepper A dolly with three small wheels on a rotating shaft.

storage in transit Temporary storage of your shipment at the moving company's warehouse.

tare weight The weight of the truck and contents prior to loading your shipment.

warehouse handling An extra charge for placing or removing items from temporary storage.

Deductible Moving Expenses

The following is based on U.S. Treasury, Internal Revenue Service Publication 521, Moving Expenses, 1997. Check with the IRS or your tax preparer for the most recent information.

Introduction

This appendix explains the deduction of certain expenses of moving to a new home because you changed job locations or started a new job. This explanation includes the following:

- ➤ Who can deduct moving expenses
- ➤ What moving expenses are deductible
- ➤ What moving expenses are not deductible
- ➤ Tax withholding and estimated tax
- ➤ How to report your moving expenses

The appendix also illustrates two examples: a move within the United States and a move to a foreign country.

You may qualify for the deduction whether you are self-employed or an employee of a company. The expenses must be related to starting work at your new job location. However, certain retirees and survivors may qualify to claim the deduction even if they are not starting work at a new job location. See the next section, "Who Can Deduct Moving Expenses."

Home defined. Your home means your main home (residence). It can be a house, apartment, condominium, houseboat, house trailer, or similar dwelling. It does not include other homes owned or kept up by you or other members of your family. It also does not include a seasonal home, such as a summer beach cottage. Your former home means your home before you left for your new job location. Your new home means your home within the area of your new job location.

Who Can Deduct Moving Expenses

You can deduct your allowable moving expenses if your move is closely related to the start of work. You also must meet the distance test and the time test. These two tests are discussed later in this appendix.

Retirees or survivors. You may be able to deduct the expenses of moving to the United States or its possessions even if the move is not related to a new job. You must have worked outside the United States or be a survivor of someone who did. See "Retirees or Survivors Who Move to the United States," later in this appendix.

Related to Start of Work

Your move must be closely related, both in time and in place, to the start of work at your new job location.

Closely related in time. You can generally consider moving expenses incurred within one year from the date you first reported to work at the new location as closely related in time to the start of work. It is not necessary that you arrange to work before moving to a new location, as long as you actually do go to work.

If you do not move within one year, you ordinarily cannot deduct the expenses unless you can show that circumstances existed that prevented the move within that time.

Example. If your family moved more than a year after you started work at a new location, or if you delayed the move for 18 months to allow your child to complete high school, you can deduct your allowable moving expenses.

Closely related in place. You can generally consider your move closely related in place to the start of work if the distance from your new home to the new job location is not more than the distance from your former home to the new job location. A move that does not meet this requirement may qualify if you can show that:

1. A condition of employment requires you to live at your new home, or
2. You will spend less time or money commuting from your new home to your new job.

Distance Test

Your move will meet the distance test if your new main job location is at least 50 miles farther from your home than your old main job location was from your former home. For example, if your old job was 3 miles from your former home, your new job must be at least 53 miles from that former home.

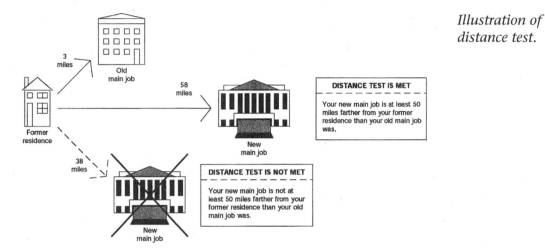

Illustration of distance test.

The distance between a job location and your home is the shortest of the more commonly traveled routes between them. The distance test considers only the location of your former home. It does not take into account the location of your new home.

Example. You moved to a new home fewer than 50 miles from your former home because you changed job locations. Your old job was 3 miles from your former home. Your new job is 60 miles from that home. Because your new job is 57 miles farther from your former home than the distance from your former home to your old job, you meet the 50-mile distance test.

First job or return to full-time work. If you go to work full time for the first time, your place of work must be at least 50 miles from your former home to meet the distance test. If you go back to full-time work after a substantial period of part-time work or unemployment, your place of work also must be at least 50 miles from your former home.

> *TIP. Exception for Armed Forces.* If you are in the Armed Forces and you moved because of a permanent change of station, you do not have to meet the distance test. See "Members of the Armed Forces," later in this appendix.

Main job location. Your main job location is usually the place where you spend most of your working time. A new job location is a new place where you will work permanently or indefinitely rather than temporarily. If you don't spend most of your working time at any one place, your main job location is the place where your work is centered, for example, where you report for work or are otherwise required to "base" your work.

Union members. If you work for several employers on a short-term basis and you get work under a union hall system (such as a construction or building trades worker), your main job location is the union hall.

More than one job. If you have more than one job anytime, your main job location depends on the facts in each case. The more important factors to be considered are

➤ The total time you spend at each place

➤ The amount of work you do at each place

➤ The money you earn from each place

Time Test

To deduct your moving expenses, you also must meet one of the following time tests.

Time test for employees. If you are an employee, you must work full time for at least 39 weeks during the first 12 months after you arrive in the general area of your new job location. For this time test, count only your full-time work as an employee; do not count any work you do as a self-employed person. You do not have to work for the same employer for the 39 weeks. You do not have to work 39 weeks in a row. However, you must work full time within the same general commuting area. Full-time employment depends on what is usual for your type of work in your area.

Temporary absence from work. You are considered full time during any week you are temporarily absent from work because of illness, strikes, lockouts, layoffs, natural disasters, or similar causes. You are also considered a full-time employee during any week you are absent from work for leave or vacation provided for in your work contract or agreement.

Seasonal work. If your work is seasonal, you are considered working full time during the off-season only if your work contract or agreement covers an off-season period and that period is less than six months. For example, a school teacher on a 12-month contract who teaches on a full-time basis for more than six months is considered a full-time employee for 12 months.

Time test for self-employed persons. If you are self-employed, you must work full time for at least 39 weeks during the first 12 months *and* for a total of at least 78 weeks during the first 24 months after you arrive in your new job location. For this time test, count any full-time work you do as an employee or as a self-employed person. You do not have to work for the same employer or be self-employed in the same trade or business for the 78 weeks.

Self-employment. You are self-employed if you work as the sole owner of an unincorporated business or as a partner in a partnership carrying on a business. You are not considered self-employed if you are semi-retired, are a part-time student, or work only a few hours each week.

Full-time work. Whether you work full time during any week depends on what is usual for your type of work in your area. For example, you are a self-employed dentist and maintain office hours 4 days per week. You are considered to perform services full time if maintaining office hours 4 days per week is usual for other self-employed dentists in the area.

Temporary absence from work. You are considered to be self-employed on a full-time basis during any week you are temporarily absent from work because of illness, strikes, natural disaster, or similar causes.

Seasonal trade or business. If your trade or business is seasonal, the off-season weeks when no work is required or available may be counted as weeks of performing services full time. The off-season must be less than six months and you must work full time before and after the off-season.

IF you are...	THEN you satisfy the time test by meeting...
An employee and become self-employed before satisfying the 39-week test for employees	The 78-week test for self-employed persons.
Self-employed and become an employee before satisfying the 78-week test	The 39-week test for employees, or using the time spent as a full-time employee to satisfy the 78-week test.
Both self-employed and an employee	The 78-week test for a self-employed person or the 39-week test for an employee. You must determine which job you spend the most time on.

Satisfying the time test for employees and self-employed persons.

For example, you own and operate a motel at a beach resort. You are considered self-employed on a full-time basis during the weeks of the off-season if the motel is closed for less than six months and you work as a full-time operator of the motel before and after the off-season.

> *TIP. Joint return.* If you are married and file a joint return and both you and your spouse work full time, either of you can satisfy the full-time work test. However, you cannot combine the weeks your spouse worked with the weeks you worked to satisfy that test.

Time test not yet met. You can deduct your moving expenses on your 1997 tax return even if you have not yet met the time test by the date your 1997 return is due. You can do this if you expect to meet the 39-week test in 1998, or the 78-week test in 1998 or 1999. If you deduct moving expenses but do not meet the time test by 1998 or 1999, you must either:

1. Report your moving expense deduction as other income on your Form 1040 for the year you cannot meet the test, or

2. Amend your 1997 return.

Use Form 1040X, "Amended U.S. Individual Income Tax Return," to amend your return.

If you do not deduct your moving expenses on your 1997 return, and you later meet the time test, you can file an amended return for 1997 to take the deduction.

Example. You arrive in the general area of your new job on September 15, 1997. You deduct your moving expenses on your 1997 return, the year of the move, even though you have not yet met the time test by the date your return is due. If you do not meet the 39-week test by September 15, 1998, you must either:

1. Report as income on your 1998 return the amount you deducted as moving expenses on your 1997 return, or

2. Amend your 1997 return.

Exceptions to the time test. You do not have to meet the time test if one of the following applies:

1. You are in the Armed Forces and you moved because of a permanent change of station—see "Members of the Armed Forces," later in this appendix.

2. You moved to the United States because you retired—see "Retirees or Survivors Who Move to the United States," later in this appendix.

3. You are the survivor of a person whose main job location at the time of death was outside the United States—see "Retirees or Survivors Who Move to the United States," later in this appendix.

4. Your job at the new location ends because of death or disability.

5. You are transferred for your employer's benefit or laid off for a reason other than willful misconduct. (For this exception, you must have obtained full-time employment, and you must have expected to meet the test at the time you started the job.)

Members of the Armed Forces

If you are a member of the Armed Forces on active duty and you move because of a permanent change of station, you do not have to meet the distance and time tests discussed earlier. You can deduct your unreimbursed allowable moving expenses.

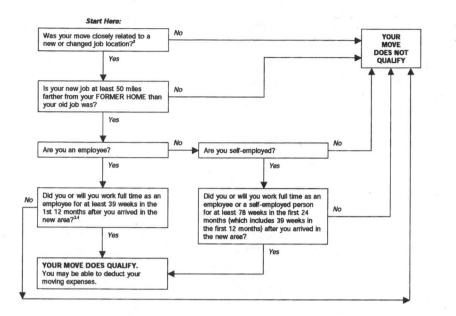

Start Here:

Was your move closely related to a new or changed job location?[2] — No →

Is your new job at least 50 miles farther from your FORMER HOME than your old job was? — No →

Are you an employee? — No → Are you self-employed? — No →

YOUR MOVE DOES NOT QUALIFY

Did you or will you work full time as an employee for at least 39 weeks in the 1st 12 months after you arrived in the new area?[3,4]

Did you or will you work full time as an employee or a self-employed person for at least 78 weeks in the first 24 months (which includes 39 weeks in the first 12 months) after you arrived in the new area? — No →

YOUR MOVE DOES QUALIFY. You may be able to deduct your moving expenses.

Qualifying moves within the United States (non-military)[1].

A permanent change of station includes:

1. A move from your home to the first post of active duty.

2. A move from one permanent post of duty to another.

3. A move from your last post of duty to your home or to a nearer point in the United States. (The move must occur within one year of ending your active duty or within the period allowed under the Joint Travel Regulations.)

Spouse and dependents. If a member of the Armed Forces deserts, is imprisoned, or dies, a permanent change of station for the spouse or dependent includes a move to

➤ Place of enlistment

➤ Member's, spouse's, or dependent's home of record

➤ Nearer point in the United States

If the military moves you and your spouse and dependents to or from separate locations, the moves are treated as a single move to your new main job location.

Services or reimbursements provided by government. Do not include in income the value of moving and storage services provided by the government because of a permanent change of station. If the total reimbursements or allowances you receive from the government because of the move are more than your actual moving expenses, the government should include the excess in your wages on Form W-2. However, the excess portion of a dislocation allowance, a temporary lodging allowance, a temporary lodging

269

expense, or a move-in housing allowance is not included in income. Do not attach Form 3903 or Form 3903-F to your Form 1040.

If your reimbursements or allowances are less than your actual moving expenses, do not include the reimbursements or allowances in income. You can deduct the expenses that exceed your reimbursements. See the section "Deductible Moving Expenses," later in this chapter.

Form 3903 for members of the Armed Forces. Take the following steps:

1. Complete lines 4 through 6, using your actual expenses. Do not reduce your expenses by any reimbursements or allowances you received from the government because of the move. Also, do not include any expenses for moving services provided by the government.

2. Enter on line 7 the total reimbursements and allowances you received from the government for the expenses in step 1. Do not include the value of moving services provided by the government. Also do not include any part of a dislocation allowance, a temporary lodging allowance, a temporary lodging expense, or a move-in housing allowance.

3. Complete line 8. If line 6 is more than line 7, subtract line 7 from line 6 and enter the result on line 8 and on Form 1040, line 25. This is your moving expense deduction. If line 6 is equal to or less than line 7, enter zero on line 8; you do not have a moving expense deduction. Subtract line 6 from line 7 and, if the result is more than zero, enter it on Form 1040, line 7.

Form 3903-F. To complete Form 3903-F, see the instructions for Form 3903-F.

If the military moves you and your spouse and dependents to or from different locations, treat these moves as a single move. Unless they exceed actual expenses, do not include income reimbursements, allowances, or the value of moving and storage services provided by the government to move you, your spouse, and your dependents to and from the separate locations.

CAUTION! Do not deduct any expenses for moving services provided by the government.

Retirees or Survivors Who Move to the United States

You can deduct your allowable moving expenses if you move to the United States or to a possession of the United States. You do not have to meet the time test discussed earlier, but you must meet these requirements:

Retirees. You can deduct moving expenses for a move to a new home in the United States when you permanently retire. However, both your former main job location and your former home must have been outside the United States.

Permanently retired. You are considered permanently retired when you cease gainful full-time employment or self-employment. If at the time you retire you intend your retirement to be permanent, you will be considered retired although you later return to work. Your intention to retire permanently will be determined by the following:

1. Your age and health.

2. Customary retirement age for people who do similar work.

3. Whether or not you receive retirement payments from a pension or retirement fund.

4. The length of time before you return to full-time work.

Survivors. You can deduct moving expenses for a move to a home in the United States if you are the spouse or the dependent of a person whose main job location at the time of death was outside the United States. The move must begin within six months after the decedent's death. It must be from the decedent's former home outside the United States. That home must also have been your home.

When a move begins. A move begins when

1. You contract for your household goods and personal effects to be moved to your home in the United States, but only if the move is completed within a reasonable time.

2. Your household goods and personal effects are packed and on the way to your home in the United States.

3. You leave your former home to travel to your new home in the United States.

Deductible Moving Expenses

If you meet the requirements discussed earlier, you can deduct the reasonable expenses of the following:

1. Moving your household goods and personal effects (including in-transit or foreign-move storage expenses).

2. Traveling (including lodging but not meals) to your new home.

However, you cannot deduct any expenses for meals.

Reasonable expenses. You can deduct only those expenses that are reasonable for the circumstances of your move. For example, the cost of traveling from your former home to your new one should be by the shortest, most direct route available by conventional transportation. If during your trip to your new home, you make side trips for sightseeing, the additional expenses for your side trips are not deductible as moving expenses.

Travel by car. If you use your car to take yourself, members of your household, or your personal effects to your new home, you can figure your expenses by deducting either of the following:

1. Your actual expenses, such as gas and oil for your car, if you keep an accurate record of each expense.

2. 10 cents per mile.

You can deduct parking fees and tolls you pay in moving. You cannot deduct any part of general repairs, general maintenance, insurance, or depreciation for your car.

Member of your household. You can deduct moving expenses you pay for yourself and members of your household. A member of your household is anyone who has both your former and new home as his or her home. It does not include a tenant or employee, unless you can claim that person as a dependent.

Location of move. There are different rules for moving within or to the United States than for moving outside the United States. These rules are discussed separately.

Moves Within or to the United States

If you meet the requirements in the section, "Who Can Deduct Moving Expenses," earlier in this chapter, you can deduct allowable expenses for a move to the area of a new main job location within the United States or its possessions. Your move may be from one United States location to another or from a foreign country to the United States.

Form 3903. Use Form 3903 to deduct your moving expenses if you moved within or to the United States or one of its possessions. An example of a filled-in Form 3903 is shown later.

Household goods and personal effects. You can deduct the cost of packing, crating, and transporting your household goods and personal effects and those of the members of your household from your former home to your new home. If you use your own car to move your things, see "Travel by car" in the section "Deductible Moving Expenses" earlier in this chapter. You can include the cost of storing and insuring household goods and personal effects within any period of 30 consecutive days after the day your things are moved from your former home and before they are delivered to your new home.

You can deduct any costs of connecting or disconnecting utilities required because you are moving your household goods, appliances, or personal effects.

You can deduct the cost of shipping your car and your household pets to your new home.

You can deduct the cost of moving your household goods and personal effects from a place other than your former home. Your deduction is limited to the amount it would have cost to move them from your former home.

Example. Paul Brown is a resident of North Carolina and has been working there for the last four years. Because of the small size of his apartment, he stored some of his furniture in Georgia with his parents. Paul got a job in Washington, D.C. It cost him $300 to move his furniture from North Carolina to Washington and $1,100 to move his furniture from Georgia to Washington. If Paul shipped his furniture in Georgia from North Carolina (his former home), it would have cost $600. He can deduct only $600 of the $1,100 he paid. He can deduct $900 ($300 + $600).

CAUTION. You cannot deduct the cost of moving furniture you buy on the way to your new home.

Travel expenses. You can deduct the cost of transportation and lodging for yourself and members of your household while traveling from your former home to your new home. This includes expenses for the day you arrive. You can include any lodging expenses you had in the area of your former home within one day after you could not live in your former home because your furniture had been moved. You can deduct expenses for only one trip to your new home for yourself and members of your household. However, all of you do not have to travel together. If you use your own car, see "Travel by car" in the section "Deductible Moving Expenses" earlier in this chapter.

Moves Outside the United States

To deduct allowable expenses for a move outside the United States, you must be a United States citizen or resident alien who moves to the area of a new place of work outside the United States or its possessions. You must meet the requirements in the section "Who Can Deduct Moving Expenses" earlier in this chapter.

Form 3903-F. Use Form 3903-F if you moved outside the United States or its possessions. A filled-in Form 3903-F is shown later. A separate Form 3903-F must be completed for each foreign move.

For an explanation of expenses that you can deduct, see the discussion "Moves Within or to the United States" earlier in this chapter. The following discussion gives additional information on expenses that you can deduct on Form 3903-F.

Storage expenses. You can deduct the reasonable expenses of moving your personal effects to and from storage. You can also deduct the reasonable expenses of storing your personal effects for all or part of the time the new job location remains your main job location. The new job location must be outside the United States.

Move in an earlier year. If you moved in an earlier year and are deducting only storage fees while you are gone from the United States, do not use Form 3903-F. Enter the net amount (after the reduction for the part that is allocable to excluded income) on line 25, Form 1040, and write "Storage Fees" to the left of the entry space.

Moving expenses allocable to excluded foreign income. If you live and work outside the United States, you may be able to exclude from income part of the income you earn in the foreign country. You may also be able to claim a foreign housing exclusion or deduction. If you claim the foreign earned income or foreign housing exclusions, you cannot deduct the part of your allowable moving expenses that relates to the excluded income.

TIP. Publication 54, Tax Guide for U.S. Citizens and Resident Aliens Abroad, discusses the foreign earned income exclusion, the foreign housing exclusion, and the foreign housing deduction. It also explains how to figure the part of your moving expenses that relates to excluded income. You can get the publication from most United States Embassies and consulates, or by writing to the IRS Forms Distribution Center for your area as shown in your income tax package.

Nondeductible Expenses

You cannot deduct the following items as moving expenses:

➤ Pre-move house-hunting expenses

➤ Temporary living expenses

➤ Meal expenses

➤ Expenses of buying or selling a home

➤ Expenses of getting or breaking a lease

➤ Security deposits (including any given up due to the move)

➤ Home improvements to help sell your home

➤ Loss on the sale of your home

➤ Mortgage penalties

➤ Losses from disposing of memberships in clubs

➤ Any part of the purchase price of your new home

➤ Real estate taxes

➤ Car tags

➤ Driver's license

➤ Refitting carpets and draperies

➤ Storage charges, except those incurred in-transit and for foreign moves

Temporary employment. You cannot take a moving-expense deduction and a business-expense deduction for the same expenses. You must decide if your expenses are deductible as moving expenses or as business expenses. For example, expenses you have for travel, meals, and lodging while temporarily working at a place away from your regular place of work may be deductible as business expenses if you are considered away from home on business. Generally, your work at a single location is considered temporary if it is realistically expected to last (and does in fact last) for one year or less.

TIP. See Publication 463, "Travel, Entertainment, Gift, and Car Expenses," for information on deducting your expenses.

Tax Withholding and Estimated Tax

Your employer must withhold income tax, Social Security tax, and Medicare tax from reimbursements and allowances paid to you that are included in your income. See "Reimbursements included in income" below.

Reimbursements excluded from income. Your employer should not include in your wages reimbursements paid under an accountable plan (explained later) for moving expenses that you

1. Could deduct if you had paid or incurred them.

2. Did not deduct in an earlier year.

These reimbursements are fringe benefits excludable from your income as qualified moving expense reimbursements. Your employer should report these reimbursements in box 13 of Form W-2.

CAUTION! You cannot claim a moving expense deduction for these reimbursed expenses (see "Reimbursements" in the section "How to Report" later in this chapter).

Expenses deducted in earlier year. If you receive reimbursement this year for moving expenses deducted in an earlier year, and the reimbursement is not included as wages in box 1 of your Form W-2, you must include the reimbursement on line 21 of your Form 1040. Your employer should show the amount of your reimbursement in box 13 of your Form W-2.

Reimbursements included in income. Your employer must include in your income any reimbursements made (or treated as made) under a nonaccountable plan, even if they are for deductible moving expenses. See "Reimbursements" in the section "How to Report" later in this chapter. Your employer must also include in your gross income as wages any reimbursements of, or payments for, non-deductible moving expenses. This includes amounts your employer reimbursed you under an accountable plan (explained below) for meals, house-hunting trips, and real estate expenses. It also includes reimbursements that exceed your deductible expenses and that you do not return to your employer.

Reimbursement for deductible and nondeductible expenses. If your employer reimburses you for both deductible and nondeductible moving expenses, your employer must determine the amount of the reimbursement that is not taxable and not subject to withholding. Your employer must treat any remaining amount as taxable wages, and withhold income tax, Social Security tax, and Medicare tax.

Amount of income tax withheld. If the reimbursements or allowances you receive are taxable, the amount of income tax your employer will withhold depends on several factors. It depends in part on whether or not income tax is withheld from your regular wages, on whether or not the reimbursements and allowances are combined with your regular wages, and on any information you have given to your employer on Form W-4, "Employee's Withholding Allowance Certificate."

Estimated tax. If you must make estimated tax payments, you need to take into account any taxable reimbursements and deductible moving expenses in figuring your estimated tax. For details about estimated tax, see Publication 505.

How to Report

The following discussions explain how to report your moving expenses and any reimbursements or allowances you received for your move.

TIP. Use Form 3903 to report your moving expenses if your move was within or to the United States or its possessions. Use a separate Form 3903 for each qualified move.

TIP. Use Form 3903-F to report your moving expenses if your move was outside the United States or its possessions. Use a separate Form 3903-F for each qualified move outside the United States or its possessions.

Where to deduct. Deduct your moving expenses on line 25 of Form 1040. The amount of moving expenses you can deduct is shown on line 8 of Form 3903, or line 7 of Form 3903-F.

CAUTION! You cannot deduct moving expenses if you file Form 1040EZ or Form 1040A.

Reimbursements

This section explains what to do when you receive a reimbursement (includes advances and allowances) for any of your moving expenses discussed in this publication.

If you received a reimbursement for your allowable moving expenses, how you report this amount and your expenses depends on whether the reimbursement was paid to you under an accountable plan or a nonaccountable plan. These plans are discussed later. For a quick overview of how to report the reimbursement, see Table 2.

Your employer should tell you what method of reimbursement is used and what records they require.

Employers. If you are an employer and you reimburse employee moving expenses, how you treat this reimbursement on your employee's Form W-2 depends in part on whether you have an accountable plan. Reimbursements treated as paid under an accountable plan are reported in box 13 with code P. For more information, see Publication 535, "Business Expenses."

Reimbursements treated as paid under nonaccountable plans, as explained later, are reported as pay. See Publication 15, Circular E, "Employer's Tax Guide," for information on employee pay.

Accountable plans. To be an accountable plan, your employer's reimbursement arrangement must require you to meet all three of the following rules:

1. Your expenses must be of the type for which a deduction should be allowed had you paid them yourself—that is, the reasonable expenses of moving your possessions from your former home to your new home, and traveling from your former home to your new home.

2. You must adequately account to your employer for these expenses within a reasonable period of time.

3. You must return any excess reimbursement or allowance within a reasonable period of time.

An excess reimbursement includes any amount you are paid or allowed that is more than the moving expenses that you adequately accounted for to your employer. See "Returning excess reimbursements," below, for information on how to handle these excess amounts.

Adequate accounting. You adequately account by giving your employer documentary evidence of your moving expenses, along with a statement of expense, an account book, a diary, or a similar record in which you entered each expense at or near the time you had it. Documentary evidence includes receipts, canceled checks, and bills.

Returning excess reimbursements. You must be required to return any excess reimbursement for your moving expenses to the person paying the reimbursement. Excess reimbursement includes any amount for which you did not adequately account within a reasonable period of time. For example, if you received an advance and you did not spend all the money on deductible moving expenses, or you do not have proof of all your expenses, you have an excess reimbursement.

Reasonable period of time. What constitutes a "reasonable period of time" depends on the facts of your situation. The IRS will consider it reasonable for you to

1. Receive an advance within 30 days of the time you have an expense.

2. Adequately account for your expenses within 60 days after the expense was paid or incurred.

3. Return any excess reimbursement within 120 days after the expense was paid or incurred.

If you are given a periodic statement (at least quarterly) that asks you to either return or adequately account for outstanding advances, and you comply within 120 days of the statement, the IRS will consider the amount adequately accounted for or returned within a reasonable period of time.

Employee meets accountable plan rules. If for all reimbursements you meet the three rules for an accountable plan, your employer should not include any reimbursements of allowable expenses in your income in box 1 of your Form W-2. Instead, your employer should include the reimbursements in box 13 of your Form W-2.

Example. You lived in Boston and accepted a job in Atlanta. You sold your home at a loss and bought a new one in Atlanta. Under an accountable plan, your employer reimbursed you for your actual traveling expenses from Boston to Atlanta and the cost of moving your furniture to Atlanta.

Your employer will include the reimbursement in box 13 of your Form W-2. If your allowable expenses are more than your reimbursement, show all of your expenses on lines 4 and 5 of Form 3903. Include the reimbursement on line 7 of Form 3903.

Employee does not meet accountable plan rules. You may be reimbursed by your employer, but for part of your expenses you may not meet all three rules.

If your deductible expenses are reimbursed under an otherwise accountable plan but you do not return, within a reasonable period, any reimbursement of expenses for which you did not adequately account, then only the amount for which you did adequately account is considered as paid under an accountable plan. The remaining expenses are treated as having been reimbursed under a nonaccountable plan (discussed below).

Reimbursement of nondeductible expenses. You may be reimbursed by your employer for moving expenses, some of which are deductible expenses and some of which are not deductible. The reimbursements received for the nondeductible expenses are treated as paid under a nonaccountable plan.

Nonaccountable plans. A nonaccountable plan is a reimbursement arrangement that does not meet the three rules listed earlier under Accountable plans.

In addition, the following payments will be treated as paid under a nonaccountable plan:

1. Excess reimbursements that you fail to return to your employer.
2. Reimbursements of nondeductible expenses. See "Reimbursement of nondeductible expenses," earlier.

If an arrangement pays for your moving expenses by reducing your wages, salary, or other pay, the amount of the reduction will be treated as a payment made under a nonaccountable plan. This is because you are entitled to receive the full amount of your pay regardless of whether you incurred any moving expenses.

If you are not sure whether the moving expense reimbursement arrangement is an accountable or nonaccountable plan, see your employer.

Your employer will combine the amount of any reimbursement paid to you under a nonaccountable plan with your wages, salary, or other pay. Your employer will report the total in box 1 of your Form W-2.

Example. To get you to work in another city, your new employer reimburses you under an accountable plan for the $7,500 loss on the sale of your home. Because this is a reimbursement of a nondeductible expense, it is treated as paid under a nonaccountable plan and must be included as pay on your Form W-2.

Completing Form 3903. Complete lines 1–3 to see whether you meet the distance test. If so, complete lines 4–6 using your actual expenses (except, if you use your own car, you can figure expenses based on a mileage rate of 10 cents per mile instead of on actual amounts for gas and oil). Enter on line 7 the total amount of your moving expense reimbursement that was excluded from your wages. This excluded amount should be identified with code P in box 13 of Form W-2.

If line 6 is more than line 7, subtract line 7 from line 6 and enter the result on line 8 and on Form 1040, line 25. This is your moving expense deduction. If line 6 is equal to or less than line 7, enter zero on line 8 (you have no moving expense deduction). Subtract line 6 from line 7 and, if the result is more than zero, include it on Form 1040, line 7.

Form 3903-F. To complete Form 3903-F, see the instructions for that form.

Form 4782. Your employer must give you an itemized list of reimbursements, payments, or allowances that have been paid to you for moving expenses. Form 4782, "Employee Moving Expense Information," shown later in this chapter, may be used for this purpose. This form shows the amount of any reimbursement, payment, or allowance made to you or to a third party for your benefit. It also shows the value of any services provided in kind to you. Your employer must provide a separate form or statement for each move for which you were reimbursed.

Uniform Relocation Assistance and Real Property Acquisition Policies Act of 1970. Do not include in income any moving expense payment you received under the Uniform Relocation Assistance and Real Property Acquisition Policies Act of 1970. These payments are made to persons displaced from their homes, businesses, or farms by federal projects.

When to Deduct Expenses

If you were not reimbursed, deduct your allowable moving expenses either in the year you had them or in the year you paid them.

Example. In December 1997, your employer transferred you to another city in the United States, where you still work. You are single and were not reimbursed for your moving expenses. In 1997 you paid for moving your furniture. You deducted these expenses in 1997. In January 1998, you paid for travel to the new city. You can deduct these additional expenses in 1998.

Reimbursed expenses. If you are reimbursed for your expenses, you may be able to deduct your allowable expenses either in the year you had them or paid them. If you use the cash method of accounting, you can choose to deduct the expenses in the year you are reimbursed even though you paid the expenses in a different year. See "Choosing when to deduct," below.

If you are reimbursed for your expenses in a later year than you paid the expenses, you may want to delay taking the deduction until the year you receive the reimbursement. If you do not choose to delay your deduction until the year you are reimbursed, you must include the reimbursement in your income, even if you are reimbursed under an accountable plan. See "Reimbursements excluded from income" and its discussion, "Expenses deducted in earlier year," under the heading "Tax Withholding and Estimated Tax," earlier in this chapter.

Choosing when to deduct. If you use the cash method of accounting, which is used by most people, you can choose to deduct moving expenses in the year your employer reimburses you if

1. You paid the expenses in a year before the year of reimbursement.

2. You paid the expenses in the year immediately after the year of reimbursement but by the due date, including extensions, for filing your return for the reimbursement year.

How to make the choice. You can choose to deduct moving expenses in the year you received reimbursement by taking the deduction on your return, or amended return, for that year.

CAUTION! You cannot deduct any moving expenses for which you received a reimbursement that was excluded from your income. Reimbursements excluded from, or included in, income are discussed under "Tax Withholding and Estimated Tax," earlier in this chapter.

Moving Within the United States

Tom Smith is married and has two children. He owned his home in Detroit where he worked. On February 8, his employer told him that he would be transferred to San Diego as of April 10 that year. His wife, Peggy, flew to San Diego on March 1 to look for a new home. She put down $25,000 on a house being built and came back to Detroit on March 4. The Smiths sold their Detroit home for $1,500 less than they paid for it. They contracted to have their personal effects moved to San Diego on April 3. The family drove to San Diego where they found that their new home was not finished. They stayed in a nearby motel until the house was ready on May 1. On April 10, Tom went to work in the San Diego plant where he still works.

His records for the move show:

1. Peggy's pre-move house-hunting trip:

Travel and lodging	$449	
Meals	75	$524

2. Down payment on San Diego home — $25,000

3. Real estate commission paid on sale of Detroit home — 3,500

4. Loss on sale of Detroit home (not including real estate commission) — 1,500

5. Amount paid for moving personal effects (furniture, other household goods, and so on) — 8,000

6. Expenses of driving to San Diego:

Mileage (Start 14,278; End 16,478)	$220	
Lodging	180	
Meals	320	$720

7. Cost of temporary living expenses in San Diego:

Motel rooms	$1,450	
Meals	2,280	$3,730
Total		$42,974

Tom was reimbursed $10,599 under an accountable plan as follows:

Moving personal effects	$6,800
Travel (and lodging) to San Diego	400
Travel (and lodging) for house-hunting trip	449
Lodging for temporary quarter	1,450
Loss on sale of home	1,500
Total reimbursement	$10,599

Tom's employer gave him Form 4782 to show him a breakdown of the amount of reimbursement. This form is shown below.

Form **4782** (Rev. July 1997) Department of the Treasury Internal Revenue Service	**Employee Moving Expense Information** Payments made during the calendar year ▶ ....97.... ▶ Instructions for employers are on the back.				OMB No. 1545-0182 **Do not file.** **Keep for your records.**
Name of employee Tom Smith					Social security number 325 : 00 : 6437
Moving Expense Payments		**(a)** Amount paid to employee	**(b)** Amount paid to a third party for employee's benefit and value of services furnished in kind		**(c)** Total (Add columns (a) and (b).)
1	Transportation and storage of household goods and personal effects 1	6,800 —			6,800 —
2	Travel and lodging payments for expenses of moving from old to new home. **Do not** include meals 2	400 —			400 —
3	All other payments (list type and amount). **Note:** *These amounts must be included in the employee's income and are subject to withholding* ▶ ..Loss on sale of home........ $1,500 Travel and lodging - Househunting............ $ 449 Lodging - Temporary quarters............ $1,450 **3**	3,399 —			3,399 —
4	Total. Add the amounts in column (c) of lines 1 through 3 . . . . ▶ **4**				10,599 —
For Paperwork Reduction Act Notice, see back of form.			Cat. No. 13079T		Form **4782** (Rev. 7-97)

The employer included this reimbursement on Tom's Form W-2 for the year. The reimbursement of deductible expenses, $7,200 for moving household goods and travel to San Diego, was included in box 13 of Form W-2. His employer identified this amount with code P.

The employer included the balance, $3,399 reimbursement of nondeductible expenses, in box 1 of Form W-2 with Tom's other wages. He must include this amount on line 7 of Form 1040. The employer withholds taxes from the $3,399, as discussed under "Nondeductible expenses," earlier. Also, Tom's employer could have given him a separate Form W-2 for his moving reimbursement.

Tom figures his deduction for moving expenses as follows:

Item 5, moving personal effects	$8,000
Item 6, driving to San Diego ($220 + $180)	400
Total deductible moving expenses	$8,400
Minus: Reimbursement included in box 13 of Form W-2	7,200
Deduction for moving expenses	$1,200

Tom enters these amounts on Form 3903 to figure his deduction. His Form 3903 is shown below. He also enters his deduction, $1,200, on line 25, Form 1040.

Form **3903**	**Moving Expenses**	OMB No. 1545-0062
Department of the Treasury Internal Revenue Service	▶ **Attach to Form 1040.**	**1997** Attachment Sequence No. **62**
Name(s) shown on Form 1040 — Tom and Peggy Smith		Your social security number 325 · 00 · 6437

Caution: *If you are a member of the armed forces, see the instructions before completing this form.*

1	Enter the number of miles from your **old home** to your **new workplace**	**1**	2,200 miles
2	Enter the number of miles from your **old home** to your **old workplace**	**2**	5 miles
3	Subtract line 2 from line 1. Enter the result but not less than zero	**3**	2,195 miles

Is line 3 at least 50 miles?

Yes. Go to line 4. Also, see **Time Test** in the instructions.

No. You **cannot** deduct your moving expenses. Do not complete the rest of this form.

4	Transportation and storage of household goods and personal effects (see instructions)	**4**	8,000 —
5	Travel and lodging expenses of moving from your old home to your new home. **Do not** include meals (see instructions)	**5**	400 —
6	Add lines 4 and 5	**6**	8,400 —
7	Enter the total amount your employer paid for your move (including the value of services furnished in kind) that is **not** included in the wages box (box 1) of your W-2 form. This amount should be identified with code **P** in box 13 of your W-2 form	**7**	7,200 —

Is line 6 more than line 7?

Yes. Go to line 8.

No. You **cannot** deduct your moving expenses. If line 6 is less than line 7, subtract line 6 from line 7 and include the result in income on Form 1040, line 7.

8	Subtract line 7 from line 6. Enter the result here and on Form 1040, line 25. This is your **moving expense deduction**	**8**	1,200 —

For Paperwork Reduction Act Notice, see back of form.   Cat. No. 12490K   Form **3903** (1997)

Nondeductible expenses. Of the $42,974 moving expenses that Tom incurred, the following items cannot be deducted:

1. Pre-move house-hunting expenses.

2. Down payment on the San Diego home. If any part of it were for payment of deductible taxes or interest on the mortgage on the house, that part would be deductible as an itemized deduction.

3. Real estate commission paid on the sale of the Detroit home. The commission is used to figure the gain or loss on the sale.

4. Loss on the sale of the Detroit home. The Smiths cannot deduct it even though Tom's employer reimbursed him for it.

6. Meal expenses while driving to San Diego. (However, the lodging and car expenses are deductible.)

7. Temporary living expenses.

Moving to a Foreign Country

Mark Green is married and has two children. He and his wife, Mary, owned their home in the Washington, D.C. area where he worked. On January 19, he was told by his employer that he would be transferred to London, England, as of March 20 that year. The Greens sold their Washington home for more than they paid for it. Mary and the children stayed in the home until the children finished the school year. Mark flew to London on March 19 and moved into a hotel. He stayed in the hotel through June 16. On March 20, Mark went to work in the London office where he still works. On May 5, Mark paid $3,000 as a security deposit on a furnished home in the London area that he could move into on June 17. Their personal effects were moved out of their old home on June 15. Most of their possessions were put in storage in Washington; the rest were shipped to London. Mary and the children stayed in a nearby motel on June 15 and flew to London on June 16, where they stayed in a hotel that night. Mark and his family moved into their leased home on June 17.

His records for the move show:

1. Expenses paid on sale of Washington home		$7,850
2. Mark's traveling expenses to London:		
Travel	$392	
Meals	19	
Lodging (in London on March 19)	<u>90</u>	$501
3. Security deposit on lease of London home		$3,000

283

4. Mark's temporary living expenses in London
from March 20 through June 16 (89 days):

Hotel room	$7,920	
Meals	3,080	$11,000

5. Amount paid that year for moving and storing personal
effects (furniture, other household goods, and so on):

Moving	$5,200	
Storage	2,900	$8,100

6. Family's traveling expenses to London:

Travel	$1,176	
Meals	90	
Lodging	160	$1,426
Total		$31,877

Mark was reimbursed under his employer's accountable plan $17,793 as follows:

Moving and storage of personal effects	$7,000
Travel (and lodging) to London	1,793
Temporary living expenses	9,000
Total reimbursement	$17,793

Mark's employer gave him Form 4782 to show him a breakdown of the amount of reimbursement.

Form **4782** (Rev. July 1997) Department of the Treasury Internal Revenue Service	**Employee Moving Expense Information** Payments made during the calendar year ▶ ...97... ▶ **Instructions for employers are on the back.**			OMB No. 1545-0182 **Do not file. Keep for your records.**
Name of employee Mark Green				Social security number 123 : 00 : 7500

Moving Expense Payments		**(a)** Amount paid to employee	**(b)** Amount paid to a third party for employee's benefit and value of services furnished in kind	**(c)** Total (Add columns (a) and (b).)
1 Transportation and storage of household goods and personal effects	**1**	7,000 —		7,000 —
2 Travel and lodging payments for expenses of moving from old to new home. **Do not** include meals	**2**	1,793 —		1,793 —
3 All other payments (list type and amount). **Note:** *These amounts must be included in the employee's income and are subject to withholding* ▶ .... Temporary living expenses............................ ....$9,000............................	**3**	9,000 —		9,000 —
4 Total. Add the amounts in column (c) of lines 1 through 3 . . . . ▶	**4**			17,793 —

For Paperwork Reduction Act Notice, see back of form. Cat. No. 13079T Form **4782** (Rev. 7-97)

The employer included this reimbursement on Mark's Form W-2 that year. The reimbursement of deductible expenses, $8,793 for moving and storing household goods and travel to London, was included in box 13 of Form W-2. His employer identified this amount with code P.

The employer included the balance, $9,000 reimbursement of nondeductible temporary living expenses, in box 1 of Form W-2 with Mark's other wages. He must include this amount on line 7 of Form 1040. The employer withholds income tax, social security tax, and Medicare tax from the $9,000. Also, Mark's employer could have given him a separate Form W-2 for his moving reimbursement.

Mark figures his deduction for moving expenses as follows:

Item 5, moving and storing personal effects	8,100
Items 2 and 6, expenses of travel to London ($392 + $90 + $1,176 + $160)	1,818
Total deductible moving expenses	$9,918
Minus: Reimbursement included in box 13 of Form W-2	8,793
Deduction for moving expenses before allocation	$1,125

Mark enters these amounts on Form 3903-F to figure the deduction. Mark also enters the deduction, $1,125, on line 25, Form 1040. He enters the amount of any moving expenses allocable to excluded income or the housing exclusion on Form 2555. Publication 54 shows how to make this allocation.

Tax treatment of expenses. The following items correspond to those in the first list of expenses (Total: $31,877) in this example. These items explain how each expense is treated:

1. Expenses paid on the sale of the Washington home are used to figure the gain or loss on the sale. The expenses are not deductible as a moving expense.

2. Mark's travel expenses to London include the cost of meals, which is not deductible as a moving expense; this also applies to the cost of his family's meals in item 6. However, Mark's other travel expenses, including lodging in London on March 19, the day he arrived, are deductible moving expenses. Mark adds Items 2 and 6 together (except meals) and enters the amount on line 4 of Form 3903-F.

3. The $3,000 security deposit on the lease of the London home is not a moving expense. See the section "Nondeductible Expenses," earlier in this chapter.

4. Mark's 89 days of temporary living expenses, from March 20 to June 16, is not deductible as a moving expense.

5. Moving and storage expenses for personal effects (furniture, other household goods, and so on) was $8,100. Mark enters this amount on line 3, Form 3903-F. Of that amount, $2,900 was paid for storing their personal effects in Washington that year. As long as Mark stays on his London job, he can deduct the amount he pays each year to store their personal effects.

6. Mark's and the children's travel expenses to London includes the cost of their meals, which is not a deductible moving expense. However, their other travel expenses are deductible. This includes lodging in the Washington area on June 15, the day their personal effects were moved out of their home. The other travel expenses also include the cost of their lodging in London on June 16, the day they arrived. Mark has already added Items 2 and 6 together (except meals) and entered the amount on line 4 of Form 3903-F.

Form **3903-F**	**Foreign Moving Expenses**	OMB No. 1545-0062
Department of the Treasury Internal Revenue Service	▶ Attach to Form 1040.	**1997** Attachment Sequence No. **63**

Name(s) shown on Form 1040	Your social security number
Mark and Mary Green	123 : 00 : 7500

Caution: *If you are a member of the armed forces, see the instructions before completing this form.*

1 City and country in which your **old** workplace was located ▶ Washington, DC USA

2 City and country in which your **new** workplace is located ▶ London, England
Also, see **Time Test** on this page.

3 Transportation and storage of household goods and personal effects (see instructions) . . .	**3**	8,100 —
4 Travel and lodging expenses of moving from your old home to your new home. **Do not** include meals (see instructions)	**4**	1,818 —
5 Add lines 3 and 4	**5**	9,918 —
6 Enter the total amount your employer paid for your move (including the value of services furnished in kind) that is **not** included in the wages box (box 1) of your W-2 form. This amount should be identified with code **P** in box 13 of your W-2 form	**6**	8,793 —

Is line 5 more than line 6?

Yes. Go to line 7.

No. You **cannot** deduct your moving expenses. If line 5 is less than line 6, subtract line 5 from line 6 and include the result in income on Form 1040, line 7.

7 Subtract line 6 from line 5. Enter the result here and on Form 1040, line 25. This is your **moving expense deduction**	**7**	1,125 —

General Instructions

Purpose of Form

Use Form 3903-F to figure your moving expense deduction if you are a U.S. citizen or resident alien who moved to a new principal place of work (workplace) **outside** the United States or its possessions. If you qualify to deduct expenses for more than one move, use a separate Form 3903-F for each move. For more details, see **Pub. 521,** Moving Expenses.

Note: *Use* **Form 3903,** *Moving Expenses, instead of this form if you moved from a foreign country to the United States or its possessions because of a change in the location of your job. Form 3903 should also be used by retirees and survivors who qualify to deduct their expenses for moving from a foreign country to the United States or its possessions.*

Another Form You May Have To File

If you sold your main home in 1997, you must file **Form 2119,** Sale of Your Home, to report the sale.

Who May Deduct Moving Expenses

If you moved to a different home because of a change in job location outside the United States or its possessions, you may be able to deduct your moving expenses. You may be able to take the deduction whether you are self-employed or an employee. But you must meet certain tests explained next.

Distance Test

Your new principal workplace must be at least 50 miles farther from your old home than your old workplace was. For example, if your old workplace was 3 miles from your old home, your new workplace must be at least 53 miles from that home. If you did not have an old workplace, your new workplace must be at least 50 miles from your old home.

The distance between the two points is the shortest of the more commonly traveled routes between them.

Time Test

If you are an employee, you must work full time in the general area of your new workplace for at least 39 weeks during the 12 months right after you move. If you are self-employed, you must work full time in the general area of your new workplace for at least 39 weeks during the first 12 months and a total of at least 78 weeks during the 24 months right after you move.

You may deduct your moving expenses even if you have not met the time test before your tax return is due. You may do this if you expect to meet the 39-week test by the end of 1998 or the 78-week test by the end of 1999. If you deduct your moving expenses on your 1997 return but do not meet the time test, you will have to either:

● Amend your 1997 tax return by filing **Form 1040X,** Amended U.S. Individual Income Tax Return, or

For Paperwork Reduction Act Notice, see back of form.　　Cat. No. 12493R　　Form **3903-F** (1997)

E-Moving

If you have access to the Internet, the following Web sites offer a wealth of information about every aspect of moving.

The American Movers Conference at **http://www.amconf.org/** has lots of information for folks considering moving.

Mobility magazine, published by the Employee Relocation Council, includes articles about relocation and children. You can e-mail them at mobility@erc.org, or visit their Web site at **http://www.erc.org**.

For information on moving with the elderly, contact the:

    American Association of Retired Persons
    Web site: **http://www.aarp.org**

You can find more about the Americans with Disabilities Act (ADA) on the Internet at **http://www.ada.ufl.edu/**.

Want to know more about your destination? Start with these addresses to search online:

    http://www.yahoo.com

    http://www.city.net

    http://www.localeyes.com

Location Guides (P.O. Box 58506, Salt Lake City UT 84158; 800/846-6310) are available for more than 200 U.S. cities and towns. The 100-page guides include local, state, and regional information and contacts. Their Web site is **http://www.locationguides.com**.

Questions about passports? Need an application? Find it at **http://travel.state.gov/passport_services.html**.

Here are some Internet addresses for moving companies:

Allied Van Lines, Inc.
Web site: **http://www.alliedvan.com**

American Red Ball Transit Co.
Web site: **http://www.americanredball.com**

Atlas Van Lines, Inc.
Web site: **http://www.atlasvanlines.com**

Bekins Van Lines
Web site: **http://www.bekins.com**

Global Van and Storage South
Web site: **http://www.globalvan.com**

Interstate Van Lines, Inc.
Web site: **http://www.invan.com**

North American Van Lines
Web site: **http://www.northamerican-vanlines.com**

Stevens Worldwide Van Lines
Web site: **http://www.stevensworldwide.com**

Wheaton Van Lines
Web site: **http://www.wheatonworldwide.com**

Here are two Internet addresses for rental truck companies:

Ryder Consumer Trucks
Web site: **http://www.ryder.inter.net**

U-Haul
Web site: **http://www.uhaul.com**

Before hiring a company, check to see if it is a member of the American Movers Conference, a professional trade association, (**http://www.amconf.org**). Also, call the Better Business Bureau near you to see if any complaints have been lodged against them and, if so, how they've been resolved. To find the location of the office nearest you, check their Web site at **http://www.bbb.org**.

If you have serious problems with your moving company, the following organizations might prove helpful:

American Movers Conference
Dispute Settlement Program
E-mail: AMC1@erols.com
Web site: **http://www.amconf.org**

American Arbitration Association
Web site: **http://www.adr.org**

For more information on tax deductions, contact the IRS at **http://www.irs.gov**.

Internet newsgroups are groups of people who exchange information and opinions on a common topic. There are newsgroups for regions, homeowners, and thousands of other topics. To learn more about newsgroups, talk with your Internet provider.

Index

D

F

N

Q-R

T